HIDDEN®

Maui

HIDDEN®

Maui

Ray Riegert

FOURTH EDITION

Ulysses Press®
BERKELEY, CALIFORNIA

Published by:
ULYSSES PRESS
P.O. Box 3440
Berkeley, CA 94703
www.ulyssespress.com

ISSN 1524-5977
ISBN 1-56975-270-2

Printed in Canada by Transcontinental Printing

10 9

EDITORIAL DIRECTOR: Leslie Henriques
MANAGING EDITOR: Claire Chun
PROJECT DIRECTOR: Lily Chou
CONTRIBUTING WRITERS: Karee Carlucci, Leslie Henriques
EDITORIAL ASSOCIATE: Marin Van Young
TYPESETTER: Lisa Kester
CARTOGRAPHY: Pease Press
COVER DESIGN: Leslie Henriques, Sarah Levin
INDEXER: Sayre Van Young
COVER PHOTOGRAPHY:
    FRONT: Laurence Parent (Hamoa Beach)
    CIRCLE: Robert Holmes (Jeeping in the Garden of the Gods)
    BACK: Leslie Henriques (Charles Ka'upu)
ILLUSTRATOR: Sandra Wong

Distributed in the United States by Publishers
Group West, in Canada by Raincoast Books,
and in Great Britain and Europe by World
Leisure Marketing

For Alice, Keith and Leslie

Acknowledgments

The drawback to being acknowledged in a book about Maui is it means you worked in the office rather than Hawaii. That's not true of my wife, Leslie Henriques, who has been helping me research Maui for years; or Claire Chun who hails from Hawaii; or Karee Carlucci, who lives in the Islands and contributed to this edition.

But consultant extraordinaire Bryce Willett, project director Lily Chou, typesetter Lisa Kester, editorial associate Marin Van Young, and indexer Sayre Van Young would all I am sure happily trade this meager thanks for a plane ticket to paradise. I am nevertheless extremely grateful to all of them and extend a huge *mahalo* to everyone who helped bring this book to press.

✳

What's Hidden?

At different points throughout this book, you'll find special listings marked with a hidden symbol:

◄ HIDDEN

This means that you have come upon a place off the beaten tourist track, a spot that will carry you a step closer to the local people and natural environment of Maui.

The goal of this guide is to lead you beyond the realm of everyday tourist facilities. While we include traditional sightseeing listings and popular attractions, we also offer alternative sights and adventure activities. Instead of filling this guide with reviews of standard hotels and chain restaurants, we concentrate on one-of-a-kind places and locally owned establishments.

Our authors seek out locales that are popular with residents but usually overlooked by visitors. Some are more hidden than others (and are marked accordingly), but all the listings in this book are intended to help you discover the true nature of Maui and put you on the path of adventure.

Write to us!

If in your travels you discover a spot that captures the spirit of Maui, or if you live in the region and have a favorite place to share, or if you just feel like expressing your views, write to us and we'll pass your note along to the author.

We can't guarantee that the author will add your personal find to the next edition, but if the writer does use the suggestion, we'll acknowledge you in the credits and send you a free copy of the new edition.

ULYSSES PRESS
P.O. Box 3440
Berkeley, CA 94703
E-mail: readermail@ulyssespress.com

Contents

Maps

OUTDOOR ADVENTURE SYMBOLS

The following symbols accompany national, state and regional park listings, as well as beach descriptions throughout the text.

Symbol	Activity	Symbol	Activity
	Camping		Surfing
	Hiking		Windsurfing
	Swimming		Canoeing/Kayaking
	Snorkeling or Scuba Diving		Fishing

ONE

The Valley Isle

Residents of Maui, Hawaii's second-largest island, proudly describe their Valley Isle by explaining that "Maui *no ka oi*." Maui is the greatest. Few of the island's visitors have disputed the claim. They return each year, lured by the enchantment of a place possessing 33 miles of public beaches, one of the world's largest dormant volcanoes, beautiful people, a breeding ground for rare humpback whales and a climate that varies from subtropic to subarctic.

Named after one of the most important demigods in the Polynesian pantheon, Maui has retained its mythic aura. The island is famous as a chic retreat and jet-set landing ground. To many people, Maui *is* Hawaii.

But to others, who have watched the rapid changes during the past several decades, Maui is no longer the greatest. They point to the 2.4 million tourists (second only to Oahu) who visited during a recent year, to the condominiums and resort hotels now lining the prettiest beaches and to the increasing traffic over once-rural roads. And they have a new slogan. "Maui is *pau*." Maui is finished. Overtouristed. Overpopulated. Overdeveloped.

Today, among the island's 103,600 population, it seems like every other person is in the real estate business. On a land mass measuring 729 square miles, just half the size of Long Island, their goods are in short supply. During the 1970s and 1980s, land prices shot up faster than practically anywhere else in the country, although the 1990s saw prices decline.

Yet over 75 percent of the island remains unpopulated. Despite pressures from land speculation and a mondo-condo mentality, Maui still offers exotic, untouched expanses for the explorer. Most development is concentrated along the south and west coasts in Kihei, Wailea and Kaanapali. The rest of the island, though more populated than neighboring islands, is an adventurer's oasis. The second-youngest island in the chain, Maui was created between one and two million years ago by two volcanoes. Haleakala, the larger, rises over 10,000 feet, and offers excellent hiking and camping within its summit caldera, the largest such dormant volcanic crater in the world. The earlier of the two firepits created the West Maui Mountains, 5788 feet at their highest elevation. Because of their relative age, and the fact they receive 400 inches of rainfall a year, they are more heavily eroded than the smooth surfaces of Haleakala. Between the two heights lies Central Maui, an isthmus formed when the lava from each volcano flowed together.

The twin cities of Kahului and Wailuku, Maui's commercial and civic centers, respectively, sit in this saddle. Until the 1990s, most of the island was planted in sugar, which became king in Maui after the decline of whaling in the 1860s. Today, a road through what remains of the cane fields leads south to the sunsplashed resorts and beaches of Kihei, Maalaea, Wailea and Makena.

Another road loops around the West Maui Mountains. It passes prime whale-watching areas along the south coast and bisects Lahaina, an old whaling town that is now the island's sightseeing capital. Next to this timeworn harbor is the resort area of Kaanapali, a two-mile stretch of beach backed by hotels, condominiums and a full range of resort facilities. Beyond Kaanapali lies eight miles of coast lined with crescent beaches and lava rock promontories with another collection of hotels, condos and homes at Honokawai, Kahana and Napili. Past Napili the Kapalua Resort adds an upscale alternative, with several hotels and condos and three of Hawaii's best golf courses. Head past Kapalua and the landscape becomes wilder, with the blue-green of pineapple mixing with a series of deep wilderness valleys and grassy headlands that offer magnificently wild coastal views. You'll want to take a break in rustic Kahakuloa, where taro is still grown and the lifestyle is reminiscent of old Hawaii. From Kahakuloa, the road continues around West Maui, returning you to Wailuku and Kahului.

The road girdling Haleakala's lower slopes passes equally beautiful areas. Along the rainswept northeast coast are sheer rock faces ribboned with waterfalls and gorges choked with tropic vegetation. The lush, somnolent town of Hana gives way along the southeast shore to a dry, unpopulated expanse that is always ripe for exploration.

On the middle slopes of Haleakala, in Maui's Upcountry region, small farms dot the landscape. Here, in addition to guavas, avocados and lychee nuts, grow the sweet Kula onions for which the Valley Isle is famous.

Because of its strategic location between Oahu and Hawaii, Maui has played a vital role in Hawaiian history. Kahekili, Maui's last king, gained control of all the islands except Hawaii before being overwhelmed by Kamehameha in 1790. Lahaina, long a vacation spot for island rulers, became a political center under Hawaii's first three kings and an important commercial center soon after Captain Cook sighted the island in 1778. It served as a supply depot for ships, then as a port for sandalwood exports. By the 1840s, Lahaina was the world capital of whaling. Now, together with the other equally beautiful sections of the Valley Isle, it is a mecca for vacationers.

Maui's magic has cast a spell upon travelers all over the world, making the island a vacation paradise. Like most modern paradises, it is being steadily gilded in plastic and concrete. Yet much of the old charm remains. Some people even claim that the sun shines longer on the Valley Isle than any other place on earth. They point to the legend of the demigod Maui who created his own daylight savings by weaving a rope from his sister's pubic hair and lassoing the sun by its gen-

Maui

PACIFIC OCEAN

Hana

Hana
Forest
Reserve

Kipahulu
Forest
Reserve

Kaupahu
Bay

Kaupo

(4-Wheel Drive
Recommended)

Pailani Hwy

Alenuihaha Channel

Koolau
Forest
Reserve

Haleakala
National Park

▲ Haleakala
8205'

Kahikinui
Forest Reserve

Wailua

Hana Hwy

Kailua

Hamakua Coast

360

Pauwela

36

365

Makawao

377

Hana Hwy

Kula Forest
Reserve

Kula Hwy

Paia

Kuau

Hana Hwy

37

Haleakala Hwy

Pukalani

Keokea

37

**Ulupalakua
Ranch**

Puunene

Kahului

380

311

Kihei

Piilani Hwy

31

Wailea

Makena

Kihei Rd

) Molokini

Wailuku

340

Kahekili Hwy

West Maui
Forest
Reserve

30

Waikapu

Iao Valley
State
Monument

Eke Crater
4480' ▲

Puu Kukui
5788' ▲

Maalaea

30

Honoapiilani Hwy

Olowalu

Auau Channel

Alalakeiki Channel

Honokohau

Kahana

Kaanapali

Lahaina

Kahoolawe

Kealaikahiki Channel

.d many hope he has one last trick to perform, one that will slow the
.e of development just as he slowed the track of the sun.

Where to Go

Quite manageable in size, Maui is a destination that can be covered entirely in the course of a short vacation. Each of the island's regions has its strengths, and the areas with the most popular hotels and restaurants are not necessarily the best places for sightseeing. You may find yourself staying on one part of the island, visiting the beaches elsewhere and then setting off in yet another direction to tour.

Lahaina, the cultural heart of the island, is a falsefront whaling town that enjoyed its heyday in the 19th century and today remains rich in tradition. More than anywhere else on the island, Lahaina balances good restaurants and attractive lodgings with nightlife and shopping possibilities. It also offers a lengthy list of historic sightseeing spots.

The neighboring **Kaanapali–Kapalua Area** is a ten-mile stretch of coast that extends along the southwest corner of the island. Some of Hawaii's prettiest beaches can be found along this corridor, along with one of the state's densest concentrations of hotels and condominiums. This is where most people stay, and where they spend luxurious days soaking up sunshine. Situated in the wind shadow of the West Maui Mountains, this area enjoys the island's best weather and offers Kodachrome views of Lanai and Molokai.

Hoteliers in the Kaanapali–Kapalua region will tell you that their biggest competitors have set up shop in the **Kihei–Wailea–Makena Area**, another strip with miles of pearly beach, this time lining Maui's southeastern quarter. Kihei, a perfect example of development run amuck, is a congeries of strip malls and condominiums. Wailea and Makena, on the other hand, are well planned, trimly manicured landscapes dotted with scalloped beaches and five-star hotels.

The commercial center of the Valley Isle sits at the northern end of the isthmus separating the West Maui Mountains and Haleakala. The **Kahului–Wailuku Area** rises from Kahului Harbor, a major shipping area, uphill to the woodframe town of Wailuku. The seat of Maui County government, Wailuku, and neighboring Kahului, lack the beaches and physical appeal of the rest of the island, but offer visitors inexpensive hotels and restaurants.

Sightseeing is spelled with a capital "H" on the **Hana Highway**. Curving along the rain-doused northeastern coast, this magnificent drive curves past rainforests, seacliffs and checkerboard taro plantations to the idyllic village of Hana. Here you'll find friendly inns, a few restaurants and some of the most absorbing scenery in Hawaii. Local residents, looking out on the luxurious flora and tumbling terrain, lovingly call it "Heavenly Hana." It's not an exaggeration.

Maui's **Upcountry**, a band of ranchland that wraps around the lower slopes of Haleakala, is where the beach culture of the coast gives way to an Old West society of cattlemen and Hawaiian-style cowboys, or *paniolos*. Angus and Hereford cattle roam these cool, moist slopes and eye-catching wildflowers grow with abandon.

You have to climb 10,000 feet, but upon arriving at the summit in **Haleakala National Park**, you may discover there is a place on Maui even more alluring than "Heavenly Hana." This is, after all, the "House of the Sun," a dormant volcano that is home to eerie occurrences, legendary sunrises and remarkable sunsets. Often standing above the clouds and vaulting high beyond the surrounding countryside, Haleakala is definitely the place on Maui closest to heaven.

Maui's environment is fragile. Part of its natural beauty comes from its geographic isolation from denser ecosystems. Bringing in plants, produce or animals could introduce pests and non-endemic species that could ruin the ecosystem forever.

As much as Maui has to offer, Maui County has something more. Two additional islands in fact. Lanai and Molokai—both long linked historically to the Valley Isle, and lying nearer to Maui than any other islands in the chain—are part of the county administered from Wailuku. Since they are so closely tied to the larger island, and offer such fascinating day-trip destinations, they have been given their own chapters in *Hidden Maui*.

Directly to the west, lying in Maui's wind shadow, sits the smallest and most secluded island. **Lanai** is an explorer's paradise, with a network of jeep trails leading to hidden beaches and scenic mountain ridges. There are only 2800 people and about 20 miles of paved road here. If you're seeking a hidden retreat, this is the place.

Molokai, slightly larger but nearly as remote, provides another extraordinary hideaway. With white-sand beaches, a mountainous interior and a large population of Hawaiians, the "Friendly Isle" retains a unique sense of old Hawaii. Here you can visit a former leper colony on the windswept Kalaupapa Peninsula, a pilgrimage that could prove to be the most inspiring of all your experiences in Hawaii.

When to Go
SEASONS

There are two types of seasons on Maui, one keyed to tourists and the other to the climate. The peak tourist seasons run from mid-December until Easter, then again from mid-June through Labor Day. Particularly around the Christmas holidays and in August, the visitors centers are crowded. Prices increase, hotel rooms and rental cars become harder to reserve and everything moves a bit more rapidly. Shop around, however; package deals that include discounts on published rates are available.

If you plan to explore the island during these seasons, make reservations several months in advance; actually, it's a good idea to make advance reservations whenever you visit. Without doubt, the off-season is the best time to hit the island. Not only are hotels more readily available, but campsites and hiking trails are also less crowded.

Climatologically, the ancient Hawaiians distinguished between two seasons—*kau*, or summer, and *hooilo*, or winter. Summer extends from May to October, when the sun is overhead and the temperatures are slightly higher. Winter brings more variable winds and cooler weather.

The important rule to remember about Maui's beautiful weather is that it changes very little from season to season but varies dramatically from place to place. The average yearly temperature is about 78°, and during the coldest weather in January and the warmest in August, the thermometer rarely moves more than 5° or 6° in either direction. Similarly, sea water temperatures range comfortably between 74° and 80° year-round.

Crucial to this luxurious semitropical environment are the trade winds that blow with welcome regularity from the northeast, providing a natural form of air conditioning. When the trades stop blowing, they are sometimes replaced by *kona* winds carrying rain and humid weather from the southwest. These are most frequent in winter, when the island receives its heaviest rainfall.

While summer showers are less frequent and shorter in duration, winter storms are sometimes quite nasty. I've seen it pour for five consecutive days, until hiking trails disappeared and local streets were awash. If you visit in winter, particularly from December to March, you're risking the chance of rain.

A wonderful factor to remember through this wet weather is that if it's raining where you are, you can often simply go someplace else. And I don't mean another part of the world, or even a different island. Since the rains generally batter the northeastern section of the island, you can usually head over to the south or west coast for warm, sunny weather. Or if you seek cooler climes, head up to the mountains; for every thousand feet in elevation, the temperature drops about 3°. If you climb high enough on Maui, you might even encounter snow!

A WEEK OF ALOHA

Hawaiian culture is celebrated island-wide during **Aloha Week** in Molokai. This ten-day-long festival, featuring hula, singing, a *poke* contest, outdoor concerts, a parade and lots more, concludes with the Royal Ball at the Hotel Molokai. Known as "Aloha Festivals" statewide, the Maui County events are held in September and October.

CALENDAR OF EVENTS

Something else to consider in planning a visit to Maui is the amazing lineup of annual cultural events. For a thumbnail idea of what's happening when, check the calendar below. You might just find that special occasion to climax an already dynamic vacation.

JANUARY

Lahaina   The beauty of Hawaiian dance is showcased during one of Maui's hula *halau* competitions that takes place at the Lahaina Cannery Mall during the **Annual Festival of Hula**.

Kaanapali–Kapalua Area   An elite field of the PGA Tour winners compete in the season opener at **Kapalua's Plantation Course Mercedes Championships**.

Molokai   **Makahiki** was traditionally a time when wars paused, taxes were paid, and partying was plentiful. Molokai celebrates this legacy with its annual **Hawaiian Games**; in addition to the sports competitions, there are crafts, food booths and entertainment.

FEBRUARY

Throughout Maui   **Chinese New Year** is celebrated at various locations throughout the island with dancing, music, martial arts demonstration, food booths and fireworks. Front Street in Lahaina is a choice spot to enjoy the festivities.

MARCH

Throughout Maui   You can volunteer to help the Pacific Whale Foundation count humpbacks during **The Great Whale Count** in late February/early March. **Prince Kuhio Day** is celebrated throughout Maui County with music and dance.

Kaanapali–Kapalua Area   Over the Easter holiday, the Ritz-Carlton, Kapalua's **Celebration of the Arts** celebrates Hawaiian culture. Artisans and members of the community offer demonstrations, workshops and entertainment.

Kahului–Wailuku Area   The **Maui Marathon** is run from the Kaahumanu Shopping Center in Kahului to Whalers Village in Kaanapali in mid-March. **Art Maui** is a month-long juried art show featuring new work by local artists. It's held at the Maui Arts and Cultural Center on Kahului Beach Road. For the eco- and creative-minded, the Kaahumanu Center in Kahului sponsors the **Trash Art Show**, a glimpse into the wonders of—what else?—trash art.

Hana Highway   The **East Maui Taro Festival** is a celebration of the staple of the Hawaiian diet, with exhibits, lectures, music, hula and, of course, food.

APRIL

Throughout Maui   Buddhist temples mark **Buddha Day**, the luminary's birthday, with special services. Included among the events are pageants, dances and flower festivals.

Lahaina Celebrations, featuring a birthday cake, displays and historical information, are held on Front Street to commemorate the planting of the historic banyan tree during the **Banyan Tree Birthday Party.**

Hana Highway The **International Board Windsurfing Competition** is a popular ten-day tournament that's held at Hookipa Beach Park. Top wavesailers compete at the five-day **Da Kine Hawaiian Pro Am Wavesailing Championship** at Hookipa Beach.

MAY

Throughout Maui **Lei Day** is celebrated by people wearing flower leis and colorful Hawaiian garb. An island-wide festival featuring lei-making contests and Hawaiian entertainment is held on May 1 at the Outrigger Wailea Resort.

Upcountry and Haleakala **Seabury Hall Crafts Fair** in Makawao offers local arts and crafts, food booths and live entertainment.

Molokai Celebrate the birth of hula on the Friendly Isle with performances, music and Hawaiian food at **Molokai Ka Hula Piko.**

JUNE

Throughout Maui **King Kamehameha Day,** honoring Hawaii's first king, is celebrated mid-June with parades, chants, hula dances and exhibits.

Kaanapali–Kapalua Area The **Maui Symphony Fest & Chamber Music Festival** features chamber music by internationally acclaimed artists.

Kahului–Wailuku Area Top guitarists come together for the **Ki hoalu (Slack Key) Guitar Festival.**

Upcountry and Haleakala Staged at the Eddie Tam Complex in Makawao, the **Upcountry Fair** is where the 4-H crowd swings into action. Enjoy the live entertainment and local delicacies and, if you're an aspiring performer, don't miss the Star Search.

JULY

Lahaina Fireworks ignite the night sky over Lahaina's roadstead during an old-fashioned **Independence Day** celebration.

Kaanapali–Kapalua Area More than 100 different wines from California, Oregon and Washington, as well as Australia, are sampled at the **Kapalua Wine & Food Symposium.**

Kihei–Wailea–Makena Area Ocean sports, music, food and crafts are showcased at the **Kihei Sea Festival.**

Kahului–Wailuku Area The Maui War Memorial Sports Complex in Wailuku hosts the **Fourth of July Fireworks Extravaganza,** which features eats, explosives and live entertainment.

Upcountry and Haleakala In addition to fireworks, Maui celebrates the Fourth of July with the **Makawao Parade and Rodeo.** Also in Makawao, the Maui County Rodeo Finals bring together the top cowboys from Molokai and Maui.

Lanai The **Pineapple Festival,** held in Lanai City, features contemporary Hawaiian music, pineapple cooking contests and arts and crafts.

Throughout Maui   Buddhists perform colorful **Bon Dances** every weekend in July and August to honor the dead.

Lahaina   **Ole Longboard Classic**, Maui's premier longboard surfing event, is held at Launiupoko Beach Park, south of Lahaina Town.

Kaanapali–Kapalua Area   In addition to a raw onion–eating contest, you'll find food booths containing onion dishes from local restaurants, live music, a farmer's market and a cookoff where people can enter their favorite Maui onion recipe at the **Maui Onion Festival**, held at the Kaanapali Beach Resort.

AUGUST

Lahaina   Food and music are the themes of **Maui Chefs Present** and **A Taste of Lahaina and The Best of Island Music**, two celebrations featuring gourmet comestibles topped off with live entertainment and games and rides.

Kaanapali–Kapalua Area   Hawaii's largest tennis purse is the prize on which everyone keeps their eyes at the **Wilson Kapalua Open Tennis Tournament**. A six-person relay across the nine-mile channel from Lanai to Kaanapali draws 50 international swimming teams to the **Maui Channel Relay Swim**.

Kahului–Wailuku Area   The six-person **Hana Relay**, a 54-mile swim from Kahului to Hana, is one of autumn's more challenging events. From late September into October, the **Maui County Fair** features agricultural exhibits, ethnic foods and arts-and-crafts displays at the Wailuku War Memorial Complex. A celebration of Hispanic and Portuguese culture takes place in Wailuku at the **Somos Amigos Hispanic & Portuguese Festival**, showcasing food, entertainment, cooking contests and arts and crafts.

Upcountry and Haleakala   **Maui Cycle to the Sun** is the ultimate uphill challenge: a 38-mile bike ride from the ocean to the 10,023-foot peak of Haleakala. Covering the same route is the **Haleakala Run to the Sun**.

SEPTEMBER

HONORING THE VOYAGE

Saluting Hawaii's rich heritage, Lahaina hosts **In Celebration of Canoes** in May, recognizing the voyaging canoes that united Polynesia. Delegations from various Pacific island nations come together with master carvers who create Polynesian canoes from wood logs. Each nation is welcomed by Hawaiians in a traditional *awa* ceremony at the beach. Cultural arts demonstrations, lessons and performances are held during the week. The highlight is The Festival of Canoes & Parade, which includes ancient warrior games, Polynesian crafts and food, a ceremonial launching of the carved canoes at sunset, and a concert under the stars. Free admission to most events.

Lanai   **Aloha Festivals** draw revelers with a parade, a block party, a beach party and activities honoring the various ethnic groups on the Pineapple Isle.

Molokai   A lantern parade and block party are two events that highlight **Aloha Festivals** in late September. More than 60 six-women outrigger canoes race across the channel from Molokai to Oahu during the **Na Wahine O Ke Kai.**

OCTOBER   **Throughout Maui**   The highlight of Hawaii's cultural season is the **Aloha Festivals,** a series of week-long celebrations featuring parades, street parties and pageants.

Lahaina   **Halloween** in Lahaina is a memorable street party with a parade, food fair, music and dancing on Front Street à la Mardi Gras.

Kaanapali–Kapalua Area   The EMC **Kaanapali Classic** tournament draws top stars from the PGA Tour.

Kahului–Wailuku Area   Folks convene for the **Kuu Home O Wailuku Hoolaulea,** a multicultural gathering featuring entertainment, food, arts-and-crafts demonstrations and much more. The highlight is the "Plate Lunch Challenge."

Molokai   An evening saluting the unique qualities of Hawaii's own music is found at the **Molokai Annual Slack Key Guitar Festival.** The **Molokai Hoe,** Men's Molokai to Oahu Race, has over 100 six-person outrigger canoes from around the world darting across the channel from Molokai to Oahu.

NOVEMBER   **Kahului–Wailuku Area**   Hawaiian and other crafts are showcased at the **Lokahi Pacific Christmas Craft Fair,** held at the War Memorial Sports Complex in Wailuku.

Hana Highway   The **Aloha Classic Windsurfing** competition at Hookipa Beach on the Hana Highway is a key event during the Pro Boardsailing Association World Tour.

DECEMBER   **Throughout Maui**   Buddha's enlightenment is commemorated with **Bodhi Day** ceremonies and religious services.

Lahaina   Held at Banyan Tree Park, flower displays, arrangements and demonstrations are showcased at the **Festival of Art**

PARADISE FOR TWO

Want to get married but can't decide where or when? Simply pick up the phone and call **A Wedding Made In Paradise.** These ready-to-please consultants will help you choose the location on Maui and the minister. They'll even plan the ceremony. ~ Kihei; 808-879-3444.

and Flowers on Front Street, along with the holiday lighting of the Banyan Tree.

Kaanapali–Kapalua Area   Hawaiian arts and crafts, music and dance are highlighted at the **Na Mele O Maui Festival**.

Kihei–Wailea–Makena Area   Santa is the center of attention at the **Wailea Christmas Festival**, staged in the Wailea Shopping Village.

Upcountry and Haleakala   Christmas arts and crafts are the star attractions at the **Hui Noeau Christmas House** in Makawao.

The **Hawaii Visitors & Convention Bureau**, a state-run agency, is a valuable resource from which to obtain free information on Maui and the rest of Hawaii. The Bureau can help plan your trip and then offer advice once you reach Maui. The Valley Isle office is called the **Maui Visitors & Convention Bureau**. ~ 1727 Wili Pa Loop, Wailuku; 808-244-3530. You can also contact the Hawaii Visitors & Convention Bureau in Honolulu. ~ 2270 Kalakaua Avenue, Suite 801, Honolulu, HI 96815; 808-923-1811, 800-464-2924; www.gohawaii.com.

Before You Go

VISITORS CENTERS

Another excellent resource is the **Hawaii State Public Library System**. With a network of libraries on Maui, this government agency provides facilities for residents and nonresidents alike. The libraries are good places to find light beach-reading material as well as books on Hawaii. Visitors can check out books by simply applying for a library card with a valid identification card.

Or boot up the computer and link up with **Maui On-Line**. A service of Channel 7, The Visitor Channel, this web page is more like a web book, with a wealth of information on lodging, dining, transportation, beaches and outdoor activities. ~ 808-661-1111, fax 808-661-6131; www.maui.net/~mol.

PACKING

When I get ready to pack for a trip, I sit down and make a list of everything I'll need. It's a very slow, exact procedure: I look in closets, drawers and shelves, and run through in my mind the activities in which I'll participate, determining which items are required for each. After all the planning is complete and when I have the entire inventory collected in one long list, I sit for a minute or two, basking in my wisdom and forethought.

Then I tear the hell out of the list, cut out the ridiculous items I'll never use, halve the number of spares among the necessary items and reduce the entire contents of my suitcase to the bare essentials.

Before I developed this packing technique, I once traveled overland from London to New Delhi carrying two suitcases and a knapsack. I lugged those damned bundles onto trains, buses, jitneys, taxis and rickshaws. When I reached Turkey, I started shipping things home, but by then I was buying so many market goods that it was all I could do to keep even.

I ended up carrying so much crap that one day, when I was sardined in a crowd pushing its way onto an Indian train, someone managed to pick my pocket. When I felt the wallet slipping out, not only was I unable to chase the culprit—I was so weighted down with baggage that I couldn't even turn around to see who was robbing me!

I will never travel that way again, and neither should you. Particularly when visiting Hawaii, where the weather is mild, you should pack very light. The airlines permit two suitcases and a carry-on bag; try to take one suitcase and maybe an accessory bag that can double as a beach bag. Dress styles are very informal in the islands, and laundromats are ubiquitous, so you don't need a broad range of clothing items, and you'll require very few extras among the essential items.

Remember, you're packing for a semitropical climate. Take along a sweater or light jacket for the mountains and something to protect against rain. But otherwise, all that travelers on Maui require are shorts, bathing suits, lightweight slacks, short-sleeved shirts and blouses and summer dresses or *muumuus*. Rarely do visitors require sport jackets or formal dresses. Wash-and-wear fabrics are the most convenient, though 100 percent cotton is more comfortable.

For footwear, I suggest soft, comfortable shoes. Low-cut hiking boots or tennis shoes are preferable for hiking; for beachgoing, there's nothing as good as sandals or Tevas, which can also be worn in the water.

There are several other items to squeeze in the corners of your suitcase—sunscreen, sunglasses, a towel and, of course, your copy of *Hidden Maui*. You might also consider packing a mask, fins and snorkel and a camera.

PACKAGE TOURS

In planning a Maui sojourn, one potential moneysaver is the package tour, which combines air transportation with a hotel room and other amenities. Generally, it is a style of travel that I avoid. However, if you can find a package that provides air transportation, a hotel or condominium accommodation and a rental car, all at one low price—it is worth considering. Just try to avoid the packages that preplan your entire visit, dragging you around on air-conditioned tour buses. Look for the package that provides only the bare necessities, namely transportation and lodging, while allowing you the greatest freedom. However you decide to go, be sure to consult a travel agent. They are professionals in the field, possessing the latest information on rates and facilities and their service to you is free.

If you plan on camping, you'll need most of the equipment required for mainland overnighting. On Maui, you can get along quite comfortably with a lightweight tent and sleeping bag. You'll also need a knapsack, canteen, camp stove and fuel, mess kit, first-aid kit (with insect repellent, water purification tablets and lip balm), toilet kit, a pocket knife, hat, waterproof matches, flash-light and ground cloth.

Accommodations on Maui range from funky cottages to highrise condominiums. You'll find inexpensive family-run hotels and bed-and-breakfast inns, run-of-the-mill tourist facilities and world-class resorts.

LODGING

Whichever you choose, there are a few guidelines to help save money. Try to visit during the off-season, avoiding the high-rate periods during the summer and from Christmas to Easter. Rooms with mountain views are less expensive than oceanview accom-modations. Generally, the farther a hotel is from the beach, the less it costs. Another way to economize is by reserving a room with a kitchen. In any case, try to reserve far in advance.

To help you decide on a place to stay, I've described the accom-modations not only by area but also according to price (prices listed are for double occupancy during the high season; prices may decrease in low season). *Budget* hotels are generally less than $60 per night for two people; the rooms are clean and comfortable, but lack luxury. The *moderately* priced hotels run $60 to $120, and provide larger rooms, plusher furniture and more attractive surroundings. At *deluxe*-priced accommodations you can expect to spend between $120 and $180 for a homey bed and breakfast or a double in a hotel or resort. You'll check into a spacious, well-appointed room with modern facilities; downstairs the lobby will be a fashionable affair, and you'll usually see a restaurant, lounge and a cluster of shops. If you want to spend your time (and money) in the island's very finest hotels, try an *ultra-deluxe* facility, which will include all the amenities and price well above $180.

Bed-and-Breakfast Inns Maui's bed-and-breakfast business be-comes more diverse and sophisticated every year. Today there are several referral services that can find you lodging on Maui or any of the other islands. Claiming to be the biggest clearinghouse in the state, **Bed & Breakfast Honolulu (Statewide)** represents over 400 properties, including about 75 on Maui. ~ 3242 Kaohinani Drive, Honolulu, HI 96817; 808-595-7533, 800-288-4666, fax 808-595-2030; www.hawaiibnb.com.

The original association, **Bed & Breakfast Hawaii**, claims more than 200 locations, many on Maui. This Kauai-based serv-ice was founded in 1979 and is well known throughout Hawaii. ~ P.O. Box 449, Kapaa, HI 96746; 808-822-7771, 800-733-1632, fax 808-822-2723; www.bandb-hawaii.com. For other possibilities contact **Hawaiian Islands Bed & Breakfast.** ~ 808-258-7895, 800-258-7895, fax 808-262-2181; www.flyhi.com.

You can also try **Affordable Accommodations Maui,** which offers help in finding all types of lodging. ~ 2825 Kauhale Street, Kihei, HI 96753; 808-879-7865, 888-333-9747, fax 808-874-0831; www.affordablemaui.com. **All Islands Bed & Breakfast,** an Oahu-based reservation service, claims to represent over 700 bed and breakfasts on Maui alone. ~ 463 Iliwahi Loop, Kailua, HI 96734; 808-263-2342, 800-542-0344, fax 808-263-0308; home.hawaii.rr.com/allislands.

The mermaid goddess Wewehi lives in the waters off Maui. You can't miss her—she'll be the only swimmer wearing *limu-loloa,* a reddish-colored seaweed.

While the properties represented by these agencies range widely in price, **Hawaii's Best Bed & Breakfasts** specializes in small, upscale accommodations on all the islands. With about 100 places to choose from, it places guests in a variety of privately owned facilities; most are deluxe in price. About two dozen of the places are on Maui. ~ P.O. Box 563, Kamuela, HI 96743; 808-885-4550, 800-262-9912, fax 808-885-0559; www.bestbnb.com.

CONDOS

Many people visiting Maui, especially those traveling with families, find that condominiums are often cheaper than hotels. While some hotel rooms come with kitchenettes, few provide all the amenities of condominiums. A condo, in essence, is an apartment away from home. Designed as studio, one-, two- or three-bedroom apartments, they come equipped with full kitchen facilities and complete kitchenware collections. Many also feature washer-dryers, dishwashers, air conditioning, color televisions, telephones, lanais and community swimming pools. Utilizing the kitchen will save considerably on your food bill; by sharing the accommodations among several people, you'll also cut your lodging bill.

DINING

A few guidelines will help you chart a course through Maui's countless dining places. Within a particular chapter, the restaurants are categorized geographically, with each restaurant entry describing the establishment as budget, moderate, deluxe or ultra-deluxe in price.

To establish a pattern for the island's parade of dining places, I've described not only the cuisine but also the ambience of each establishment. Restaurants listed offer lunch and dinner unless otherwise noted.

Dinner entrées at *budget* restaurants usually cost $8 or less. The ambience is informal café style and the crowd is often a local one. *Moderately* priced restaurants range between $8 and $16 at dinner and offer pleasant surroundings, a more varied menu and a slower pace. *Deluxe* establishments tab their entrées above $16, featuring sophisticated cuisines, plush decor and more personalized service. *Ultra-deluxe* restaurants generally price above $24.

Vacation Rentals in Maui, Lanai and Molokai

AA Oceanfront Condominium Rentals   800-488-6004;
www.aaoceanfront.com

Affordable Accommodations Maui   888-333-9747;
www.affordablemaui.com

All Globe Travel & Vacations   800-688-2254; www.allglobetravel.com

Aloha Destinations Vacations   808-893-0388;
www.alohadestinations.com

Aloha Paradise Vacation Rentals   800-613-5400;
www.alohavacationhomes.com

Aston   800-922-7866; www.astonhotels.com

CyberRentals   www.cyberrentals.com

Direct by Owner   www.dbomauicondos.com

Island Resort Rentals   888-382-8320; www.islandresortrentals.com

Maui & All Islands Condominiums & Cars   www.mauiallislands.com

Maui Condominium and Home Realty   800-822-4409; www.resort
questmaui.com

Maui Organics Vacation Rentals   866-628-4674; www.mauiorganics
vacationrentals.com

Maui Resort Vacation Rentals   800-441-3187; www.mauiresort4u.com

Sullivan Properties, Inc.   800-332-1137

Tropical Villa Vacations   888-875-2818; www.tropicalvillavacations.com

VacationHosts.com   800-754-0905; www.vacationhosts.com

Villa Network of Hawaii   800-262-9013; www.villanetworkhawaii.com

Breakfast and lunch menus vary less in price from restaurant to restaurant. Even deluxe-priced kitchens usually offer light breakfasts and lunch sandwiches, which place them within a few dollars of their budget-minded competitors. These early meals can be a good time to test expensive restaurants.

TRAVELING WITH CHILDREN

Maui is an ideal vacation spot for family holidays. The pace is slow, the atmosphere casual. A few guidelines will help ensure that your trip to the islands brings out the joys rather than the strains of parenting, allowing everyone to get into the *aloha* spirit.

Use a travel agent to help with arrangements; they can reserve spacious bulkhead seats on airlines and determine which flights are least crowded. They can also seek out the best deals on inexpensive condominiums, saving you money on both room and board.

Planning the trip with your kids stimulates their imagination. Books about travel, airplane rides, beaches, whales, volcanoes and Hawaiiana help prepare even a two-year-old for an adventure. This preparation makes the "getting there" part of the trip more exciting for children of all ages.

And "getting there" means a long-distance flight. Plan to bring everything you need on board the plane—diapers, food, toys, books and extra clothing for kids and parents alike. I found it helpful to carry a few new toys and books as treats to distract my son and daughter when they got bored. When they were young children, I also packed extra snacks.

Allow extra time to get places. Book reservations in advance and make sure that the hotel or condominium has the extra crib, cot or bed you require. It's smart to ask for a room at the end of the hall to cut down on noise. And when reserving a rental car, inquire to see if they provide car seats and if there is an added charge. Hawaii has a strictly enforced car seat law.

Besides the car seat you may have to bring along, also pack shorts and T-shirts, a sweater, sun hat, bathing suits, sundresses and waterproof sandals. A stroller with sunshade for little ones helps on sightseeing sojourns; a shovel and pail are essential for

IT'S RAINING, IT'S POURING

There are plenty of indoor activities to keep kids amused when the rains come. Check out all the sea creatures at the Maui Ocean Center in Maalaea Harbor Village (see page 147), or view the island's wildlife and underwater sealife on a three-story-high movie screen at the Hawaii Experience domed theater in Lahaina (see page 96), or investigate the whaling artifacts and 30-foot-long skeleton at The Whalers Village Museum in Kaanapali (see page 100).

sandcastle building. Most important, remember to bring a good sunblock. The quickest way to ruin a family vacation is with a bad sunburn. Also plan to bring indoor activities such as books and games for evenings and rainy days.

Most towns have stores that carry diapers, food and other essentials. However, prices are much higher than on the mainland. To economize, some people take along an extra suitcase filled with diapers and wipes, baby food, peanut butter and jelly, etc.

A first-aid kit is always a good idea. Also check with your pediatrician for special medicines and dosages for colds and diarrhea. If your child does become sick or injured on Maui, contact a local doctor or the **Maui Memorial Hospital** at 808-242-2343. On Molokai there's **Molokai General Hospital**. ~ 808-553-5331. There is also a **Hawaii Poison Center** in Honolulu, which can be reached at 800-362-3585 or 808-941-4411.

Hotels often provide access to babysitters and some resorts and hotels have daily programs for kids during the summer and holiday seasons. Hula lessons, lei making, storytelling, sandcastle building and various sports activities keep *keikis* (kids) over six happy while also giving Mom and Dad a break. As an added bonus, these resorts offer family plans, providing discounts for extra rooms or permitting children to share a room with their parents at no extra charge. Check with your travel agent.

WOMEN TRAVELING ALONE

Traveling solo grants an independence and freedom different from that of traveling with a partner, but single travelers are more vulnerable to crime and should take additional precautions. An option for those who are alone but prefer not to be is to join a tour group. A multitude abound that are tailored to your specific interests; see "The New Travel" section in Chapter Two for ideas.

It's unwise to hitchhike and probably best to avoid inexpensive accommodations; the money saved does not outweigh the risk. Bed and breakfasts, youth hostels and YWCAs are generally your safest bet for lodging, and they also foster an environment ideal for bonding with fellow travelers.

Keep all valuables well-hidden and hold onto cameras and purses. Avoid late-night treks or strolls through undesirable parts of town, but if you find yourself in this situation, continue walking with a confident air until you reach a safe haven. A fierce scowl never hurts.

These hints should by no means deter you from seeking out adventure. Wherever you go, stay alert, use your common sense and trust your instincts. If you are hassled or threatened in some way, never be afraid to call for assistance. It's also a good idea to carry change for a phone call and to know a number to call in case of emergency. You can call **Women Helping Women**, a domestic

violence shelter that can provide referrals. ~ 808-579-9581; www.
whwmaui.net.

For more helpful hints, get a copy of *Safety and Security for
Women Who Travel* (Travelers' Tales, 1998).

**GAY &
LESBIAN
TRAVELERS**

The island of Maui is at the cutting edge of gay culture in at least
one regard: It has been home for years to **Royal Hawaiian Wed-
dings**. This Valley Isle institution arranges beautiful gay wedding
ceremonies set in lush tropical surroundings. (Straight couples are
welcome, too.) ~ P.O. Box 424, Puunene, HI 96784; 800-659-1866.

Local wags also point out that ever since the days of Hawaiian royalty, Maui has been a favorite playground for island queens.
Seriously now, after Oahu, Maui has more exclusively gay and
gay-friendly facilities than any other island. This includes an impressive concentration of gay and lesbian bed and breakfasts.
Maui also offers some of Hawaii's best beaches, including **Little
Beach**, a gay nude beach in the Kihei–Wailea–Makena district.

For information on the gay and lesbian scene on Maui, contact
Both Sides Now. They can provide details on lodging, upcoming
events and social gatherings. ~ P.O. Box 5042, Kahului, HI 96733;
808-244-4566, fax 808-573-0045; www.maui-tech.com/glom. Les-
bians can also call **Contact Dykes**. ~ 808-879-2971.

Women can contact the **Women's Events Information Line**
for goings-on around the island. ~ 808-573-3077.

The Valley Isle is even home to "the only gay and lesbian surfing school in the world," the **Maui Surfing School**. Lessons are
held at the south end of Lahaina. ~ P.O. Box 424, Puunene, HI
96784; 808-875-0625. (See "Surfing" in Chapter Two for more
information.)

Organized nightlife on the island centers around **Hapa's Brew-
house and Restaurant**'s Tuesday night gay and lesbian deejay dancing. ~ 808-572-0220. Every Thursday night, **Casanova Italian Restaurant** in Makawao offers a full bar, dinner and music for a gay
crowd. The gay and lesbian bed-and-breakfast accommodations

CRUISING THE ISLANDS

You once were able to cruise to Maui County's smaller islands on an ocean-
liner. Nowadays, the only way to shuttle between the islands of Maui,
Molokai and Lanai is to hop aboard a sailboat charter, a swift-moving
catamaran or a local ferry. To get to Molokai by ferry, contact the
Moloka'i Princess. ~ 808-667-6165, 800-275-6969; www.molokai
ferry.com. **Expeditions**, a Lahaina-based ferry service to Lanai, makes
five roundtrips a day. ~ 808-661-3756.

are concentrated in Kihei, along the Hana Highway and in the Upcountry region.

For more information on nightlife and lodging see "Gay and lesbian travelers" in the index.

SENIOR TRAVELERS

Maui is a hospitable place for senior citizens to visit. Countless museums, historic sights and even restaurants and hotels offer senior discounts that can cut a substantial chunk off vacation costs. For a small fee, the national park system's Golden Age Passport, which must be applied for in person, allows free admission for anyone 62 and older to the national park facilities on the island. Once purchased, the passport is good for life.

The **American Association of Retired Persons** (AARP) offers membership to anyone over 50. AARP's benefits include travel discounts with car-rental agencies, hotel chains and many other firms. ~ 601 E Street NW, Washington, DC 20049; 800-424-3410; www.aarp.org.

Elderhostel offers reasonably priced, all-inclusive educational programs in a variety of locations throughout the year. ~ 11 Avenue de Lafayette, Boston, MA 02111; 877-426-8056, fax 617-426-0701; www.elderhostel.org.

Be extra careful about health matters. Consider carrying a medical record with you—including your medical history and current medical status as well as your doctor's name, phone number and address. Make sure your insurance covers you while you are away from home. It is wise to have your doctor write out extra prescriptions in case you lose your medication. Always carry your medications on board your planes, not in your luggage.

DISABLED TRAVELERS

The **Commission on Persons with Disabilities** publishes a survey of the city, county, state and federal parks in Hawaii that are accessible to disabled people. They also provide "Aloha Guides to Accessibility," which covers Maui as well as the other islands, and gives information on various hotels, shopping centers and restaurants that are accessible. ~ 919 Ala Moana Boulevard, Room 101, Honolulu, HI 96814; 808-586-8121, fax 808-586-8129; e-mail accesshi@aloha.net.

The **Maui Center for Independent Living** offers helpful information for travelers with disabilities. ~ 220 Imi Kala Street, Suite 103, Wailuku, HI 96793; 808-242-4966; e-mail mcilogg@gte.net. The **Society for Accessible Travel & Hospitality** also provides information. ~ 347 5th Avenue #610, New York, NY 10016; 212-447-7284, fax 212-725-8253; www.sath.org. **Travelin' Talk**, a network of people and organizations, provides assistance as well. ~ P.O. Box 1796, Wheat Ridge, CO 80034; 303-232-2979; www.travelintalk.net. **Access-Able Travel Source** has worldwide information online. ~ 303-232-2979; www.access-able.com.

Be sure to check in advance when making room reservations. Some hotels feature facilities for those in wheelchairs.

FOREIGN TRAVELERS

Passports and Visas   Most foreign visitors are required to have a passport and a tourist visa to enter the United States. Contact your nearest United States Embassy or Consulate well in advance to obtain a visa and to check on any other entry requirements.

Customs Requirements   Foreign travelers are allowed to carry in the following: 200 cigarettes (1 carton), 50 cigars, or 2 kilograms (4.4 pounds) of smoking tobacco; one liter of alcohol for personal use only (you must be 21 years of age to bring in alcohol); and US$100 worth of duty-free gifts that include an additional quantity of 100 cigars. You may bring in any amount of currency, but must fill out a form if you bring in over US$10,000. Carry any prescription drugs in clearly marked containers. (You may have to produce a written prescription or doctor's statement for the customs officer.) Meat or meat products, seeds, plants, fruits and narcotics are not allowed to be brought into the United States. Contact the **United States Customs Service** for further information. ~ 1301 Constitution Avenue NW, Washington, DC 20229; 202-927-6724; www.customs.treas.gov.

Check out the bargains and shop with the local crowd in Kahului at the Maui Swap Meet on Saturdays. ~ 808-877-3100.

Driving   If you plan to rent a car, an international driver's license should be obtained prior to arrival. Some rental car companies require both a foreign license and an international driver's license. Many car rental agencies require that the lessee be at least 25 years of age; all require a major credit card. Seat belts are mandatory for the driver and all passengers. Children under the age of 5 or weighing less than 40 pounds should be in the back seat in approved child safety restraints.

Currency   United States money is based on the dollar. Bills come in six denominations: $1, $5, $10, $20, $50 and $100. Every dollar is divided into 100 cents. Coins are the penny (1 cent), nickel (5 cents), dime (10 cents), quarter (25 cents), half-dollar (50 cents) and dollar (100 cents).

You may not use foreign currency to purchase goods and services in the United States. Consider buying traveler's checks in dollar amounts. You may also use credit cards affiliated with an American company such as Interbank, Barclay Card, VISA and American Express.

Electricity and Electronics   Electric outlets use currents of 110 volts, 60 cycles. For appliances made for other electrical systems, you need a transformer or adapter. Travelers who use laptop computers for telecommunication should be aware that modem configurations for U.S. telephone systems may be different from their

European counterparts. Similarly, the U.S. format for videotapes is different from that in Europe; U.S. Park Service visitors centers and other stores that sell souvenir videos often have them available in European format.

Weights and Measurements   The United States uses the English system of weights and measures. American units and their metric equivalents are as follows: 1 inch = 2.5 centimeters; 1 foot (12 inches) = 0.3 meter; 1 yard (3 feet) = 0.9 meter; 1 mile (5280 feet) = 1.6 kilometers; 1 ounce = 28 grams; 1 pound (16 ounces) = 0.45 kilogram; 1 quart (liquid) = 0.9 liter.

▼ ▼ ▼ ▼ ▼ ▼ ▼ ▼ ▼ ▼

Transportation

AIR

Chances are you'll be flying through Honolulu on your way into Maui. The **Honolulu International Airport** is served by Air New Zealand, American Airlines, Canada 3000, Canadian Airlines, China Airlines, Continental Airlines, Delta Air Lines, Hawaiian Airlines, Korean Air, Northwest Airlines, Quantas, Philippine Airlines and United.

Three airports serve Maui—Kahului Airport, Kapalua–West Maui Airport and Hana Airport. The latter two are exclusively interisland.

The **Kahului Airport** is the main landing facility and should be your destination if you're staying in the Central Maui region or on the southeast coast in the Kihei–Wailea–Makena area. American Airlines, Delta Air Lines, Hawaiian Airlines, United Airlines and a couple of charter companies offer nonstop service from the mainland.

If you land in Kahului, you'll arrive at a bustling airport. I never realized how popular Maui was until I first pushed through the mobs of new arrivals here. In addition to the masses, you'll find a coffee shop and lounge, newsstand, gift shop, lei stand, baggage service and information booth (808-872-3893).

Kapalua–West Maui Airport serves the Lahaina–Kaanapali area. Island Air flies into the facility.

Hana Airport, really only a short landing strip and a one-room terminal, sits near the ocean in Maui's lush northeastern corner. Island Air lands in this isolated community. And don't expect very much ground transportation waiting for you. There is no bus service, though there is a car rental agency.

During the 19th century, sleek clipper ships sailed from the West Coast to Hawaii in about 11 days. Today, you'll be traveling by a less romantic but far swifter conveyance—the jet plane. Rather than days at sea, it will be about five hours in the air from California, nine hours from Chicago or around 11 hours if you're coming from New York.

(For airline information on Molokai and Lanai, see the end of those chapters.)

Whichever carrier you choose, ask for the economy or excursion fare and try to fly during the week; weekend flights are generally higher in price. To qualify for lower-price fares, it is sometimes necessary to book your flight two weeks in advance and to stay over a Saturday night. Generally, however, the restrictions are minimal. Children under two years of age can fly for free, but they will not have a seat of their own. Each passenger is permitted two large pieces of luggage plus a carry-on bag. Shipping a bike or surfboard will cost extra. (Be sure to check on length restrictions.)

GETTING BETWEEN ISLANDS

Since cruise ships are the only commercial boats serving Maui and all five of the other Hawaiian Islands, most of the transportation between islands is by plane. **Aloha Airlines** and **Hawaiian Airlines**, the state's major carriers, provides frequent interisland jet service. If you're looking for smooth, rapid, comfortable service, this is certainly it. You'll be buckled into your seat, offered a free soft drink or low-cost cocktail and whisked to your destination within about 20 minutes.

Holo-holo is Hawaiian for "day tripping."

Without doubt, the best service aboard any interisland carrier is on Aloha Airlines. They have an excellent reputation for flying on time. I give them my top recommendation.

Now that you know how to fly quickly and comfortably, let me tell you about the most exciting way to get from Honolulu to Maui or to fly from Maui to other neighbor islands. **IslandAir** flies twin-engine propeller planes. These small airplanes travel at low altitudes and moderate speeds over the islands. Next to chartering a helicopter, they are the finest way to see Hawaii from the air.

Expeditions ferry services operates out of Maui and links Lahaina with Manele Bay on Lanai. There are five boats per day in each direction. The 45-minute trip is a unique way to travel between the islands. ~ P.O. Box 10, Lahaina, HI 96767; 808-661-3756.

CAR RENTALS

Renting a car is as easy in Maui as anywhere. Every island supports at least several rental agencies, which compete fiercely with one another in price and quality of service. So before renting, shop around: check the listings in this book, and also look for special temporary offers that many rental companies sometimes feature.

There are several facts to remember when renting a car. First of all, a major credit card is essential. Also, many agencies don't rent at all to people under 25. Regardless of your age, many companies charge several dollars a day extra for insurance. The insurance is optional and expensive, and in many cases, unnecessary (many credit cards provide the same coverage when a rental is charged to the card). Find out if you credit card company offers this coverage. Your personal insurance policy may also provide for rental cars and, if necessary, have a clause added that will include rental car protection. Check on this before you leave home. But remember, whether you have insurance or not, you are liable for the first several thousand dollars in accident damage.

Rates fluctuate with the season; slack tourist seasons are great times for good deals. Also, three-day, weekly and monthly rates are almost always cheaper than daily rentals; cars with standard shifts are generally less than automatics; and compacts are more economical than the larger four-door models.

Naturally, the most convenient means of renting a car is through one of the outfits at the airport. The problem with these companies, however, is that you pay for the convenience. In Kahului, the airport car-rental agencies are as follows: **Avis Rent A Car** (808-871-7575, 800-331-1212), **Budget Rent A Car** (808-871-8811, 800-527-0700), **Dollar Rent A Car** (808-877-2731, 800-800-4000), **Hertz Rent A Car** (808-877-5167, 800-654-3131) and **National Car Rental** (808-871-8851, 800-227-7368).

Then there are the agencies located away from the airport. Some of them will provide airport pick-up service when your plane arrives. I recommend that you check in advance and reserve a car from an outfit that extends this service. The others might be a little cheaper, but I've never considered the inconvenience worth the savings. Without a ride you'll be confronted with the Catch-22 situation of getting to your car. Do you rent a car in which to pick up your rental car? Take a bus? Or are you supposed to hitchhike?

Enough said. The rental agencies outside the airport include companies that rent older model cars at very competitive rates. One of these is **Word of Mouth Rent A Used Car**, which strongly recommends reservations. ~ 808-877-2436, 800-533-5929; www.mauirentacar.com, e-mail word@maui.net.

Budget travelers might want to consider **Maui Cruisers, Inc.** Located in Wailuku, they rent used cars, primarily Toyotas (always reliable), for a bargain. (Their claim is that if you rent from them, you'll look like a local rather than a tourist—good as an anti-theft device.) If you rent the car for at least a week, they'll pick you up at the airport for free. ~ 808-249-2319; www.mauicruisers.net.

If you find yourself in the Lahaina–Kaanapali area wanting to rent a car, try **Avis Rent A Car** (808-661-4588, 800-331-1212), **Budget Rent A Car** (808-661-8721, 800-527-0700), **Dollar Rent A Car** (808-667-2651, 800-800-4000), **Hertz Rent A Car** (808-661-7735, 800-654-3131) or **National Car Rental** (808-667-9737, 800-227-7368). All of these agencies have courtesy phones at the Kapalua–West Maui Airport.

Dollar Rent A Car is the sole company in Hana. ~ 808-248-8237, 800-800-4000.

Kihei is served by **Avis Rent A Car**. ~ 808-874-4077, 800-331-1212. For a cheaper alternative, try **Kihei Rent A Car**. ~ 808-879-7257, 800-251-5288.

Note: Many rental agencies will forbid you from driving the road from Hana around the southeast side of the island because it is sometimes in poor condition.

(For car and jeep rentals on Molokai or Lanai, see the individual chapters.)

JEEP RENTALS

Generally, I don't recommend renting a jeep. They're more expensive and less comfortable than automobiles, and won't get you to very many more interesting spots. In addition, the rental car collision insurance provided by most credit cards does not cover jeeps. If you hit the rainy season though, and want to explore the back roads, it can't hurt. Except in extremely wet weather when roads are muddy, all the places mentioned in this book can be reached by conventional car.

Log on to www.visit maui.com for extensive visitor websites and information.

If, like most visitors to Maui, you arrive at the airport in Kahului, you certainly won't want for car rental agencies. There are quite a few with booths right at the airport. A number of others are located around town.

There are several companies on the island of Maui that rent four-wheel-drive vehicles. Some outfits offering jeeps are **Adventures Rent A Jeep** (190 Papa Place, Kahului; 808-877-6626, 800-701-5337) and **Budget Rent A Car** (808-871-8811, 808-661-8721, 800-527-0700).

MOTOR SCOOTER RENTALS

A & B Moped Rental rents mopeds by the hour. These vehicles provide an exhilarating and economical way to explore the area. Though they are not intended for long trips or busy roadways, they're ideal for short jaunts to the beach. ~ 3481 Lower Honoapiilani Highway, Honokowai; 808-669-0027.

PUBLIC TRANSIT

There is almost no general transportation on Maui and the little that is provided lies concentrated in one small sector of the island. The **West Maui Shuttle** travels between Wailea, Lahaina, Kaanapali and Kapalua with stops at major resorts, Lahaina Harbor, the Sugar Cane Train and Whalers Village. ~ 808-877-7308. **Akina Bus Service** (808-879-2828) operates buses in the Wailea area.

Speedy Shuttle (808-875-8070) offers transportation from Kahului Airport to resorts on the west to the southside of the island. (It's recommended that you call at least a day in advance, though last-minute pickups are available.)

AERIAL TOURS

Much of Maui's best scenery is reached via serpentine roads or steep mountain drives. While the views are stunning, the best way to get a bird's-eye view is from the air. Helicopters, fixed-wing aircraft and gliders all make it easy to see the volcanic uplands, waterfall splashed cliffs and dreamy back-country beaches.

There's also a west Maui/Molokai flight highlighting the tallest waterfall in the state, Molokai's Kahiwa. **Hawaii Helicopters** offers tours ranging from 30 minutes to three hours. The longer tours stop in Hana for 45 minutes to three hours, offering a chance to explore this verdant area's beaches and waterfalls via limousine van. ~ Kahului Heliport; 808-877-3900.

AlexAir, a Maui-based helicopter-tour company, offers pilot-to-passenger radio communication on all of its flights. They also offer choreographed CD music on the trips, and a free (two-for-one) sunset catamaran cruise. ~ Kahului Heliport; 808-871-0792, 888-418-8458.

If you prefer to see Maui and a bit more, check out **Paragon Air**. Travel aboard a nine-passenger Piper Navajo Chieftain or a six-passenger Partenavia over Maui to the Big Island or Molokai. On Molokai, passengers land and journey by foot or mule to visit Kalaupapa, the leper colony made famous by the work of Father Damien. ~ Kahului Airport; 808-244-3356, 800-428-1231, fax 808-573-8218.

Sunshine Helicopters offers tours that include whale watching when in season, waterfalls, island circumnavigation and private charters. ~ Kahului Heliport; 808-871-0722, 800-544-2520.

Another option is **Blue Hawaiian Helicopters**, a company that has accumulated its share of accolades. They offer a standard roster of tours. ~ Kahului Heliport; 808-871-8844, 800-745-2583.

TWO

The Land
and Outdoor Adventures

Maui is part of the Hawaiian archipelago that stretches more than 1500 miles across the North Pacific Ocean. Composed of 132 islands, Hawaii has eight major islands, including Maui, clustered at the southeastern end of the chain. Together these larger islands are about the size of Connecticut and Rhode Island combined. Only seven are inhabited: the eighth, Kahoolawe, served until recently as a bombing range for the U.S. Navy. Another island, Niihau, is privately owned and off-limits to the public.

Located 2500 miles southwest of Los Angeles, Maui is on the same 20th latitude as Hong Kong and Mexico City. It's two hours earlier in Maui than in Los Angeles, four hours before Chicago and five hours earlier than New York. Since Hawaii does not practice daylight-saving, this time difference becomes one hour greater during the summer months.

Maui, in a sense, is a small continent. Volcanic mountains rise in the interior, while the coastline is fringed with coral reefs and white-sand beaches. The northeastern face, buffeted by trade winds, is the wet side. The contrast between this side and the island's southwestern sector is sometimes startling. Maui's Hana region, for instance, is one of the wettest spots in the United States, but the southern side of the island resembles Arizona. Dense rainforests in the northeast are teeming with exotic tropical plants, while across the island you're liable to see cactus growing in a barren landscape!

For years, sugar was king in Maui, the most lucrative part of the island's economy. Today, pineapple remains the surviving plantation crop, with flower farms, onion farms and other produce venues being small-scale replacements to sugar. Statewide, tourism is number one. More than 2.4 million travelers worldwide visit Maui every year. It's now a $10.9 billion business that expanded exponentially during the 1970s and 1980s.

Marijuana is now Hawaii's foremost cash crop, flourishing on Maui, Hawaii and Kauai and representing a $3.4 billion business. Of course, no Chamber of

Commerce report will list the demon weed as Hawaii's prime crop. But while the $200 million sugar industry is small potatoes compared with tourism, Hawaii remains one of America's largest sugar-producing states. However, sugar, like everything on Maui and elsewhere in the islands, is threatened by urban development. A ton of water is required to produce a pound of sugar.

Pineapple's future remains uncertain. Stiff competition from the Philippines, where labor is cheap and easily exploitable, has reduced pineapple plantations on Maui and other islands to a few relatively small operations.

The islands do a booming business in macadamia nuts, orchids, anthuriums, guava nectar and passion-fruit juice. Together, with the cattle business, these industries have created a viable economy in the 50th state, though an economy many consider too dependent on tourism. The per capita income on Maui and throughout Hawaii is greater than the national average, and the standard of living is generally higher.

More than 25 million years ago a fissure opened along the Pacific **GEOLOGY** floor. Beneath tons of seawater molten lava poured from the rift. This liquid basalt, oozing from a hot spot in the earth's center, created a crater along the ocean bottom. As the tectonic plate that comprises the ocean floor drifted over the earth's hot spot, numerous other craters appeared. Slowly, in the seemingly endless procession of geologic time, a chain of volcanic islands, now stretching almost 2000 miles and including the idyllic island of Maui, has emerged from the sea.

On the continents it was also a period of terrible upheaval. The Himalayas, Alps and Andes were rising, but these great chains would reach their peaks long before the Pacific mountains even touched sea level. Not until about 25 million years ago did the first of these underwater volcanoes, today's Kure and Midway atolls, break the surface and become islands. It was not until about five million years ago that the first of the main islands of the archipelago, Niihau and Kauai, broke the surface to become high islands.

Maui's first volcano, now the West Maui Mountains, rose above the waves about two million years ago. It was another million years before Haleakala first appeared. Gradually, lava flows from these two firepits joined together, creating the archipelago's second-largest island.

For many millennia, the mountains continued to grow. The forces of erosion cut into them, creating knife-edged cliffs and deep valleys. Then plants began germinating: mosses and ferns, springing from windblown spores, were probably first, followed by seed plants carried by migrating birds and on ocean currents. The steep-walled valleys provided natural greenhouses in which unique species evolved, while transoceanic winds swept insects and other life from the continents.

Some islands never survived this birth process: the ocean simply washed them away. The first islands that did endure, at the northwestern end of the Hawaiian chain, proved to be the smallest. Today these islands, with the exception of Midway, are barren uninhabited atolls. The volcanoes of Maui and its sister islands, far to the southeast, became the mountainous archipelago generally known as the Hawaiian Islands.

FLORA   Many of the plants you'll see on Maui are not indigenous. In fact, much of the lush vegetation of this tropical island found its way here from locations all over the world. Sea winds, birds and seafaring settlers brought many of the seeds, plants, flowers and trees from the islands of the South Pacific, as well as from other, more distant regions. Over time, some plants adapted to Maui's unique ecosystem and climate, creating strange new lineages and evolving into a completely new ecosystem. This process has long interested scientists, who consider the Hawaiian Islands one of the best natural labs for studies of plant evolution.

With several distinct biological regions, there's much more to Maui than lush tropics. Rainforests give way to dry forests, and to coastal habitats where the vegetation is specially suited to withstand wind and salt. Higher in altitude are the bogs, pools of standing water containing rare life forms that have been forced to adapt to a difficult environment. Highest in altitude is the alpine zone, consisting of bare volcanic surfaces scattered with clumps of low-growing herbs and shrubs. Subzero temperatures, frost and even snow help keep this region desolate.

Sugar cane arrived in Hawaii with the first Polynesian settlers, who appreciated its sweet juices. By the late 1800s, sugar cane was well established as a lucrative crop. The pineapple was first planted on Maui in 1903 and the island now harvests over 50 percent of the state's pineapples. A member of the bromeliad family, this spiky plant is actually a collection of beautiful pink, blue and purple flowers, each of which develops into a fruitlet. The pineapple is a collection of these fruitlets, grown together into a single fruit that takes 14 to 17 months to mature. Sugar cane and pineapple are still the main crops on Maui, although competition from other countries and environmental problems caused by pesticides have taken their toll.

Visitors to Maui will find the island a perpetual flower show. Two flowers the island is particularly known for are the protea and the carnation. Originally from Australia and South Africa, the protea comes in varying shapes, sizes and colors, each unique. They are found mostly on the leeward slopes of Haleakala, where the altitude, cool nights and dry volcanic soil provide the perfect growing conditions for this exotic plant. Carnations grow in abundance in the Kula area, where the fields are filled with color and the air is often heady with the flowers' distinctive perfume. But it is the sweetly scented plumeria, delicate orchids, exotic ginger, showy birds of paradise, highly fragrant gardenias and the brightly hued hibiscus that run riot on Maui and add color and fragrance to the island. Scarlet and purple bougainvillea vines, and the aromatic lantana, with its dense clusters of flowers, are also found in abundance.

One of Maui's unique plants is the silversword. Delicate looking, this silvery green plant is actually very hardy. It thrives on the moonscape of Haleakala, 6000 to 10,000 feet above sea level. Very adaptable, it can survive in extreme hot and cold temperatures with little moisture. Its silvery hairs reflect the sun and its leaves curl inward, protecting the stalk and creating a sort of bowl where rain is collected and stored. The plant lives from five to more than thirty years, waiting until the right moment before sprouting a three- to six-foot stalk composed of hundreds of small, reddish flowers—and then it dies. In the same family as the sunflower, this particular type of silversword lives only on Haleakala and has been close to extinction for many years. Now protected, it is currently making a comeback.

> Each Hawaiian island has its own official flower; the Valley Isle's blossom is the pink Maui rose.

Although many people equate the tropics with the swaying palm tree, Maui is home to a variety of exotic trees. The famed banyan tree, known for pillarlike aerial roots that grow vertically downward from the branches, spreads to form a natural canopy. When the roots touch the ground, they thicken, providing support for the tree's branches to continue expanding. The candlenut tree, originally brought to Hawaii from the South Pacific islands, is big, bushy and prized for its nuts, which can be used for oil or polished and strung together to make leis. With its cascades of bright yellow or pink flowers, the cassia tree earns its moniker—the shower tree. Covered with tiny pink blossoms, the canopied monkeypod tree has fernlike leaves that close up at night.

Found in a variety of shapes and sizes, the ubiquitous palm does indeed sway to the breezes on white-sand beaches, but it also comes in a short, stubby form featuring more frond than trunk. The fruit, or nuts, of these trees are prized for their oil, which can be utilized for making everything from margarine to soap. The wood (rattan, for example) is often used for making furniture.

FRUITS AND VEGETABLES There's a lot more to Maui's tropical wonderland than gorgeous flowers and overgrown rainforests. The island is also teeming with edible plants. Roots, fruits, vegetables, herbs and spices grow like weeds from the shoreline to the mountains. Following is a list of some of the more commonly found.

Avocado: Covered with either a tough green or purple skin, this pear-shaped fruit can weigh as much as three pounds. It grows on 10- to 40-foot-high trees, and ripens from June through November.

Bamboo: The bamboo plant is actually a grass with a sweet root that is edible and a long stem frequently used for making furniture. Often exceeding eight feet in height, bamboo is green until picked, when it turns a golden brown.

Banana: Polynesians use banana trees not only for food but also for clothing, medicines, dyes and even alcohol. The fruit, which grows upside down on broad-leaved trees, can be harvested as soon as the first banana in the bunch turns yellow.

Breadfruit: This large round fruit grows on trees that reach up to 60 feet in height. Breadfruit must be boiled, baked or fried.

Coconut: The coconut tree is probably the most important plant in the entire Pacific. Every part of the towering palm is used. Most people are concerned only with the hard brown nut, which yields delicious milk as well as a tasty meat. If the coconut is still green, the meat is a succulent jellylike substance. Otherwise, it's a hard but delicious white rind.

Guava: A roundish yellow fruit that grows on a small shrub or tree, guavas are extremely abundant in the wild. They ripen between June and October.

Mango: Known as the king of fruits, the mango grows on tall shade trees. The oblong fruit ripens in the spring and summer.

Maui onion: Resembling an ordinary yellow onion in size and color, these bulbs are uncommonly sweet and mild. They are grown on the south side of Haleakala in rich volcanic soil, and enjoy enough sun and altitude to make them very sweet. A member of the lily family, the Maui onion is best eaten raw.

Mountain apple: This sweet fruit grows in damp, shaded valleys at an elevation of about 1800 feet. The flowers resemble fluffy crimson balls; the fruit, which ripens from July to December, is also a rich red color.

SHORELINE HARVEST

Few Westerners think of seaweed as food, but it's very popular among the Japanese, and it once served as an integral part of the Hawaiian diet. It's extremely nutritious, easy to gather and very plentiful. Rocky shores are the best places to find the edible species of seaweed. Some of them float in to shore and can be picked up; other species cling stubbornly to rocks and must be freed with a knife; still others grow in sand or mud. Low tide is the best time to collect seaweed: more plants are exposed, and some can be taken without even getting your feet wet.

Papaya: This delicious fruit, which is picked as it begins to turn yellow, grows on unbranched trees. The sweet flesh can be bright orange or coral pink in color. Summer is the peak harvesting season.

Passion fruit: Known as *lilikoi* on the islands, this tasty yellow fruit is oval in shape and grows to a length of about two or three inches. It's produced on a vine and ripens in summer or fall.

Taro: The tuberous root of this Hawaiian staple is pounded, then made into a grayish-purple paste known as *poi*. One of the most nutritious foods, it has a rather bland taste. The plant has wide, shiny, thick leaves with reddish stems; the root is white with purple veins.

FAUNA

On Maui, it seems there is more wildlife in the water and air than on land. A scuba diver's paradise, the ocean is a promised land for many creatures. Coral, colorful fish and migrating whales are only part of this underwater community. Sadly, many of Hawaii's coral reefs have been dying mysteriously in the last few years. No one is sure why, but many believe this is partially due to runoff from pesticides used in agriculture.

Not many wild four-footed creatures roam the island. Deer, feral goats and pigs were brought to the islands early on and have found a home in the forests. Some good news for people fearful of snakes: There is nary a serpent (or a sea serpent) on the island, although lizards such as skinks and geckos abound.

One can only hope that with the renewed interest in Hawaiian culture, and growing environmental awareness, Hawaii's plants and animals will continue to exist as they have for centuries.

WHALES AND DOLPHINS   For adventure lovers, Maui, and to a lesser extent the Big Island, offer excellent opportunities for whale watching. Every year, humpback whales converge in the warm waters off the islands to give birth to their calves. Beginning their migration in Alaska, they can be spotted in Hawaiian waters from November through May. The humpback, named for its practice of showing its dorsal fin when diving, is quite easy to spy. They feed in shallow waters, usually diving for periods of no longer than 15 minutes. They often sleep on the surface and breathe fairly frequently. Unlike other whales, humpbacks have the ability to sing. Loud and powerful, their songs carry above and below the water for miles. The songs change every year, yet, incredibly, all the whales always seem to know the current one. Quite playful, they can be seen leaping, splashing and flapping their 15-foot tails over their backs. The best time for whale watching is from January to April.

Spinner dolphins are also favorites among visitors. Named for their "spinning" habit, they can revolve as many as six times during one leap. They resemble the spotted dolphin, another frequenter of Hawaiian waters, but are more likely to venture closer to the shore. Dolphins have clocked in with speeds ranging from 9 to 25 mph, a feat they often achieve by propelling themselves out of the water (or even riding the bow wave of a ship). Their thick, glandless skin also contributes to this agility. The skin is kept smooth by constant renewal and sloughing (bottlenoses replace their epidermis every two hours). Playful and intelligent, dolphins are a joy to watch. Many research centers are investigating the mammals' ability to imitate, learn and communicate; some believe that dolphin intelligence may be comparable to that of humans.

FISH It'll come as no surprise to anyone that Maui's waters literally brim with an extraordinary assortment of fish—over 400 different species, in fact.

The goatfish, with more than 50 species in its family worldwide, boasts at least ten in Maui waters. This bottom dweller is recognized by a pair of whiskers, used as feelers for searching out food, that are attached to its lower jaw. The *moano* sports two stripes across its back and has shorter whiskers. The red-and-black banded goatfish has a multihued color scheme that also includes yellow and white markings; its light yellow whiskers are quite long. The head of the goatfish is considered poisonous and is not eaten.

Occasionally found on the sharper end of your line is the bonefish, or *oio*. One of the best game fish in the area, its head extends past its mouth to form a somewhat transparent snout. The *awa*, or milkfish, is another common catch. This silvery, fork-tailed fish can grow longer than three feet and puts up a good fight.

A kaleidoscope of brilliantly colored specimens can be viewed around the reefs of Maui; you'll feel like you're in a technicolor movie when snorkeling. Over 30 known species of butterfly fish are found in this area. Highlighted in yellow, orange, red, blue, black and white, they swim in groups of two and three. The long, tubular body of the needlefish, or *aha*, can reach up to 40 inches in length; this greenish, silvery species is nearly translucent. The masked angelfish flits around in deeper waters on the outer edge of reefs. The imperial angelfish is distinguishable by fantastic color patterns of dark blue hues. The Hawaiian fish with the longest name, the colorful *humuhumunukunukuapuaa*, is found in the shallow waters along the outer fringes of reefs.

Sharks, unlike fish, have skeletons made of cartilage; the hardest parts of their bodies are their teeth (once used as tools by the Hawaiians). If you spend a lot of time in the water, you may spot a shark. But not to worry; Hawaiian waters are just about the safest around. The harmless, commonly seen blacktipped and whitetipped reef sharks (named for the color of their fins) are as concerned about your activities as you are about theirs. The gray reef shark (gray back, white belly with a black tail) and tiger shark, however, are predatory and aggressive, but they are rarely encountered.

Another cartilaginous creature you might see in shallow water near the shoreline is the manta ray, a "winged" plankton feeder with two appendages on either side of its head that work to direct food into its mouth. The eagle ray, a bottom dweller featuring "wings" and a tail longer than its body, feeds in shallow coastal waters. When it's not feeding, it lies on the ocean floor and covers itself with a light layer of sand. Since some eagle rays have stingers, take precautions by shuffling the sand as you walk. Not only will you not be impaled, you will also be less likely to squash smaller, unsuspecting sea creatures.

While on Maui, you'll inevitably see fish out of water as well—on your plate. The purple-blue-green-hued mahimahi, or dolphin fish, can reach six feet and 70 pounds. The *opakapaka* is another common dish and resides in the deeper, offshore waters beyond the reef. This small-scaled snapper is a reddish-olive color and can grow up to four feet long. Elongated with a sharply pointed head, the *ono* (also known as the wahoo) is a carnivorous, savage striped fish with dark blue and silver coloring. Perhaps the most ubiquitous fish is the ahi, or tuna, often used for sashimi.

REPTILES   Green sea turtles are common on all of the Hawaiian islands, although this was not always the case. Due to the popularity of their shells, they spent many years on the endangered species list, but are now making a comeback. Measuring three to four feet in diameter, these large reptiles frolic in saltwater only, and are often visible from the shore.

BIRDS   Maui is also home to many rare and endangered birds. Like the flora, the birds on this island are highly specialized. Hawaii's state bird, the nene, or Hawaiian goose, is a cousin to the Canadian goose and has strong pair bondings. Extinct on Maui for many years, several nenes were reintroduced here in the late 1960s. There's still some doubt as to whether they will produce a self-sustaining wild population. They currently live in the wild

PRESERVING MAUI

With the current interest in ecology, even Maui's resorts are becoming environmentally aware. Most have instituted recycling and conservation programs. The Maui Land and Pineapple Company, owner of Kapalua, has awarded The Nature Conservancy a conservancy easement on 8000 acres on the slopes of Puu Kukui, a western Maui summit. The Ritz-Carlton hotel offers a variety of "eco-packages," where a dollar of each guest's bill is donated to The Nature Conservancy, and the Aston Wailea Resort saves seven million gallons of water annually by recycling and is a pesticide-free resort.

in the West Maui Mountains, on the Big Island and on Kauai. Once thought to be native to high-elevation habitats, biologists now believe that these rare birds may be more suited to a sea-level environment. The slopes of Haleakala are also home to two other endangered birds: the crested honeycreeper and the parrotbill.

There *are* a few birds native to Hawaii that have thus far avoided the endangered species list. Two of the most common birds are the yellow-green *amakihi* and the red *iiwi*.

Known in Hawaiian mythology for its protective powers, the *pueo*, or Hawaiian owl, a brown-and-white-feathered bird, resides in Haleakala crater. The *koae kea*, or "tropic bird," also lives on Haleakala and in the crater. Resembling a seagull in size, it has a long, thin white tail and a striking striping pattern on the back of the wings.

If you see an *iwa* (frigate), be careful not to point at it. Legend has it that it's bad luck.

Another common bird is the *iwa*, or frigate, a very large creature measuring three to four feet in length, with a wing span averaging seven feet. The males are solid black, while the females have a large white patch on their chest and tail. A predatory bird, they're easy to spot raiding the nesting colonies of other birds along the offshore rocks. Other birds that make Maui their home are the Hawaiian stilt and the Hawaiian coot—both water birds—along with the black noddy, American plover and wedge-tailed shearwater.

Outdoor Adventures

The opportunities for adventuring on the Valley Isle are numerous and the conditions for several activities are outstanding. Whale watching, for example, is top-notch on Maui as humpbacks return each year to the waters off Lahaina to give birth. For cyclists, there are thrilling rides down the slopes of Haleakala and challenging courses on Hana's curving coast. Maui is also home to several of the world's premier windsurfing spots including Hookipa Beach on the island's north shore. In addition, Maui has more miles of swimmable beach than any of the other islands in the chain.

CAMPING

Camping on Maui usually means pitching a tent, reserving a cabin or renting a camper. Throughout the island there are secluded spots and beaches, and numerous county, state and federal parks. All the campsites, together with hiking trails, are described in the following chapters; it's a good idea to consult those detailed listings when planning your trip.

Before you set out to camp, there are a few very important matters that I want to explain more fully. First, bring a campstove: firewood is scarce in most areas and soaking wet in others.

Another problem that you're likely to encounter are those nasty varmints that buzz in your ear just as you're falling asleep —mosquitoes. Maui contains neither snakes nor poison ivy, but it has plenty of these dive-bombing pests. Like me, you probably consider that it's always open season on the little bastards.

With most of the archipelago's other species, however, you'll have to be a careful conservationist. You'll be sharing the wilderness with pigs, goats, tropical birds, deer and mongooses, as well as a spectacular array of exotic and indigenous plants. They exist in one of the world's most delicate ecological balances. There are more endangered species in Hawaii than in all the rest of the United States. So keep in mind the maxim that the Hawaiians try to follow. *Ua mau ke ea o ka aina i ka pono:* The life of the land is preserved in righteousness.

Though extremely popular with adventurers, Maui has very few official campsites. The laws restricting camping here are more strictly enforced than on other islands. The emphasis on this boom island favors condominiums and resort hotels rather than outdoor living, but you can still escape the concrete congestion at several parks and unofficial campsites (including one of the most spectacular tenting areas in all Hawaii—Haleakala Wilderness Area).

Camping at **county parks** requires a permit. These are issued for a maximum of three consecutive nights at each campsite, and cost $3 per person per night, children 50¢. Permits can be obtained at War Memorial Gym adjacent to Baldwin High School, Route 32, Wailuku, or by writing the Department of Parks and Recreation Permit Department, 1580 Kaahumanu Avenue, Wailuku, Maui, HI 96793; 808-270-7389.

State park permits are free and allow camping for five days. They can be obtained at the Division of State Parks in the State Building, High Street, Wailuku, or by writing the Division of State Parks. ~ 54 South High Street, Room 101, Wailuku, Maui, HI 96793. You can also rent cabins at Waianapanapa and Polipoli state parks through this office.

If you plan on camping in the Haleakala Wilderness Area, you must obtain a permit on the day you are camping from Haleakala National Park headquarters, located on the way to the valley. These permits are allocated on a first-come, first-served basis.

Remember, rainfall is heavy along the northeast shore around Hana, but infrequent on the south coast. Also, Haleakala gets quite cold; you'll need heavy clothing and sleeping gear.

It is best to bring along your own camping gear, but in a pinch check **Gaspro Inc.** ~ 365 Hanakai Street, Kahului; 808-877-0056. **Sears** at Kahului's Kaahumanu Center also carries camping gear. ~ 275 Kaahumanu Avenue, Kahului; 808-877-2206.

More and more adventure tours are becoming eco-tours. Combining the usual tourist activities with a dose of conservation, eco-tours are a lovely way to soak up the beauty and culture of Hawaii while "leaving only footprints." **ECO-TOURS**

Mango Mitch Tropical Ecotours, a pioneer of Hawaiian nature tours, will tailor their tours to you but they won't take groups of more than five—the better to keep it personal. They have snorkeling, whale watching and various rainforest excursions. ~ 220 Ulana Street, Makawao; 808-573-1848; www.mauigateway.com/~mangos.

The flora and fauna of Maui, as well as traces of the ancient Polynesians, are the focus of **Paths in Paradise**. The company's owner/operator is an environmentalist who will lead you on hikes to explore Hawaii's endangered nature. They have seven- and fourteen-day trips that include accommodations, hiking, snorkeling and a luau show. Shorter trips are also available, as are cultural trips to a hula school. ~ P.O. Box 667, Makawao, HI 96768; 808-573-0094; www.mauibirdhikes.com.

An excellent educational opportunity awaits you at the **Ocean Project**, a marine research center studying the coral reefs of Maui. They have extensive knowledge and will build their events around your interests. At the beach, they'll give you a "class" in the subject of your choice (for example, identification of fish and coral species or the behavior of giant green sea turtles), and then take you snorkeling for an up-close look at what you just learned. The sessions are about two to three hours long and will change the way you view those pretty-colored fish. ~ Lahaina; 808-661-6706.

DIVING   Maui offers a wide variety of snorkeling and diving opportunities ranging from Black Rock off Kaanapali to Honolua Bay not to mention Olowalu, Ahihi–Kinau Natural Area Reserve and Ulua Beach. While most of the dive operators are located near the island's south coast resorts, there are also good diving and snorkeling opportunities on the north shore at Paia's Baldwin Beach Park, as well as Hana's Waianapanapa State Park. From Maui it's also easy to reach neighboring destinations such as the Molokini Crater Marine Preserve and reefs off Lanai.

Molokini, a crescent-shaped crater off Maui's southern coast, offers one of the island's great snorkeling adventures. Every day dozens of boatloads of people pull up to dive the remarkably clear waters. Visibility typically ranges between 80 and 150 feet, conditions so clear you can spot fish before even entering the water. During winter months, you're also likely to see the humpback whales cavorting nearby.

LAHAINA   **Extended Horizons** offers half-day excursions to the Molokini crater and Lanai's west coast. Dive through caverns and lava tubes in search of dolphins, turtles and whales. ~ Mala Wharf, Lahaina; 808-667-0611, 888-348-3628; www.scubadive maui.com.

Ocean Riders Adventure Rafting specializes in snorkeling trips; set out from Maui to Lanai or Molokai on full-day snorkel

The New Travel

Travel today is becoming a personal art fo... longer serves as just a place to relax: it'... To many, this new wave in travel customs is... and involves trekking glaciers or sweeping ... others, it connotes nothing more daring than a restful spell in a ... resort. Actually, it's a state of mind, a willingness not only to accept but seek out the uncommon and unique.

Few places in the world are more conducive to this imaginative new travel than Maui. Several organizations on the island cater specifically to people who want to add local customs and unusual adventures to their vacation itineraries.

The Nature Conservancy of Hawaii conducts natural history day hikes of Maui and Molokai. Led by expert guides, small groups explore untrammeled beaches, a rainforest and an ancient bog. The tours provide a singular insight into the plant and animal life of the islands. Reservations should be made at least one month in advance. ~ P.O. Box 1716, Makawao, Maui, HI 96768, 808-572-7849; and P.O. Box 220, Kuala-puu, Molokai, HI 96757, 808-553-5236; www.nature.org.

Hawaiian Adventure Tours features a ten-day tour of Kauai, Maui and the Big Island, including hiking and snorkeling. It offers daily whale-watching trips. ~ P.O. Box 1269, Kapaa, HI 96755; 808-889-0227, 800-659-3544; www.hawaiianadventuretours.com.

Maui Hiking Safaris sets out from Kahului at 8 a.m. and 2 p.m. on full- and half-day adventures. With a guide and no more than six hikers, they explore the 1790 lava flow as well as rainforests and natural pools. The guides identify local flora and talk about Hawaiiana and volcanology. ~ P.O. Box 11198, Lahaina, HI 96761; 808-573-0168, 888-445-3963, fax 808-572-3037; www.mauihikingsafaris.com, e-mail mhs@maui.net.

Open Eye Tours & Photos, led by nature photographer Barry Fried, provides custom-designed educational walking tours from a base in Maui's Upcountry. On the menu of outdoor adventures are visits to sacred healing places, gardens, petroglyphs, rainforests and, of course, some very photogenic waterfalls. ~ P.O. Box 324, Makawao, HI 96768; 808-572-3483 or 808-280-5299; www.openeyetours.com, e-mail barry@openeyetours.com.

When you're ready to take up the challenge of this new style of free-wheeling travel, check with these outfits. Or plan your own trip.

ps accompanied by schools of tropical fish and topped with a continental breakfast and lunch. ~ Mala Wharf, Lahaina; 808-661-3586.

Lahaina Divers Inc. is another well-liked dive operator. Their retail store provides equipment and accessories. Scuba classes and trips are available year round depending on the weather. Equipment repair and service are also available. ~ 143 Dickenson Street, Lahaina; 808-667-7496.

KIHEI–WAILEA–MAKENA AREA **Maui Classic Charters** offers half-day dives into the Molokini crater along with schooner excursions. ~ 1215 South Kihei Road, Kihei; 808-879-8188; www.mauicharters.com.

Another recommended tour operator that also rents snorkel and scuba equipment is **Maui Dive Shop**, which has six locations in Maui. ~ 1455 South Kihei Road, Kihei; 808-879-1175, 800-542-3483; www.mauidiveshop.com.

Well-known by underwater photographers, **Mike Severns Diving** runs trips for certified divers to Molokini and Makena. Dives focus on the southwest rift of Haleakala, a fascinating place to study marine life. Led by informative biologists, these trips are an excellent way to see Maui's hidden marine life. ~ Kihei Boat Ramp, Kihei; 808-879-6596; www.mikesevernsdiving.com.

Scuba Shack features scuba and snorkeling trips to Molokini Crater. Visibility of 150 feet makes this marine reserve a favorite place to splash down. ~ 2349 South Kihei Road, Kihei; 808-891-0500; www.scubashack.com.

Maui Sun Divers provides all gear and offers everything from beginner trips to certification classes to night dives. A true part

SNORKELING SAFETY TIPS

Don't miss out on an opportunity to explore the depths of Maui's busy ocean life. You're apt to find fish and coral in a dazzling array of colors, sizes and shapes. But take the following precautions before you dip into the water:

- always snorkel with someone else
- avoid big waves, surfers and windy conditions
- bring a flotation device like an inner tube, noodle or life jacket, especially if you are with kids or are a novice swimmer
- don't poke your hands into crevices or cracks in a reef (an eel hangout)
- look up now and again to watch the weather conditions—if you're having trouble getting back to shore because the waves are too high, wait for the set to break
- wear lots of waterproof sunscreen (and perhaps a T-shirt) because your back will be lobster red if you don't!

of "Hidden Hawaii," you won't find them on land. They will take you anywhere around the island, weather permitting. ~ Kihei; 877-879-3337; www.mauisundivers.com.

Experienced divers should sign on with **Ed Robinson's Diving Adventures**. A prominent oceanic photographer, Robinson leads half-day scuba excursions aboard the *Seadiver II* and *Sea Spirit* to the Lanai Cathedrals, Molokini and other favored dive sites. ~ Kihei; 808-879-3584; www.mauiscuba.com.

Makena Boat Partners operates the 46-foot *Kai Kanani,* which departs from Makena Beach, and goes closer to the largely submerged volcano than other touring vessels. Prices include all equipment, food and drink. ~ 808-879-7218.

If you must go down to the sea again, why not do it on a board? For surfing, Maalaea, Honolua Bay and Hookipa are consistent world-class spots. La Perouse is an expert's heaven.

Pro windsurfers and kitesurfers (a relatively new sport, this one is just what it sounds like) will want to head to Hookipa. Pros at other things should confine their windsurfing and kitesurfing to Kanaha, Kihei and Spreckelsville.

SURFING, WIND-SURFING & KITE-SURFING

LAHAINA   **Goofy Fool** has a portable surfing site they'll outfit you from; they also give beginner- to advanced-level lessons and lead surf safaris. ~ 505 French Street, Lahaina; 808-244-9283.

KAANAPALI-KAPALUA AREA   **Maui Ocean Activities** offers surfing and windsurfing lessons on the adjacent beach. Ninety-minute windsurfing lessons come with a guarantee of success. Four-person surfing classes are also offered, weather permitting. Rentals are available. ~ Whalers Village, Kaanapali; Maui Ocean Activities reservations 808-667-2001, fax 808-667-5164; www.mauiwatersports.com, e-mail beaches@maui.net.

KAHULUI-WAILUKU AREA   **Maui Windsurf Company** can help work windsurfing into your visit, either with a car rack and sails or with lessons. Instruction is held in the calmer waters at Kanaha, near the airport. Hookipa's more powerful winds are recommended only for experts. ~ 22 Hana Highway, Kahului; 808-877-4816, 800-872-0999; www.mauiwindsurf.com.

At **Second Wind Sail Surf & Kite**, you can get everything you need for a day (or longer) of surfing, windsurfing or kitesurfing. They offer equipment rental and sales, extensive instruction and even car rentals. ~ 111 Hana Highway, Kahului; 808-877-7467; www.secondwindmaui.com.

You can buy surfing gear at **Lightning Bolt**, the oldest surf shop on Maui. ~ 55 Kaahumanu Avenue, Kahului; 808-877-3484.

HANA AREA   **Kai Nalu Surf Tours** will take you on a four-day excursion to lesser-known Maui and Oahu surfing spots. ~ 536 Kahua Place, Paia; 808-579-9937.

FISHING The deep blue sea around Maui can be nirvana for sportfishing enthusiasts. For deep-sea fishing you'll have to charter a boat, and freshwater angling requires a license, which can be obtained at sportfishing stores. For information on seasons, licenses and official regulations, check with the Aquatic Resources Division of the State Department of Land & Natural Resources. Choose between party boats, diesel cruisers and yachts custom-designed for trolling. All outfits provide equipment and bait. Just bring your own food and drinks and you're in business. Occasionally, your skipper may head for the productive game fishing waters between Maui and the Big Island. It's a treacherous channel, however, so you're more likely to fish the leeward side of the island or off neighboring Lanai.

There is also good fishing from the shore in many places. For information on the best spots, ask at local fishing stores, or try the following beaches: Hoaloha Park, Launiupoko State Wayside Park, Honokowai Beach Park, D. T. Fleming Park, Honokohau Beach, Keawakapu Beach, Poolenalena Beach Park, Black Sands Beach, Little Beach and Waianapanapa State Park.

Beaches and rocky points are usually good places to surf-cast; the best times are during the incoming and outgoing tides. Successful baits include octopus, eel, lobster, crab, frozen shrimp and sea worms. You can also fish with lures. The ancient Hawaiians used pearl shells to attract the fish and hooks, some made from human bones, to snare them. Your friends will probably be quite content to see you angling with store-bought artificial lures.

LAHAINA Ideal for groups up to four, **Robalo-One** is a stable 23-foot vessel that hits speeds up to 40 miles per hour in pursuit of bottomfish. You'll catch snapper, wrasse, barracuda or jack crevalle on half-day trips. ~ 645 Lahaina Harbor; 808-661-0480.

SPELUNKING

Lava tubes form when surface lava hardens and the flowing lava continues to drain downslope through a tube. **Hana Cave Tours** offers excursions through a two-mile-long lava tube that winds its way 30 to 40 feet below the surface. You'll be fully outfitted with a hard hat, gloves, a fanny pack with water, and a powerful flashlight that illuminates even the largest caverns in this long, linear cave. There are one- and two-hour tours, each taking in more of the cave system, all with plenty of interesting detail about what you're passing through. Snacks or meals are provided. Turn toward the ocean when you hit Ulaino Road, which is just before the Hana Airport Road. ~ P.O. Box 40, Hana, HI 96713; 808-248-7308; www.mauicave.com.

Luckey Strike Charters fishes for marlin, mahimahi, wahoo and tuna with light and medium tackle. Light-tackle bottom fishing is also available. ~ Lahaina Harbor; 808-661-4606; www.luckeystrike.com.

Hinatea is a sportfishing boat that offers trips into coastal waters. On half- and full-day trips you'll fish for marlin, tuna, mahimahi, wahoo and shark. ~ Lahaina Harbor; 808-667-7548.

KIHEI-WAILEA-MAKENA AREA   In the Kihei area, contact Carol Ann Charters for four-, six- and eight-hour fishing trips great for catching marlin, tuna, mahimahi and *ono*. She runs a 33-foot Bertrum. ~ Maalaea Harbor; 808-877-2181.

Rascal Charters fishes for ahi, *ono*, mahimahi and marlin. They also run four-, six- and eight-hour trips aboard a Bertrum, only Rascal's is 31 feet. Trips can include game or bottom fishing. ~ Maalaea Harbor; 808-874-8633.

TORCH-FISHING

The old Hawaiians often fished at night by torchlight. They fashioned torches by inserting nuts from the *kukui* tree into the hollow end of a bamboo pole, then lighting the flammable nuts. When fish swam like moths to the flame, the Hawaiians speared, clubbed or netted them. Today, locals use flashlights.

CRABBING

There are several important crab species in Hawaii. The most sought after are the Kona and Samoan varieties. Kona crabs are found in relatively deep water, and can usually be caught only from a boat. Samoan crabs inhabit sandy and muddy areas in bays and near river mouths. All that most local people use to catch them is a boat plus a net fastened to a round wire hoop secured by a string. The net is lowered to the bottom; then, after a crab has gone for the bait, the entire contraption is raised to the surface.

SQUIDDING

Between June and December, squidding is a popular Hawaiian sport. Actually, the term is a misnomer: squid inhabit deep water and are not usually hunted. What you'll really be after are octopuses. There are two varieties in Hawaii, both of which are commonly found in water three or four feet deep: the *hee*, a grayish-brown animal that changes color like a chameleon, and the *puloa*, a red-colored mollusk with white stripes on its head. Both are nocturnal and live in holes along coral reefs. The Hawaiians used to pick up the octopus, letting it cling to their chest and shoulders. When they were ready to bag their prize, they'd dispatch the creature by biting it between the eyes. Today, most people feel more comfortable spearing the beast.

SHELLFISH GATHERING

Among Hawaii's many natural food sources are the shellfish that inhabit coastal waters. Oysters and clams, which use their muscular feet to burrow into sand and soft mud, are collected along the bottom of Hawaii's bays. Spiny lobsters, rarely found in Hawaii waters, are illegal to spear but can be taken with short poles to which cable leaders and baited hooks are attached. You can also just grab them with a gloved hand but be careful—spiny lobsters live up to their name! Locals also gather limpets. These tiny black shellfish, locally known as *opihi*, cling tenaciously to rocks in the tidal zone. In areas of very rough surf, the Hawaiians gather them by leaping into the water after one set of waves breaks, then jumping out before the next set arrives. Being a coward myself, I simply order them in Hawaiian restaurants.

SHELL HUNTING

With over 1500 varieties of shells washing up on its beaches, Hawaii has some of the world's finest shelling. The miles of sandy beach along Maui's south shore are a prime area for handpicking free souvenirs. Along the shores are countless shell specimens with names like horned helmet, Hebrew cone, Hawaiian olive and Episcopal miter. Or you might find glass balls from Japan and sunbleached driftwood.

Hawkfish have eyes that work independently, allowing them to trick their prey.

Beachcombing is the easiest method of shell gathering. Take along a small container and stroll through the backwash of the waves, watching for ripples from shells lying under the sand. You can also dive in shallow water where the ocean's surge will uncover shells.

It's tempting to walk along the top of coral reefs seeking shells and other marine souvenirs, but these living formations maintain a delicate ecological balance. Reefs in Hawaii and all over the planet are dying because of such plunder. In order to protect this underwater world, try to collect only shells and souvenirs that are adrift on the beach and no longer necessary to the marine ecology.

The best shelling spots along Maui's south shore are Makena, Kihei beaches, Maalaea Bay, Olowalu, the sandy stretch from Kaanapali to Napili Bay, D. T. Fleming Park and Honolua Bay. On the north coast, the stretch from Waiehu to Waihee (west of Kahului) and the beaches around Hana are the choicest hunting grounds.

After heavy rainfall, watch near stream mouths for Hawaiian olivines and in stream beds for Maui diamonds. Olivines are small, semiprecious stones of an olive hue. Maui diamonds are quartz stones and make beautiful jewelry. The best places to go diamond hunting are near the Kahului Bay hotel strip and in Olowalu Strea.

SAILING & WHALE WATCHING

From mid-December until the middle of May, it is prime whale-watching season on Maui. Humpback whales, measuring about 40 feet and weighing over 40 tons, migrate as many as 4000 miles from their summer home in Alaska. On the journey south, they

Ocean Safety

For swimming, surfing and scuba diving, there's no place quite like Maui. With endless miles of white-sand beach, the island attracts aquatic enthusiasts worldwide. They come to enjoy Maui's colorful coral reefs and matchless surf conditions. Many water lovers, however, don't realize how dangerous the sea can be. Particularly in Hawaii, where waves can reach 30-foot heights and currents flow unobstructed for thousands of miles, the ocean is sometimes as treacherous as it is spectacular. Dozens of people drown every year in Hawaii, many others are dragged from the crushing surf with broken backs, and countless numbers sustain minor cuts and bruises.

These accidents can be avoided entirely if you approach the ocean with a respect for its power as well as an appreciation of its beauty. Just heed a few simple guidelines. First, never turn your back on the sea. Waves come in sets: one group may be small and quite harmless, but the next could be large enough to sweep you out to sea. Never swim alone.

Don't try to surf, or even bodysurf, until you're familiar with the sports' techniques and precautionary measures. Be extremely careful when the surf is high.

If you get caught in a rip current, don't swim against it: swim across it, parallel to the shore. These currents, running from the shore out to sea, can often be spotted by their ragged-looking surface water and foamy edges.

Around coral reefs, wear something to protect your feet against cuts. Recommended are inexpensive Japanese *tabis*, or reef slippers. If you do get a coral cut, clean it with hydrogen peroxide, then apply an antiseptic or antibiotic substance. This is also a good procedure for octopus bites.

When stung by a Portuguese man-of-war or a jellyfish, rub on Adolph's unseasoned meat tenderizer, leave it on the sting for 10 or 20 minutes, then rinse it off with alcohol. The old Hawaiian remedies, which are reputedly quite effective, involve applying urine or green papaya.

If you step on the sharp, painful spines of a sea urchin, soak the affected area in very hot water for 15 to 90 minutes. Another remedy calls for applying urine or undiluted vinegar. If the pain persists for more than a day, or you notice swelling or other signs of infection, consult a doctor.

Oh, one last thing. The chances of encountering a shark are about as likely as sighting a UFO. But should you meet one of these ominous creatures, stay calm. Simply swim quietly to shore. By the time you make it back to terra firma, you'll have one hell of a story to tell.

consume tons of krill and tiny fish, then fast while in Hawaii. It is in the waters off Maui that they give birth to their young, babies that can weigh as much as three tons and gain up to 100 pounds a day.

Eager to protect the whales who winter in these waters, local officials have forced power craft to keep their distance from these cetaceans. But these restrictions are not so severe as to unduly interfere with the many sailing vessels that offer whale-watching opportunities off the Maui coast. You can also enjoy dive trips or pure performance rides on these beautiful vessels.

A prime area for whale watching lies along Honoapiilani Highway between Maalaea Bay and Lahaina, particularly at McGregor Point. So while you're visiting Maui, always keep an eye peeled seaward for vaporous spume and a rolling hump. The place you're standing might suddenly become an ideal crow's-nest.

Between 2000 and 3000 of the world's 10,000 humpbacks make the annual migration to Maui's southwestern coast each year. Today they are an endangered species, protected by federal law from whalers. Several local organizations study these leviathans and serve as excellent information sources.

The **Pacific Whale Foundation** issues daily reports over local radio stations during whale season. This same organization conducts "eco-adventure cruises," the profits from which help fund their whale protection projects. They have snorkeling tours to Molokini and whale-watching cruises, both led by marine naturalists. Most interesting is their dolphin adventure, where you snorkel Lanai's untouched coral reefs and see spinner and bottlenose dolphins in one of the island's many hidden coves. ~ 101 North Kihei Road, Kihei; 808-879-8860; www.pacificwhale.org. Whale hotline: 800-942-5311.

LAHAINA Trilogy Excursions specializes in half- and full-day sailing adventures. They also offer whale-watching trips aboard a 41-foot sloop, as well as snorkeling excursions, scuba trips, instruction and joysailing. Special trips include Molokini crater and Lanai. Trilogy receives high praise from repeat clients who climb aboard the 50-foot catamaran for excursions to Lanai. Once on the nearby island, they can swim and snorkel Hulopoe Bay Marine Reserve, enjoy a Hawaiian barbecue and tour Lanai City. Trips depart from Lahaina and Maalaea harbors and Kaanapali Resort beach. ~ Lahaina Harbor; 808-661-4743.

Scotch Mist Sailing Charters offers half-day snorkeling trips. Whale watching, sailing and champagne-and-chocolate sunset sails are also available. ~ Lahaina Harbor; 808-661-0386.

Windjammer Cruises has a 70-foot, three-masted schooner ideal for whale watching in addition to brunch and sunset dinner sails. You can dine on island cuisine, enjoy traditional Polynesian entertainment and take in the vistas of Kahoolawe, Molokai and

Lanai. Sunset dinner cruises daily, brunch cruises on Friday and Sunday. ~ Lahaina Harbor; 808-661-8600, 800-732-4852.

For an intimate experience, try the six-passenger **Cinderella**, a 50-foot luxury sailboat. ~ Maalaea Harbor; 808-244-0009.

Operating out of Maalaea Bay, which boasts some of the best sailing in the world, **Hawaiian Charters Inc.** has several options. You can take a morning sail/snorkel intended for all levels (although they specialize in beginners), an afternoon sail/whale watch or a sunset sail. ~ P.O. Box 959, Kihei, HI 96753; 808-244-6655; www.mauisailing.net.

Island Marine Activities offers whale-spotting cruises from mid-December to May. They also have fine-dining sunset dinner cruises, Molokini Crater snorkel tours, and four package tours to Molokai, from a walking tour to a car rental package. ~ 113 Prison Street, Lahaina; 808-661-8397.

KAANAPALI–KAPALUA AREA **Kapalua Kai** is a popular catamaran offering picnic-and-snorkeling and sunset sails. It sails Maui's most scenic waters and features whale-watching excursions in winter months. Scuba trips also available. ~ Kaanapali; 808-667-5980; www.sailingmaui.com.

PARA-SAILING & HANG GLIDING

Lahaina and Kaanapali Beach are perfect places to become airborne. Wonderful views of Maui's west side and neighboring Molokai add to the fun. The typical parasailing trip includes 30 to 45 minutes shuttling out and back to the launch point and eight to ten minutes in the air.

Parasail Kaanapali riders rise as high as 900 feet, single or tandem. Closed mid-December to mid-May. ~ Mala Wharf, Lahaina; 808-669-6555. **UFO Parasail** lets you ascend up to 800 feet and also fly with a companion. Open mid-May to mid-December. ~ Whalers Village, Kaanapali; 808-661-7836.

AUTHOR FAVORITE

There was a time when a Zodiac boat ride was synonymous with roughing it out on the open sea. But the 48-foot Explorer-class craft has lent new meaning to the experience. In the case of the **Maui Nui Explorer**, a 35-passenger craft that cruises at 20 knots, it translates into cushioned seating and canopy shading. Step aboard and they'll take you whale watching in season or on a half-day eco-adventure combing the coast of Lanai and snorkeling along its coral reefs. Among the top-notch crew on board this "luxury raft" is a marine life naturalist from the Hawaii Wildlife Fund. ~ Lahaina Harbor, Lahaina; 808-873-3475.

For hang gliding from some of the most beautiful spots on the island, try **Hang Gliding Maui**. They also operate motorized hanggliding out of Hana Airport. Reservations required. ~ Makawao; 808-572-6557; www.hangglidingmaui.com.

KAYAKING   A sport that's grown tremendously in popularity, kayaking is an up-close way to explore Maui's waters.

KAANAPALI–KAPALUA AREA   Kayaks are available from **Kaanapali Windsurfing School**. Trips are offered through the Hyatt Regency. ~ Whalers Village, Kaanapali; Maui Ocean Activities reservations 808-667-1964.

KIHEI–WAILEA–MAKENA AREA   An easy-going kayaking excursion along the Makena–La Perouse area can be had with **Kelii's Kayak Tours**. Rising early in the morning, you get a quick lesson on ocean kayaking, and then venture off the shoreline in search of Maui's sea life. Those lazy-looking sea turtles bobbing alongside you don't have to work as hard as you do. The trip concludes with a dip in the sea for an up-close-and-personal snorkeling adventure. Kelii's also offers north shore tour excursions in the Honolua Bay/Honokohau area. ~158 Lanakila Place, Kihei; 808-874-7652, 888-874-7652; e-mail kelii@maui.net. Kayak rentals and tours can also be arranged through **South Pacific Kayaks**. Their naturalist-guided trips include snorkeling, and you're likely to see whales, sea turtles and dolphins, depending on the season. ~ 2439 South Kihei Road, Kihei; 808-875-4848; www.mauikayak.com, e-mail seakayaks@maui.net.

KAHULUI–WAILUKU AREA   In Central Maui, **Maui Sea Kayaking** offers day trips to Maui and Lanai and full-moon trips to Molokini. Or they'll lead you on an overnight "romance" retreat, for which a guide will arrange a seaside campsite that is off the beaten track and inaccessible by car. In the morning, the guide will return to prepare your breakfast and lead the way back to civilization. They also lead kayak and wave-ski surfers to beaches good for surfing. Maximum four people. ~ Puunene; 808-572-6299; www.maui.net/~kayaking.

BE A CONTENDER

Imagine the thrill of big-time yacht racing when you sail aboard **America II**, a 65-foot America's Cup contender. There are morning whale-watching excursions from December 15 through April and afternoon tradewind and sunset sails the rest of the year. The trips last two hours and include soft drinks and snacks. ~ Lahaina Harbor; 808-677-2195.

Rafting trips are the adventurous way to enjoy the Maui coast. **RAFTING**
Easily combined with dive and whale-watching trips, these sturdy
craft are a great way to reach hidden coves and beaches.

LAHAINA   Hawaiian Rafting Adventures operates half- and full-
day trips to Lanai and Lanai dive trips. Whale-watching excursions are great fun in the winter months. ~ 1223 Front Street,
Lahaina; 808-661-7333; www.thesupersites.com/hirafting.

Ocean Riders Adventure Rafting will take you out to Lanai
and, weather permitting, Molokai, for a glorious day of snorkeling, as well as whale watching during whale season. All trips are
aboard rigid-hull inflatable boats. ~ Mala Wharf, Lahaina; 808-
661-3586; www.mauioceanriders.com.

Another company offering tours is Captain Steve's Rafting
Excursions, which heads out regularly in search of tropical fish,
dolphins and exotic birdlife. One trip not to miss circumnavigates
Lanai. ~ Mala Wharf, Lahaina; 808-667-5565; e-mail office@
captainsteves.com.

Full- and half-day trips are offered aboard Hawaii Ocean Rafting's vessel, a motorized raft that takes you to a variety of different snorkeling spots while spinner dolphins leap picturesquely
in your wake. ~ P.O. Box 381, Lahaina, HI 96767; 808-667-2191.

KIHEI–WAILEA–MAKENA AREA   Blue Water Rafting offers both
rafting and snorkeling trips to Molokini. ~ Kihei Boat Ramp, Kihei;
808-879-7238; www.bluewaterrafting.com.

Maui's volcanic landscape, beaches and sculptured valleys are **RIDING**
choice sites for equestrian excursions. A variety of rides are avail- **STABLES**
able across the island—from the shoreline of Hana to the slopes
of Haleakala, you can count on seeing wildlife, lava fields and
those famous Maui sunsets.

KIHEI–WAILEA–MAKENA AREA   Makena Stables leads trail rides
across the scenic 20,000-acre Ulupalakua Ranch on the south
slope of Haleakala. Mountain trails cross a 200-year-old lava flow.
Choose among two-hour, three-hour and all-day rides. Possibilities
include visiting La Perouse Bay or Kalua Olapa, which is an old,
inactive volcanic vent, and sunset rides. ~ 8299 South Makena
Road, Makena; 808-879-0244; www.makenastables.com.

HANA HIGHWAY   Oheo Stables offers outings up the back slope
of Haleakala. Trips ascend through a tropical rainforest and include views of waterfalls and the Kipahulu Valley. Highlights include the view from Pipiwai lookout above Oheo Gulch. Six riders maximum. ~ Hana Highway, one mile south of National Park
Headquarters at Pools of Ohea; 808-667-2222.

UPCOUNTRY AND HALEAKALA   Hit the trail on Maui's north
shore with Adventures on Horseback and you will ride along 300-

foot cliffs, see lush rainforests and take a break to swim in water-fall-fed pools. Six riders maximum. ~ Makawao; 808-242-7445.

Ironwood Ranch in Napili offers some easy, scenic excursions including a jaunt through a pineapple plantation and a sunset view from horseback. Most of the trips are three-and-a-half hours. ~ Lahaina; 808-669-4991.

At **Thompson Ranch and Riding Stables** ride through pasture-land on short day and sunset trips that offer views of the other islands. Trips are suitable for children. ~ Thompson Road, Kula; 808-878-1910.

For tours of Haleakala National Park, contact **Pony Express Tours**, which leads half- and full-day horseback trips to the crater. Rides in the Haleakala Ranch are available, as is a one-hour introduction to horse riding. Closed Sunday. ~ 808-667-2200; www.ponyexpresstours.com. On the weekends **Charlie's Trail Rides and Pack Trips** provides overnight horseback trips from Kaupo through Haleakala. There is a six-person maximum on overnight trips. Two- and four-hour trips outside the Park are also available. Meals are included in the travel package. ~ 808-248-8209.

GOLF
With more than a dozen public and private courses, Maui is golf heaven. Choices on the Valley Isle range from country club links to inexpensive community courses. Also, several resorts offer a choice of championship courses ideal for golfers looking for a change of pace. These are open to the public for a hefty fee. Consider reserving tee-times before your visit, especially during the high season. Some courses allow you to book up to a month in advance.

KAANAPALI–KAPALUA AREA   The **Kaanapali Golf Courses** are among the island's finest. The championship par-71 North Course, designed by golf course architect Robert Trent Jones, Sr., has a slight incline. The easier South Course is intersected by Maui's popular sugar cane train. ~ Kaanapali Beach Resort, Kaanapali; 808-661-3691; www.kaanapali-golf.com.

With three courses, the **Kapalua Golf Club** is one of the best places to golf on Maui. For a real challenge, try the par-73 Plantation Course built in the heart of pineapple country. The oceanfront Bay Course, and the Village Course, which ascends into the foothills, were created by Arnold Palmer himself. ~ 300 Kapalua Drive, Kapalua; 808-669-8044.

KIHEI–WAILEA–MAKENA AREA   The **Wailea Golf Club**, located in the heart of the Wailea Resort complex, offers three courses, all with ocean views. The 18-hole "blue course" heads uphill along the slopes of Haleakala. The least-challenging "emerald course" is also the shortest. The "gold course" is the longest and most challenging, with 93 bunkers. There are two clubhouses on the premises. ~ 100 Wailea Golf Club Drive; 808-879-2966.

Located next to the Maui Prince Hotel, **Makena Golf Club** has two 18-hole courses. Designed by Robert Trent Jones, Jr., the "North" and "South" courses are intended to blend into the natural Hawaiian landscape while offering high-challenge golf. Rolling terrain and beautiful views of the neighbor islands make these links a treat. ~ 5415 Makena Alanui, Makena; 808-879-3344; www.makenagolf.com.

KAHULUI–WAILUKU AREA **Waiehu Municipal Golf Course** is the island's only publicly owned course. With a front nine on the shoreline and a challenging back nine along the mountains, this course offers plenty of variety. Other amenities include a driving range and practice green. ~ Kahekili Highway, Waiehu; 808-244-5934.

The somewhat hilly, par-72 **Sandalwood** was designed by Nelson and Wright. Three holes have lakes or ponds. There's a restaurant and pro shop on the premises, as well as a practice range, a chipping green and two putting greens. ~ 2500 Honoapiilani Highway, Waikapu; 808-242-7090.

HANA HIGHWAY The **Maui Country Club** is a relatively easy nine-hole course open to the public on Mondays. ~ 48 Nonohe Place, Paia; 808-877-7893.

UPCOUNTRY AND HALEAKALA The upcountry **Pukalani Country Club**, on the slopes of Haleakala, is an 18-hole public course. Bring a jacket or sweater because these links can get cool. Boasting the highest elevation of all Maui's courses, this one is a sleeper (with great views). ~ 360 Pukalani Street; 808-572-1314.

TENNIS

If you're an avid tennis fan, or just in the mood to whack a few balls, you're in luck. Public tennis courts are easily found through-

HELP PROTECT THE REEF

Exploring underwater in Maui is one of the most wonderful experiences available in the islands. But we must protect that environment while we enjoy it. Did you know that coral reefs are living animals that live in large colonies? They are also home to hundreds of sea creatures, including fish and invertebrates. It takes years and years for coral reefs to regenerate themselves when damaged, and if they are badly damaged they die. We can help to protect the reefs by not touching them (they are protected by Hawaiian law—it is illegal to take live coral from their beds); not walking upon or standing on them; keeping anchors away from them; and by not feeding the fish that inhabit them—that upsets the eco-balance.

out the island. Almost all are lighted and convenient to major resort destinations.

LAHAINA   In the Lahaina area, you'll enjoy the courts at the **Lahaina Civic Center** ~ 1840 Honoapiilani Highway; or at **Maluulu-olele Park** ~ Front and Shaw streets. For more information call the Parks and Recreation Department in Lahaina. ~ 808-661-4685.

KAANAPALI–KAPALUA AREA   There are several resorts in the area that open their courts to the public for a fee. One is the **Hyatt Regency Maui**. ~ 200 Nohea Kai Drive, Kaanapali; 808-661-1234. Another is the **Maui Marriott**. ~ 100 Nohea Kai Drive, Kaanapali; 808-667-1200.

The **Kapalua Tennis Garden** offers ten courts. Fee. ~ 100 Kapalua Drive, Kapalua; 808-669-5677.

KIHEI–WAILEA–MAKENA AREA   There are public courts at **Kalama Park** on Kihei Road and **Maui Sunset Condominiums** on Waipulani Road. ~ 808-879-4364.

Makena Resort Tennis Club is a favorite resort that lets the public use its courts. Fee. ~ Makena Resort, 5400 Makena Alanui, Makena; 808-879-8777.

Wailea Tennis Club has 11 courts. Fee. ~ 131 Wailea Iki Place, Wailea; 808-879-1958.

KAHULUI–WAILUKU AREA   In the Kahului area, try the courts at the **Kahului Community Center** on Onehee and Uhu streets and the **Maui Community College** on Kaahumanu and Wakea avenues. In Wailuku, try **Wailuku War Memorial** at 1580 Kaahumanu Avenue, or the public courts at Wells and Market streets. ~ 808-270-7389.

HANA HIGHWAY   In the Hana area try the **Hana Ball Park**.

UPCOUNTRY AND HALEAKALA   Popular Upcountry courts are found at the **Eddie Tam Memorial Center** in Makawao and the **Pukalani Community Center** in Pukalani. ~ 808-572-8122.

BIKING

If you've ever wanted to zip down a mountainside or go off-road in volcanic highlands, you've come to the right place. While Maui is best known for its downhill cycling trips, there are also many other challenging adventures. For example, you can enjoy the remote route from Hana to Ulupalakua or head from Kapalua to Wailuku via Kahakuloa.

For a friendly cruise down Haleakala on single-gear beach cruisers, contact **Maui Mountain Cruisers**. They serve breakfast or lunch on sunrise or midday rides, stopping for lunch at the Sunrise Market and Protea Farm. ~ 15 South Wakea Street, Kahului; 808-871-6014, 800-232-6284.

Chris' Adventures runs such intriguing trips as the Haleakala Wine Trek, a tour of the mountain's remote backside and a trip along the island's hidden northwest coast, complete with off-road biking. Unlike other bike tours, this company lets at their own pace. Other tour options include boa Molokai and a "volcano bike" trip. ~ Kula; 808-

Aloha Bicycle Tours is a family-run operatio as a ride-at-your-own-pace tour company. Sounds good idea along these gorgeous routes. The vol ample, swings through Haleakala National Parl farm and Keokea (a.k.a. China Town) and descends to a Minimum age is 14. ~ Kula; 808-249-0911, 800-749-1564.

At **Maui Downhill**, you'll enjoy sunrise daytrips and mid-morning runs on Haleakala. The sunrise run is a beautiful 38-mile trip from the crater to sea level. The longer trips include a meal; helmets, windbreakers, suits and insulated gloves are provided for all rides. ~ 199 Dairy Road, Kahului; 808-871-2155, 888-661-6887; www.mauidownhill.com.

Family-owned and -operated, **Cruiser Phil's Volcano Rides** also runs Haleakala downhill tours. Phil's has custom-built low-rider, single-gear cruisers and included with the uniform of safety gear are Kevlar motorcycle jackets. ~ 552 Keolani Place, Kahului; 808-893-2332.

HIKING

Many people complain that Maui is overdeveloped. The wall-to-wall condominiums lining the Kaanapali and Kihei beachfront can be pretty depressing to the outdoors lover. But happily there is a way to escape. Hike right out of it.

The Valley Isle has many fine trails that lead through Hana's rainforest, Haleakala's magnificent valley, up to West Maui's peaks and across the south shore's arid lava flows. Any of them will carry you far from the madding crowd. It's quite simple on Maui to trade the tourist enclaves for virgin mountains, untrammeled beaches and eerie volcanic terrain.

Most trails you'll be hiking are composed of volcanic rock. This is a very crumbly substance, so be extremely cautious when climbing rock faces. In fact, you should avoid steep climbs if pos-

AUTHOR FAVORITE

Hike Maui has been offering hiking tours longer than anyone else on the island. They emphasize natural history, and their affection for their subject matter shows. One of the hikes wanders through Kipahula Valley, on the track of waterfalls and streams. You can swim through clear pools past ferns and hanging vines, then lunch at the top of a 200-foot waterfall. They also have volcano and coastline hikes. ~ P.O. Box 330969, Kahului, HI 96733; 808-879-5270.

sible. Stay on the trails: Maui's dense undergrowth makes it very easy to get lost. If you get lost at night, stay where you are. Because of the low latitude, night descends rapidly here; there's practically no twilight. Once darkness falls, it can be very dangerous to move around. You should also be careful to purify all drinking water. And be extremely cautious near streambeds as flash-flooding sometimes occurs, particularly on the windward coast. This is particularly true during the winter months, when heavy storms from the northeast lash the island.

It's advisable to wear long pants when hiking in order to protect your legs from rock outcroppings, insects and spiny plants. Also, if you're going to explore Haleakala volcano, be sure to bring cold-weather gear; temperatures are often significantly lower than at sea level and this peak occasionally receives snow.

One note: A number of trails pass preserved cultural or historical sites. Please do not disturb these in any way.

For more information, contact the Division of Forestry and Wildlife, Na Ala Hele Trails and Access Program. ~ 54 South High Street, Room 101, Wailuku, HI 96793; 808-984-8100, 808-873-3509, fax 808-984-8111.

You might want to obtain hiking maps; they are available on Oahu from **Hawaii Geographic Maps & Books**. They also sell informational guides and books useful for hiking. ~ P.O. Box 1698, Honolulu, HI 96806; 808-538-3952, 800-538-3950.

If you're uncomfortable about exploring solo, you might consider an organized tour. The **National Park Service** provides information to hikers interested in exploring Haleakala or other sections of the island. What follows is a basic guide to most of Maui's major trails. ~ Haleakala National Park, P.O. Box 369, Makawao, Maui, HI 96768; 808-572-4400, fax 808-572-1304.

All distances listed for hiking trails are one way unless otherwise noted.

KAHULUI–WAILUKU AREA The main hiking trails in this region lie in Iao Valley, Kahului and along Kakekili Highway (Route 340).

Iao Stream Trail (1 mile) leads from the Iao Valley State Monument parking lot for half a mile along the stream. The second half of the trek involves wading through the stream or hopping across the shoreline rocks. But your efforts will be rewarded with some excellent swimming holes en route. You might want to plan your time so you can relax and swim. (See "You're Not Alone—Beware!" sidebar before swimming in the river.)

Not far from Kahului Airport on Route 360, birders will be delighted to find a trail meandering through the **Kanaha Pond Wildlife Sanctuary** (2 miles). This jaunt follows two loop roads, each one mile long, and passes the natural habitat of the rare

Hawaiian stilt, the Hawaiian duck (a species re-introduced to Maui in 1991) and the Hawaiian coot. The trails in the Kanaha Pond area are closed during bird-breeding season (April–August). The pond-kiosk area, which has a short observation "peninsula," is open year-round, but to hike on the trail, you'll need a permit from the State Division of Forestry. ~ 808-984-8100.

Northwest of Kahului, along the Kahekili Highway, are two trails well worth exploring, the **Waihee Ridge Trail** and **Kahakuloa Valley Trail**.

Waihee Ridge Trail (3 miles) begins just below Maluhia Boy Scout Camp outside the town of Waihee. The trail passes through a guava thicket and scrub forest and climbs 1500 feet en route to a peak overlooking West and Central Maui. The trail summit is equipped with a picnic table rest stop.

KIHEI–WAILEA–MAKENA AREA King's Highway Coastal Trail (5.5 miles) follows an ancient Hawaiian route over the 1790 lava flow and is considered a desert region. The trail begins near La Perouse Bay at the end of the rugged road that connects La Perouse Bay with Makena Beach and Wailea. It heads inland through groves of *kiawe* trees, then skirts the coast and finally leads to Kanaloa Point. From this point the trail continues across private land. Because segments of the trail pass through the Ahihi-Kinau Natural Area Reserve, which has stricter regulations, call Na Ala Hele Trails and Access Program for more information. ~ 808-243-5352.

HANA HIGHWAY Hana-Waianapanapa Coastal Trail (3 miles), part of the ancient King's Highway, skirts the coastline between Waianapanapa State Park and Hana Bay. Exercise extreme caution near the rocky shoreline and cliffs. The trail passes a *heiau*, sea arch, blowhole and numerous caves while winding through lush stands of *hala* trees.

Waimoku Falls Trail (2 miles) leads from the bridge at Oheo Gulch up to Waimoku Falls. On the way, it goes by four pools and traverses a bamboo forest. (Mosquito repellent advised.)

YOU'RE NOT ALONE—BEWARE!

For those ready to take a dip in Iao Stream, beware that you might be in the water with *leptospirosis*. This bacterium penetrates the body through broken skin or such orifices as the nose, mouth and ears. Flu-like symptoms are the results ... unless you have a severe case, which can lead to kidney, liver or heart damage. Consult the Hawaii State Department of Health at 808-244-4288 for further information.

Contact Haleakala National Park Headquarters for information on this trail.

UPCOUNTRY The main trails in Maui's beautiful Upcountry lie on Haleakala's southern slopes. They branch out from Polipoli Spring State Recreation Area through the Kula and Kahikinui Forest Reserves.

Redwood Trail (1.7 miles) descends from Polipoli's 6200-foot elevation through impressive stands of redwoods to the ranger's cabin at 5300 feet. There is a dilapidated public shelter in the old CCC camp at trail's end. A four-wheel drive is required to reach the trailhead.

Brrrr... the lowest recorded temperature in the Hawaiian Islands was 11°F, in 1961, atop Haleakala!

Plum Trail (1.7 miles) begins at the CCC camp and climbs gently south to Haleakala Ridge Trail. The route passes plum trees as well as stands of ash, redwood and sugi pine. There are shelters at both ends of the trail.

Tie Trail (0.5 mile) descends 500 feet through cedar, ash and sugi pine groves to link Redwood and Plum Trails. There is a shelter at the Redwood junction.

Polipoli Trail (0.6 mile) cuts through cypress, cedars and pines en route from Polipoli Campground to Haleakala Ridge Trail.

Boundary Trail (4 miles) begins at the cattle guard marking the Kula Forest Reserve boundary along the road to Polipoli. It crosses numerous gulches planted in cedar, eucalyptus and pine. The trail terminates at the ranger's cabin.

Waiohuli Trail (1.4 miles) descends 800 feet from Polipoli Road to join Boundary Trail. Along the way it passes young pine and grasslands, then drops down through groves of cedar, redwood and ash. There is a shelter at the Boundary Trail junction.

Skyline Road (6.5 miles) begins at 9750 feet, near the top of Haleakala's southwest rift, and descends more than 3000 feet to the top of Haleakala Ridge Trail. The trail passes a rugged, treeless area resembling the moon's surface. Then it drops below timberline at 8600 feet and eventually into dense scrub. The unobstructed views of Maui and the neighboring islands are awesome. Bring your own water.

Haleakala Ridge Trail (1.6 miles) starts from Skyline Trail's terminus at 6550 feet and descends along Haleakala's southwest rift to 5600 feet. There are spectacular views in all directions and a shelter at trail's end.

THREE

History and Culture

POLYNESIAN ARRIVAL   The history of Maui, complex and dynamic as it is, actually began after that of other islands in the chain. Perhaps as early as the third century, Polynesians sailing from the Marquesas Islands, and then later from Tahiti, landed on the southern tip of the Big Island. By about A.D. 800, Polynesians from the Marquesas and Society Islands arrived on Maui. In Europe, mariners were rarely venturing outside the Mediterranean Sea, and it would be centuries before Columbus happened upon the New World. Yet in the Pacific, entire families were crossing 2500 miles of untracked ocean in hand-carved canoes with sails woven from *hala* (pandanus) leaves. The boats were formidable structures, catamaran-like vessels with a cabin built on the platform between the wooden hulls. Some were a hundred feet long and could do twenty knots, making the trip to Hawaii in a month.

The Polynesians had originally come from the coast of Asia about 3000 years before. They had migrated through Indonesia, then pressed inexorably eastward, leapfrogging across archipelagoes until they finally reached the last chain, the most remote—Hawaii.

These Pacific migrants were undoubtedly the greatest sailors of their day and stand among the finest in history. When close to land they could smell it, taste it in the seawater, see it in a lagoon's turquoise reflection on the clouds above an island. They knew the courses of 150 stars. From the color of the water they determined ocean depths and current directions. They had no charts, no compasses, no sextants; sailing directions were simply recorded in legends and chants. Yet Polynesians discovered the Pacific, from Indonesia to Easter Island, from New Zealand to Hawaii. They made the Vikings and Phoenicians look like landlubbers.

On Maui, the seaborne colonizers established a line of kings who ruled the island for several centuries. Among them was Hua, a 12th-century monarch who earned a reputation for being a fierce warrior. According to legend, he angered the Hawaiian gods by murdering a priest and felt the holy wrath in the form of an island-wide drought. In desperation, Hua moved to the Big Island in search of fresh water, but the gods made sure the drought traveled with him.

CAPTAIN COOK   They were high islands, rising in the northeast as the sun broke across the Pacific. First one, then a second, and finally, as the tall-masted ships drifted west, a third island loomed before them. Landfall! The British crew was ecstatic. It meant fresh water, tropical fruits, solid ground on which to set their boots and a chance to carouse with the native women. For their captain, James Cook, it was another in an amazing career of discoveries. The man whom many call history's greatest explorer was about to land in one of the last spots on earth to be discovered by the West.

He would name the place for his patron, the British earl who became famous by pressing a meal between two crusts of bread. The Sandwich Islands. Later they would be called Owhyhee, and eventually, as the Western tongue glided around the uncharted edges of a foreign language, Hawaii.

It was January 1778. The English army was battling a ragtag band of revolutionaries for control of the American colonies, and the British Empire was still basking in a sun that never set. The Pacific had been opened to Western powers over two centuries before, when a Portuguese sailor named Magellan crossed it. Since then, the British, French, Dutch and Spanish had tracked through in search of future colonies.

They happened upon Samoa, Fiji, Tahiti and the other islands that spread across this third of the globe, but somehow they had never sighted Hawaii. Even when Cook finally spied it, he little realized how important a find he had made. Hawaii, quite literally, was a jewel in the ocean, rich in fragrant sandalwood, ripe for agricultural exploitation and crowded with sea life. But it was the archipelago's isolation that would prove to be its greatest resource. Strategically situated between Asia and North America, it was the only place for thousands of miles where whalers, merchants and bluejackets could go for provisions and rest.

Cook was 49 years old when he shattered Hawaii's quiescence. The Englishman hadn't expected to find islands north of Tahiti. Quite frankly, he wasn't even trying. It was his third Pacific voy-

MAUI THE GOD

So many legends have grown up around the demigod Maui, the island's namesake, that many believe the mischievous deity actually existed. According to popular legend, he created the Hawaiian chain by hooking the islands and pulling them up from the bottom of the ocean. It was also Maui who learned the secrets of firemaking from a mud hen and shared them with men and women across the island.

age and Cook was hunting bigger game, the fabled Northwest Passage that would link this ocean with the Atlantic.

But these mountainous islands were still an interesting find. He could see by the canoes venturing out to meet his ships that the lands were inhabited; when he finally put ashore on Kauai, Cook discovered a Polynesian society. He saw irrigated fields, domestic animals and high-towered temples. The women were bare-breasted, the men wore loincloths. As his crew bartered for pigs, fowls and bananas, he learned that the natives knew about metal and coveted iron like gold.

If iron was gold to these "Indians," then Cook was a god. He soon realized that his arrival had somehow been miraculously timed, coinciding with the Makahiki festival, a months-long celebration highlighted by sporting competitions, feasting, hula and exaltation of the ruling chiefs. Even war ceased during this gala affair. Makahiki honored the roving deity Lono, whose return to Hawaii on "trees that would move over seas" was foretold in ancient legend. Cook was a strange white man sailing tall-masted ships—obviously he was Lono. The Hawaiians gave him gifts, fell in his path and rose only at his insistence.

But even among religious crowds, fame is often fickle. After leaving Hawaii without ever visiting Maui, Cook sailed north to the Arctic Sea, where he failed to discover the Northwest Passage.

As the winter of 1778 approached, the British sea captain determined to steer a course south once more, spending the season in the Sandwich Islands. On November 25, at a latitude of 20° 55', as day broke across the Pacific, he first sighted Maui. To Western eyes it was an exotic locale, vaulting 10,000 feet above the waves with a peak that rose through the clouds.

By noon, canoes filled with local natives, including the great Maui chief, Kahekili, visited the English explorers, presenting them with elaborate feather cloaks and small pigs. By the next day, Cook had departed, sailing east to the Big Island.

He arrived at the tail end of another exhausting Makahiki festival. By then the Hawaiians had tired of his constant demands for provisions and were suffering from a new disease that was obviously carried by Lono's archangelic crew—syphilis. This Lono was proving to be something of a freeloader.

Tensions ran high. The Hawaiians stole a boat. Cook retaliated with gunfire. A scuffle broke out on the beach and in a sudden violent outburst, which surprised the islanders as much as the interlopers, the Hawaiians discovered that their god could bleed. The world's finest mariner lay face down in foot-deep water, stabbed and bludgeoned to death.

Cook's end marked the beginning of an era. He had put the Pacific on the map, his map, probing its expanses and defining its fringes. In Hawaii he ended a thousand years of solitude. The archipelago's geographic isolation, which has always played a crucial role in Hawaii's development, had finally failed to protect it, and a second theme had come into play—the islands' vulnerability. Together with the region's "backwardness," these conditions would now mold Hawaii's history. All in turn would be shaped by another factor, one which James Cook had added to Hawaii's historic equation: the West.

KAMEHAMEHA AND KAAHUMANU   The next man whose star would rise above Hawaii was present at Cook's death. Some say he struck the Englishman, others that he took a lock of the great leader's hair and used its residual power, its mana, to become king of all Hawaii.

Kamehameha was a tall, muscular man with a furrowed face, a lesser chief on the powerful island of Hawaii. When he began his career of conquest a few years after Cook's death, he was a mere upstart, an ambitious, arrogant young chief. But he fought with a general's skill and a warrior's cunning, often plunging into the midst of a melee. He had an astute sense of technology, an intuition that these new Western metals and firearms could make him a king.

Hawaiian craftsmen produced the world's finest featherwork, weaving thousands of tiny feathers into golden cloaks and ceremonial helmets.

In Kamehameha's early years, Maui and the other islands were composed of many fiefdoms. Several kings or great chiefs, continually warring among themselves, ruled individual islands. At times, a few kings would carve up one island or a lone king might seize several. Never had one monarch controlled all the islands.

Among the most powerful was the Maui chief, Kahekili. He was, according to the historian Gavan Daws, "one of the last of the older generation of chiefs, raised in the tradition of warriors who roasted their enemies and used the skulls of the dead for filth pots." With the Valley Isle as a power base, he seized Oahu, torturing its chiefs and killing his own foster son. By 1786 he also controlled Molokai and Lanai.

During that same year, Captain Jean-François de La Pérouse, sailing under orders from the king of France, became the first Westerner to set foot on Maui.

Other players were entering the field: Westerners with ample firepower and towering ships. During the decade following Cook, only a handful arrived, mostly Englishmen and Americans, and they did not yet possess the influence they soon would wield. However, even a few foreigners were enough to upset the balance of power. They sold weapons and hardware to the great chiefs, making several of them more powerful than any of the others had ever been. War was imminent.

Kamehameha stood in the center of the hurricane. Like any leader suddenly caught up in the terrible momentum of history, he never quite realized where he was going or how fast he was moving. And he cared little that he was being carried in part by Westerners who would eventually want something for the ride. Kamehameha was no fool. If political expedience meant Western intrusion, then so be it. He had enemies among chiefs on the other islands; he needed the guns.

During the 1780s, Kahekili thwarted two attacks on Maui. But when two white men came into Kamehameha's camp in 1790, he had the military advisers to complement a fast expanding arsenal. Within months he cannonaded Maui. Attacking also with war canoes, he drove the forces of Kahekili's son, Kalanikupule, from Kahului up into the sharp-walled confines of Iao Valley.

In 1792, Kamehameha seized the Big Island by inviting his main rival to a peaceful parley, then slaying the hapless chief. By 1795, he had consolidated his control of Maui, grasped Molokai and Lanai and begun reaching greedily toward Oahu. He struck rapidly, landing near Waikiki and sweeping inland, forcing his enemies to their deaths over the precipitous cliffs of the Nuuanu Pali.

The warrior had become a conqueror, establishing his new capital in Lahaina and controlling all the islands except Kauai, which he finally gained in 1810 by peaceful negotiation. Kamehameha proved to be as able a bureaucrat as he had been a general. He became a benevolent despot who, with the aid of an ever-increasing number of Western advisers, expanded Hawaii's commerce, brought peace to the islands and moved his people inexorably toward the modern age.

He came to be called Kamehameha the Great, a wise and resolute leader who gathered a war-torn archipelago into a kingdom. But with the revisionist history of the 1960s and 1970s, as Third World people questioned both the Western version of events and the virtues of progress, Kamehameha began to resemble Benedict Arnold. He was seen as an opportunist, a megalomaniac who permitted the Western powers their initial foothold in Hawaii. He used their technology and then, in the manner of great men who depend on stronger allies, was eventually used by them.

As long a shadow as Kamehameha cast across the islands, the event that most dramatically transformed Hawaiian society occurred after his death in 1819. The kingdom had passed to Kamehameha's son Liholiho, but Kamehameha's favorite wife, Kaahumanu, usurped the power. Liholiho was a prodigal son, dissolute, lacking self-certainty, a drunk. A native of Maui, Kaahumanu was a woman for all seasons, a canny politician who combined brilliance with boldness, the feminist of her day. She had infuriated Kamehameha by eating forbidden foods and sleeping with other chiefs, even when he placed a taboo on her body and executed her lovers. She drank liquor, ran away, proved completely uncontrollable and won Kamehameha's love.

It was only natural that when he died, she would take his mana, or so she reckoned. Kaahumanu gravitated toward power with the drive of someone whom fate has unwisely denied. She carved her own destiny, announcing that Kamehameha's wish had been to give her a governmental voice. There would be a new post and she would fill it, becoming in a sense Hawaii's first prime minister.

And if the power, then the motion. Kaahumanu immediately marched against Hawaii's belief system, trying to topple the old idols. For years she had bristled under a polytheistic religion regulated by taboos, or *kapus*, which severely restricted women's rights. Now Kaahumanu urged the new king, Liholiho, to break a very strict *kapu* by sharing a meal with women.

Since the act might help consolidate Liholiho's position, it had a certain appeal to the king. Anyway, the *kapus* were weakening: these white men, coming now in ever greater numbers, defied them with impunity. Liholiho vacillated, went on a two-day drunk before gaining courage, then finally sat down to eat. It was a last supper, shattering an ancient creed and opening the way for a radically new divinity. As Kaahumanu had willed, the old order collapsed, taking away a vital part of island life and leaving the Hawaiians more exposed than ever to foreign influence.

> Hawaii is the only state in the union to have been ruled by a monarchy—from Kamehameha the Great in 1758 until Liliuokalani's overthrow in 1893. In all, eight monarchs reigned over the kingdom.

Already Western practices were gaining hold. Commerce from Lahaina, Honolulu and other ports was booming. In the 1840s, more American ships visited Hawaii than any other port in the world. There was a fortune to be made dealing sandalwood to China-bound merchants, and the chiefs were forcing the common people to strip Hawaii's forests. The grueling labor might make the chiefs rich, but it gained the commoners little more than a barren landscape. Western diseases struck virulently. The Polynesians in Hawaii, who numbered 300,000 in Cook's time, were extremely susceptible. By 1866, their population had dwindled to less than 60,000. It was a difficult time for the Hawaiian people.

MISSIONARIES AND MERCHANTS Hawaii was not long without organized religion. The same year that Kaahumanu shattered tradition, a group of New England missionaries boarded the brig *Thaddeus* for a voyage around Cape Horn. It was a young company—many were in their twenties or thirties—and included a doctor, a printer and several teachers. They were all strict Calvinists, fearful that the second coming was at hand and possessed of a mission. They were bound for a strange land called Hawaii, 18,000 miles away.

Hawaii, of course, was a lost paradise, a hellhole of sin and savagery where men slept with several wives and women neglected to wear dresses. To the missionaries, it mattered little that the

Hawaiians had lived this way for centuries. The churchmen would save these heathens from hell's everlasting fire whether they liked it or not.

The delegation arrived in Kailua on the Big Island in 1820 and then spread out, establishing important missions in Lahaina and Honolulu. Soon they were building schools and churches, conducting services in Hawaiian and converting the natives to Christianity.

The missionaries rapidly became an integral part of Hawaii, despite the fact that they were a walking contradiction to everything Hawaiian. They were a contentious, self-righteous, fanatical people whose arrogance toward the Hawaiians blinded them to the beauty and wisdom of island lifestyles. Where the natives lived in thatch homes open to the soothing trade winds, the missionaries built airless clapboard houses with New England–style fireplaces. While the Polynesians swam and surfed frequently, the new arrivals, living near the world's finest beaches, stank from not bathing. In a region where the thermometer rarely drops much below 70°, they wore long-sleeved woolens, ankle-length dresses and claw-hammer coats. At dinner they preferred salt pork to fresh beef, dried meat to fresh fish. They considered coconuts an abomination and were loath to eat bananas.

And yet the missionaries were a brave people, selfless and God-fearing. Their dangerous voyage from the Atlantic had brought them into a very alien land. Many would die from disease and overwork; most would never see their homeland again. Bigoted though they were, the Calvinists committed their lives to the Hawaiian people. They developed the Hawaiian alphabet, rendered Hawaiian into a written language and, of course, translated the Bible. Theirs was the first printing press west of the Rockies. They introduced Western medicine throughout the islands and created such an effective school system that, by the mid-19th century, 80 percent of the Hawaiian population was literate. Unlike almost all the other white people who came to Hawaii, they not only took from the islanders, they also gave.

But to these missionaries, *giving* meant ripping away everything repugnant to God and substituting it with Christianity. They would have to destroy Hawaiian culture in order to save it. Though instructed by their church elders not to meddle in island politics, the missionaries soon realized that heavenly wars had to be fought on earthly battlefields. Politics it would be. After all, wasn't government just another expression of God's bounty?

They allied with Kaahumanu and found it increasingly difficult to separate church from state. Kaahumanu converted to Christianity, while the missionaries became government advisers and helped pass laws protecting the sanctity of the Sabbath. Disgusting practices such as hula dancing were prohibited.

Politics can be a dangerous world for a man of the cloth. The missionaries were soon pitted against other foreigners who were quite willing to let the clerics sing hymns, but were adamantly opposed to permitting them a voice in government. Hawaii in the 1820s had become a favorite way station for the whaling fleet. As the sandalwood forests were destroyed, the island merchants began looking for other industries. By the 1840s, when over 500 ships a year anchored in Hawaiian ports, whaling had become the islands' economic lifeblood. On Maui, the population soared to 35,000 and the economy boomed.

Like the missionaries, the whalers were Yankees, shipping out from bustling New England ports. But they were a different cut of Yankee: rough, crude, boisterous men who loved rum and music and thought a lot more of fornicating with island women than saving them. After the churchmen forced the passage of laws prohibiting prostitution, the sailors rioted along the waterfront and fired cannons at the mission homes. When the smoke cleared, the whalers still had their women. When the authorities tried to crack down on debauchery in Lahaina, a band of sailors from the whaling ship *Daniel*, brandishing a black flag, forced the local missionary to barricade himself in his house. Fearing for his life, he was finally rescued by a group of Hawaiians who drove the sailors back to their ship.

It was during the 1840s that Maui, led by a governor who placed money before mores, became a center for wild living. Lahaina, according to the missionaries, was the capital of sin, something of a seaside Sodom.

Religion simply could not compete with commerce, and other Westerners were continuously stimulating more business in the islands. By the mid-19th century, as Hawaii adopted a parliamentary form of government, American and British fortune hunters were replacing missionaries as government advisers. It was a time when anyone, regardless of ability or morality, could travel to the islands and become a political powerhouse literally overnight. A consumptive American, fleeing the mainland for reasons of health, became chief justice of the Hawaiian Supreme Court while still in his twenties. Another lawyer, shadowed from the East Coast by a checkered past, became attorney general two weeks after arriving.

The situation was no different internationally. Hawaii was subject to the whims and terrors of gunboat diplomacy. The archipelago was solitary and exposed, and Western powers were beginning to eye it covetously. In 1843, a maverick British naval officer actually annexed Hawaii to the Crown, but the London government later countermanded his actions. Then, in the early 1850s, the threat of American annexation arose. Restless Californians, fresh from the gold fields and hungry for revolution, plotted un-

successfully in Honolulu. Even the French periodically sent gun-
boats in to protect their small Catholic minority.

Finally, the three powers officially stated that they wanted to
maintain Hawaii's national integrity. But independence seemed
increasingly unlikely. European countries had already begun claiming other Pacific islands, and with the influx of Yankee missionaries and whalers, Hawaii was being steadily drawn into the
American orbit.

THE SUGAR PLANTERS   There is an old Hawaiian saying that
describes the 19th century: The missionaries came to do good,
and they did very well. Actually the early evangelists, few of whom
profited from their work, lived out only half the maxim. Their sons
would give the saying its full meaning.

This second generation, quite willing to sacrifice glory for gain,
fit neatly into the commercial society that had rendered their fa-
thers irrelevant. They were shrewd, farsighted young Christians
who had grown up in Hawaii and knew both the islands' pitfalls
and potentials. They realized that the missionaries had never
found Hawaii's pulse, and they watched uneasily as whaling became the lifeblood of the islands. Certainly it brought wealth, but
whaling was too tenuous—there was always a threat that it might
dry up entirely. A one-industry economy would never do; the mission boys wanted more. Agriculture was the obvious answer, and
eventually they determined to bind their providence to a plant
that grew wild in the islands—sugar cane.

In the years following the California gold rush of 1849, Maui's
agricultural products were in particularly high demand. Prevailing
winds persuaded many captains rounding Cape Horn en route to
San Francisco to reprovision in Maui. Fresh fruits and vegetables,
not to mention sugar cane plants, were plentiful and business for

SPRECKELSVILLE

You have doubtless been losing sleep wondering how the old plantation town
of Spreckelsville got its name. The moniker derives from Claus Spreckels,
known locally as the Sugar King. This 19th-century robber baron combined
business with politics, won the hearts and votes of Hawaii's leaders and
came to dominate the islands' sugar industry. Once, when the Hawaiian
cabinet refused to grant him water rights, Spreckels lent a sum of
money to King Kalakaua, who reciprocated by naming another cabinet.
Spreckels also put His Majesty heavily into debt at the card table,
forcing the legislature to retire the king's gambling debts with a
special loan.

Upcountry farms expanded until the region earned the nickname *Nu Kaliponi*, or New California.

The first sugar plantation was actually started on Kauai in 1835 and on Maui in 1849, but not until the 1870s did the new industry blossom. By then, the Civil War had wreaked havoc with the whaling fleet, and a devastating winter in the Arctic whaling grounds practically destroyed it. The mission boys, who had prophesied the storm, weathered it comfortably. They had already begun fomenting an agricultural revolution.

The entire island of Niihau, which is still owned by the same family, sold for $10,000 in the mid-19th century.

By the early 1860s, James Campbell had built Maui's first large sugar mill. Soon the center of island activity moved from Lahaina to the plantation town of Paia. A narrow-gauge railroad began operating between Kahului and Paia, and the island's population, which had been largely Polynesian and Caucasian, became increasingly Asian.

THE GREAT MAHELE Agriculture, of course, means land, and until the 19th century all Hawaii's acreage was held by chiefs. So in 1848, the mission sons, together with other white entrepreneurs, pushed through the Great Mahele, one of the slickest real estate laws in history. Rationalizing that it would grant chiefs the liberty to sell land to Hawaiian commoners and white men, the mission sons established a Western system of private property.

The Hawaiians, who had shared their chiefs' lands communally for centuries, had absolutely no concept of deeds and leases. What resulted was the old $24-worth-of-beads story. The benevolent Westerners wound up with the land, while the lucky Hawaiians got practically nothing. Large tracts were purchased for cases of whiskey; others went for the cost of a hollow promise. It was a bloodless coup, staged more than 40 years before the revolution that would topple Hawaii's monarchy. In a sense it made the 1893 uprising anticlimactic. By then Hawaii's future would already be determined: white interlopers would own four times as much land as Hawaiian commoners.

On Maui, James Makee established a plantation on the slopes of Haleakala that sprawled across 1000 acres and produced up to 800 tons of sugar a year. His Rose Ranch, at Ulupalakua, became a lavish center of fashionable living. A piano and an organ were imported to entertain those guests uninterested in the bowling alley and tennis court.

Following the Great Mahele, the mission boys, along with other businessmen like Makee, were ready to become sugar planters. The mana once again was passing into new hands. Obviously, there was money to be made in cane, a lot of it, and now that they had land, all they needed was labor. The Hawaiians would never do. Cook might have recognized them as industrious, hardworking people, but the sugar planters considered them shiftless. Disease was killing them off anyway, and the Hawaiians who survived seemed to lose the will to live. Many made appointments with death, stating that in a week they would die; seven days later they were dead.

Foreign labor was the only answer. In 1850, the Masters and Servants Act was passed, establishing an immigration board to import plantation workers. Cheap Asian labor would be brought over. It was a crucial decision, one that would ramify forever through Hawaiian history and change the very substance of island society. Between 1850 and 1930, 180,000 Japanese, 125,000 Filipinos, 50,000 Chinese and 20,000 Portuguese immigrated. They transformed Hawaii from a chain of Polynesian islands into one of the world's most varied and dynamic locales, a meeting place of East and West.

The Chinese were the first to come, arriving in 1852 and soon outnumbering the white population. Initially, with their long pigtails and unusual habits, the Chinese were a joke around the islands. They were poor people from southern China whose lives were directed by clan loyalty. They built schools and worked hard so that one day they could return to their native villages in glory. They were ambitious, industrious and—ultimately—successful.

Too successful, according to the sugar planters, who found it almost impossible to keep the coolies down on the farm. The Chinese came to Hawaii under labor contracts, which forced them to work for five years. After their indentureship, rather than re-enlisting as the sugar bosses had planned, the Chinese moved to the city and became merchants. Worse yet, they married Hawaiian women and were assimilated into the society.

These coolies, the planters decided, were too uppity, too ready to fill social roles that were really the province of white men. So in the 1880s, they began importing Portuguese. But the Portuguese thought they already *were* white men, while any self-respecting American or Englishman of the time knew they weren't.

The Portuguese spelled trouble, and in 1886 the sugar planters turned to Japan, with its restricted land mass and burgeoning population. The new immigrants were peasants from Japan's southern islands, raised in an authoritarian, hierarchical culture in which the father was a family dictator and the family was strictly defined by its social status. Like the Chinese, they built schools to protect their heritage and dreamed of returning home someday; but unlike their Asian neighbors, they only married other Japanese. They sent home for "picture brides," worshiped their ancestors and emperor and paid ultimate loyalty to Japan, not Hawaii.

The Japanese, it soon became evident, were too proud to work long hours for low pay. Plantation conditions were atrocious;

workers were housed in hovels and frequently beaten. The Japanese simply did not adapt. Worst of all, they not only bitched, they organized, striking in 1909.

So in 1910, the sugar planters turned to the Philippines for labor. For two decades the Filipinos arrived, seeking their fortunes and leaving their wives behind. They worked not only with sugar cane but also with pineapples, which were becoming a big business in the 20th century. They were a boisterous, fun-loving people, hated by the immigrants who preceded them and used by the whites who hired them. The Filipinos were given the most menial jobs, the worst working conditions and the shoddiest housing. In time, another side of their character began to show— a despondency, a hopeless sense of their own plight, their inability to raise passage money back home. They became the untouchables of Hawaii.

The sugar industry on Maui, and throughout the islands, was dominated by a sugar refiner named Claus Spreckels, from San Francisco. Buying in to a Maui sugar plantation in 1877, he set his sights on the isthmus that separates Haleakala from the West Maui Mountains. Two other sugar planters, Samuel T. Alexander and Henry P. Baldwin, sons of missionaries, who founded Alexander & Baldwin, one of Hawaii's largest companies, were already digging a 17-mile-long irrigation ditch to their Haiku plantation.

Spreckels, also known as the "Sugar King," manipulated Hawaii's real monarch with bribes and loans into granting him invaluable water rights. Neither Baldwin nor Alexander was any match for "His Royal Saccharinity." By 1880, Maui began yielding the Sugar King's first crop.

REVOLUTIONARIES AND ROYALISTS Sugar, by the late 19th century, was king. It had become the center of island economy, the principal fact of life for most islanders. Like the earlier whaling industry, it was drawing Hawaii ever closer to the American sphere. The sugar planters were selling the bulk of their crops in California; having already signed several tariff treaties to protect their American market, they were eager to further strengthen mainland ties. Besides, many sugar planters were second-, third- and fourth-generation descendants of the New England missionaries; they had a natural affinity for the United States.

There was, however, one group that shared neither their love for sugar nor their ties to America. To the Hawaiian people, David Kalakaua was king, and America was the nemesis that had long threatened their independence. The whites might own the land, but the Hawaiians, through their monarch, still held substantial political power. During Kalakaua's rule in the 1870s and 1880s, anticolonialism was rampant.

The sugar planters were growing impatient. Kalakaua was proving very antagonistic; his nationalist drumbeating was becoming louder in their ears. How could the sugar merchants convince the United States to annex Hawaii when all these silly Hawaiian royalists were running around pretending to be the Pacific's answer to the British Isles? They had tolerated this long enough. The Hawaiians were obviously unfit to rule, and the planters soon joined with other businessmen to form a secret revolutionary organization. Backed by a force of well-armed followers, they pushed through the "Bayonet Constitution" of 1887, a self-serving document that weakened the king and strengthened the white landowners. If Hawaii was to remain a monarchy, it would have a Magna Carta.

But Hawaii would not be a monarchy long. Once revolution is in the air, it's often difficult to clear the smoke. By 1893, Kalakaua was dead and his sister, Liliuokalani, had succeeded to the throne. She was an audacious leader, proud of her heritage, quick to defend it and prone to let immediate passions carry her onto dangerous ground. At a time when she should have hung fire, she charged, proclaiming publicly that she would abrogate the new constitution and reestablish a strong monarchy. The revolutionaries had the excuse they needed. They struck in January, seized government buildings and, with four boatloads of American marines and the support of the American minister, secured Honolulu. Liliuokalani surrendered.

The first president of Hawaii, Sanford Dole, was a missionary boy whose name eventually became synonymous with pineapples.

It was a highly illegal coup; legitimate government had been stolen from the Hawaiian people. But given an island chain as isolated and vulnerable as Hawaii, the revolutionaries reasoned, how much did it really matter? It would be weeks before word reached Washington of what a few Americans had done without official sanction, then several more months before a new American president, Grover Cleveland, denounced the renegade action. By then the revolutionaries would already be forming a republic.

Not even revolution could rock Hawaii into the modern age. For years, an unstable monarchy had reigned; now an oligarchy composed of the revolution's leaders would rule. Officially, Hawaii was a democracy; in truth, the Chinese and the Japanese were hindered from voting, and the Hawaiians were encouraged not to bother. Hawaii, reckoned its new leaders, was simply not ready for democracy.

More than ever before, the sugar planters, alias revolutionaries, held sway. By the early 20th century, they had linked their plantations into a cartel, the Big Five. It was a tidy monopoly composed of five companies that owned not only the sugar and pineapple industries, but also the docks, shipping companies and many of the stores. Most of these holdings, happily, were the property of a few interlocking, intermarrying mission families—

the Doles, Thurstons, Alexanders, Baldwins, Castles, Cookes and others—who had found heaven right here on earth. They golfed together and dined together, sent their daughters to Wellesley and their sons to Yale. All were proud of their roots, and as blindly paternalistic as their forefathers. It was their destiny to control Hawaii, and they made very certain, by refusing to sell land or provide services, that mainland firms did not gain a foothold in their domain.

What was good for the Big Five was good for Hawaii. Competition was obviously not good for Hawaii. Although the Chinese and the Japanese were establishing successful businesses in Honolulu and some Chinese were even growing rich, they posed no immediate threat to the Big Five. And the Hawaiians had never been good at capitalism. By the early 20th century, they had become one of the world's most urbanized groups. But rather than competing with white businessmen in Honolulu, unemployed Hawaiians were forced to live in hovels and packing crates, cooking their poi on stoves fashioned from empty oil cans.

Political competition was also unhealthy. Hawaii was ruled by the Big Five, so naturally it should be run by the Republican Party. After all, the mission families were Republicans. Back on the mainland, the Democrats had always been cool to the sugar planters, and it was a Republican president, William McKinley, who eventually annexed Hawaii. The Republicans, quite simply, were good for business.

The Big Five set out deliberately to overwhelm any political opposition. When the Hawaiians created a home-rule party around the turn of the century, the Big Five shrewdly co-opted it by running a beloved descendant of Hawaii's royal family as the Republican candidate. On the plantations they pitted one ethnic group against another to prevent the Asian workers from organizing. Then, when labor unions finally formed, the Big Five attacked them savagely. In 1924, police killed 16 strikers on Kauai. Fourteen years later, in an incident known as the "Hilo massacre," the police wounded 50 picketers.

The Big Five crushed the Democratic Party by intimidation. Polling booths were rigged. It was dangerous to vote Democratic —workers could lose their jobs, and if they were plantation workers, that meant losing their houses as well. Conducting Democratic meetings on the plantations was about as easy as holding a hula dance in an old missionary church. The Democrats went underground.

Those were halcyon days for both the Big Five and the Republican Party. In 1900, only five percent of Hawaii's population was white. The rest comprised races that rarely benefited from Republican policies. But for the next several decades, even during the Depression, the Big Five kept the Republicans in power.

While the New Deal swept the mainland, Hawaii clung to its colonial heritage. The islands were still a generation behind the rest of the United States—the Big Five preferred it that way. There was nothing like the status quo when you were already in power. Other factors that had long shaped Hawaii's history also played into the hands of the Big Five. The islands' vulnerability, which had always favored the rule of a small elite, permitted the Big Five to establish a formidable cartel. Hawaii's isolation, its distance from the mainland, helped protect their monopoly.

THE JAPANESE AND THE MODERN WORLD   All that ended on December 7, 1941. The Japanese bombers that attacked Pearl Harbor sent shock waves through Hawaii that are still rumbling today. World War II changed all the rules of the game, upsetting the conditions that had determined island history for centuries.

Ironically, no group in Hawaii would feel the shift more thoroughly than the Japanese. When the emperor declared war on the United States, 160,000 Japanese-Americans were living in Hawaii, fully one-third of the islands' population. On the mainland, Japanese-Americans were rounded up and herded into relocation camps. But in Hawaii that was impossible; there were simply too many, and they made up too large a part of the labor force.

Many were second-generation Japanese, *nisei*, who had been educated in American schools and assimilated into Western society. Unlike their immigrant parents, the *issei*, they felt few ties to Japan. Their loyalties lay with America and, when war broke out, they determined to prove it. They joined the U.S. armed forces and formed a regiment, the 442nd, which became the most frequently decorated outfit of the war. The Japanese were heroes, and when the war ended many heroes came home to the United States and ran for political office. Men like Daniel Inouye and Spark Matsunaga began winning elections and would eventually become U.S. senators.

By the time the 442nd returned to the home front, Hawaii was changing dramatically. The Democrats were coming to power. Leftist labor unions won crucial strikes in 1941 and 1946. Jack Burns, an ex-cop who dressed in tattered clothes and drove around Honolulu in a beat-up car, was creating a new Democratic coalition.

TORA! TORA! TORA!

Although Oahu was devastated by the Japanese attack on Pearl Harbor, Maui suffered but a single casualty. A week after the Pacific war began, the Maui Pineapple Company was hit by a pair of Japanese submarine shells. Total damage: $700.

Burns, who would eventually become governor, recognized the potential power of Hawaii's ethnic groups. Money was flowing into the islands—first military expenditures and then tourist dollars—and nonwhites were rapidly becoming a new middle class. The Filipinos still constituted a large part of the plantation workforce, and the Hawaiians remained disenchanted, but the Japanese and the Chinese were moving up fast. Together they constituted a majority of Hawaii's voters.

While in 1939 about 500 people flew to Hawaii, now about seven million visitors land every year.

Burns organized them, creating a multiracial movement and thrusting the Japanese forward as candidates.

By 1954, the Democrats controlled the legislature, with the Japanese filling one out of every two seats in the capital. Then, when Hawaii attained statehood five years later, the voters elected the first Japanese ever to serve in Congress. Today one of the state's U.S. senators and a congressman are Japanese. On every level of government, from municipal to federal, the Japanese predominate. They have arrived. The mana, that legendary power coveted by the Hawaiian chiefs and then lost to the sugar barons, has passed once again—to a people who came as immigrant farm-workers and stayed to become the leaders of the 50th state.

The Japanese and the Democrats were on the move, but in the period from World War II until the present day, everything was in motion. Hawaii was in upheaval. Jet travel and a population boom shattered the islands' solitude. The military population escalated as Oahu became a key base not only during World War II but throughout the Cold War and the Vietnam War as well. Hawaii's overall population exploded from about a half-million just after World War II to over one million today.

No longer did the islands lag behind the mainland; they rapidly acquired the dubious quality of modernity. Hawaii became America's 50th state in 1959, Honolulu grew into a bustling highrise city, and hotels and condominiums mushroomed along Maui's beaches. In 1961, the Kaanapali area of Maui became the first resort complex to be built on a neighbor island.

Outside investors swallowed up two of the Big Five corporations, and several partners in the old monopoly began conducting most of their business outside Hawaii. Everything became too big and moved too fast for Hawaii to be entirely vulnerable to a small interest group. Now, like the rest of the world, it would be prey to multinational corporations.

By the 1980s, Hawaii would also be of significant interest to investors from Japan. In a few short years they succeeded in buying up a majority of the state's luxury resorts, including every major beachfront hotel in Waikiki and a number of resorts on Maui, sending real estate prices into an upward spiral that did not level off until the early 1990s. During the rest of the decade, the economy was stagnant, with real estate prices dropping, agriculture declining and tourism leveling off at seven million visitors annually; but by the year 2000 Hawaii was beginning to experience yet another boom.

One element that did not plateau during the last decade was the Native Hawaiian movement. Nativist sentiments were spurred in January 1993 by the 100th anniversary of the American overthrow of the Hawaiian monarchy. Over 15,000 people turned out to mark the illegal coup. Later that year, President Clinton signed a statement issued by Congress formally apologizing to the Hawaiian people. Then in 1994, the United States Navy returned the island of Kahoolawe to the state of Hawaii. Long a rallying symbol for the Native Hawaiian movement, the unoccupied island had been used for decades as a naval bombing target. By 1996, efforts to clean away bomb debris and make the island habitable were well under way, although completion of the clean-up is still years off. Then in 1998, the issue of Hawaii's monarchy arose again when demonstrators marched around the entire island of Oahu and staged rallies to protest the 100th anniversary of the United States' annexation of Hawaii.

Today, numerous perspectives remain to be reconciled, with grassroots movements working to secure a degree of autonomy for Hawaii's native people. The most common goal seems to be a status similar to that accorded the American Indians by the federal government, although there are still those who seek a return to an independent Hawaii, either as a restored monarchy or along democratic lines. Also pending resolution is the distribution of land to native Hawaiians with documented claims, as well as a financial settlement with the state government. It's a complex situation involving the setting right of injustices of a century past.

Culture

Hawaii, according to Polynesian legend, was discovered by Hawaii-loa, an adventurous sailor who often disappeared on long fishing trips. On one voyage, urged along by his navigator, Hawaii-loa sailed toward the planet Jupiter. He crossed the "many-colored ocean," passed over the "deep-colored sea," and eventually came upon "flaming Hawaii," a mountainous island chain that spewed smoke and lava.

History is less romantic. The Polynesians who found Hawaii were probably driven from their home islands by war or some similar calamity. They traveled in groups, not as lone rangers, and shared their canoes with dogs, pigs and chickens, with which they planned to stock new lands. Agricultural plants such as coconuts, yams, taro, sugar cane, bananas and breadfruit were also stowed on board.

Most important, they transported their culture, an intricate system of beliefs and practices developed in the South Seas. After undergoing the stresses and demands of pioneer life, this traditional lifestyle was transformed into a new and uniquely Hawaiian culture.

It was based on a caste system that placed the *alii*, or chiefs, at the top and the slaves, *kauwas*, on the bottom. Between these two groups were the priests, *kahunas*, and the common people, *makaainanas*. The chiefs, much like feudal lords, controlled all the land and collected taxes from the commoners who farmed it. Each island was divided like a pie into wedge-shaped plots, *ahu-puaas*, which extended from the ocean to the mountain peaks. In that way, every chief's domain contained fishing spots, village sites, arable valleys and everything else necessary for the survival of his subjects.

Life centered around the *kapu*, a complex group of regulations that dictated what was sacred or profane. For example, women were not permitted to eat pork or bananas; commoners had to prostrate themselves in the presence of a chief. These strictures were vital to Hawaiian religion; *kapu* breakers were directly violating the will of the gods and could be executed for their actions. And there were a lot of gods to watch out for, many quite vindictive. The four central gods were *Kane*, the creator; *Lono*, the god of agriculture; *Ku*, the war god; and *Kanaloa*, lord of the underworld. They had been born from the sky father and earth mother, and had in turn created many lesser gods and demigods who controlled various aspects of nature.

It was, in the uncompromising terminology of the West, a stone-age civilization. Though the Hawaiians lacked metal tools, the wheel and a writing system, they managed to include within their inventory of cultural goods everything necessary to sustain a large population on a chain of small islands. They fashioned fish nets from native *olona* fiber, made hooks out of bone, shell and ivory, and raised fish in rock-bound ponds. The men used irrigation in their farming. The women made clothing by pounding mulberry bark into a soft cloth called tapa, dyeing elaborate patterns into the fabric. They built peak-roofed thatch huts from native *pili* grass and *hala* leaves. The men fought wars with spears, slings, clubs and daggers. The women used mortars and pestles to pound the roots of the taro plant into poi, the islanders' staple food. Breadfruit, yam and coconut were other menu standards.

The West labeled these early Hawaiians "noble savages." Actually, they often lacked nobility. The Hawaiians were cannibals who practiced human sacrifice during religious ceremonies and often used human bone to fashion fish hooks. They constantly warred among themselves and would mercilessly pursue a retreating army, murdering as many of the vanquished soldiers as possible.

Sovereignty

Since the "Hawaiian Renaissance" began several decades ago, the call among native Hawaiians for island sovereignty has increased in volume.

The mistrust many Hawaiians feel toward the U.S. government goes back to the overthrow of the monarchy in 1893. Many are outspoken in their demands that Washington right the wrong that was done to them.

There is confusion, however, among various Hawaiian groups as to what exactly should be done. Some activists see the sovereignty movement as a struggle to elevate the native Hawaiian people socially and economically within the context of American society. Many believe in compromise, calling for reparations for native Hawaiians. Other more radical voices demand that Hawaii secede from the United States, reinstate the monarchy and declare itself an independent country.

To those of us watching this struggle from the outside, it's easy to become confused by the different approaches and factions. Even Hawaiians calling simply for reparations are divided as to what constitutes a "native Hawaiian." Does that mean pure Hawaiian, 50 percent Hawaiian blood, or 25 percent?

As with all political movements, there are many issues the Hawaiians are trying to work out. But amid the ambiguity there is a unanimous sense of love for their islands, a passion for their culture and a belief that justice ultimately will prevail.

But they weren't savages either. The Hawaiians developed a rich oral tradition of genealogical chants and created beautiful lilting songs to accompany their hula dancing. The Hawaiians helped develop the sport of surfing. They also swam, boxed, bowled and devised an intriguing game called *konane*, a cross between checkers and the Japanese game of *go*. They built networks of trails across lava flows, and created an elemental art form in the images—petroglyphs—that they carved into lava rock along the trails.

They also achieved something far more outstanding than their varied arts and crafts, something that the West, with its awesome knowledge and advanced technology, has never duplicated. The Hawaiians on Maui and other islands created a balance with nature. They practiced conservation, establishing closed seasons on certain fish species and carefully guarding their plant and animal resources. They led a simple life, without the complexities the outside world would eventually thrust upon them. It was a good life: food was plentiful, people were healthy and the population increased. For a thousand years, the Hawaiians lived in delicate harmony with the elements. It wasn't until the West entered the realm, transforming everything, that the fragile balance was destroyed. But that is another story entirely.

PEOPLE   Because of its unique history and isolated geography, Hawaii is truly a cultural melting pot. It's one of the few states in the union in which white people are a minority group. Whites, or *haoles* as they're called in the islands, comprise only about 22 percent of Hawaii's 1.2 million population. Japanese constitute 18 percent, Filipinos 13 percent, Hawaiians and part-Hawaiians account for 21 percent, Chinese about 3 percent and other racial groups 24 percent. The population of Maui is a little more than 100,000 and the ethnic mix is similar to that in the rest of the islands.

It's a very vital society, with one-fifth of the people born of racially mixed parents.

One trait characterizing many of these people is Hawaii's famous spirit of aloha, a genuine friendliness, an openness to strangers, a willingness to give freely. Undoubtedly, it is one of the finest qualities any people has ever demonstrated. Aloha originated with the Polynesians and played an important role in ancient Hawaiian civilization.

The aloha spirit is alive and well in the islands, although bad attitudes toward *haoles*, the pejorative term used for whites, are not unknown. All parties, however, seem to understand the crucial role tourism has come to play in Hawaii's economy, which means you're not likely to experience unpleasantness from the locals you'll meet.

CUISINE   Nowhere is the influence of Hawaii's melting pot population stronger than in the kitchen. While on Maui, you'll probably eat not only with a fork, but with chopsticks and fingers as well. You'll sample a wonderfully varied cuisine. In addition to standard American fare, hundreds of restaurants serve Hawaiian, Japanese, Chinese, Korean, Portuguese and Filipino dishes. There are also fresh fruits aplenty—pineapples, papayas, mangoes, bananas and tangerines—plus native fish such as mahimahi, marlin and snapper.

The mainstay of the traditional Hawaiian diet is poi, a purplish paste pounded from baked or steamed taro tubers. It's pretty bland fare, but it does make a good side dish with *imu*-cooked pork or tripe stew. You should also try *laulau*, a combination of fish, pork and taro leaves wrapped in a *ti* leaf and steamed. And don't neglect to taste baked *ulu* (breadfruit) and *opihi* (limpets).

Among the other Hawaiian culinary traditions are *kalua* pig, a shredded pork dish baked in an *imu*; *lomilomi* salmon, which is salted and mixed with onions and tomatoes; and chicken *luau*, prepared in taro leaves and coconut milk.

A good way to try all these dishes at one sitting is to attend a luau. This Hawaiian tradition is maintained by community organizations, which advertise the events in the newspaper, and, in a manner of speaking, by major resorts, who sponsor splashy shows.

I suggest that you take in the local color at a neighborhood feast. If you decide instead on one of the commercial events, consider the **Old Lahaina Luau**. It's a small event, staged on the waterfront in a historic region favored by Hawaiian monarchs. Cast members offer a succession of entertaining traditional Hawaiian dances. The *lomilomi* salmon is first rate. Daily. ~ 1251 Front Street, Lahaina; 808-667-1998.

Japanese dishes include sushi, sukiyaki, teriyaki and tempura, plus an island favorite—sashimi, or raw fish. On most any menu, including McDonald's, you'll find *saimin*, a noodle soup filled with meat, vegetables and *kamaboko* (fishcake).

You can count on the Koreans for *kim chi*, a spicy salad of pickled cabbage, and *kalbi*, barbecued beef short ribs prepared with soy and sesame oil. The Portuguese serve up some delicious sweets including *malasadas* (donuts minus the holes) and *pao doce*, or sweet bread. For Filipino fare, I recommend *adobo*, a pork or chicken dish spiced with garlic and vinegar, and *pochero*, a meat entrée cooked with bananas and several vegetables. In addition to a host of dinner dishes, the Chinese have contributed treats such as *manapua* (a steamed bun filled with barbecued pork) and oxtail soup. They also introduced crack seed to the islands. Made from dried and preserved fruit, it provides a treat as sweet as candy.

As the Hawaiians say, *"Hele mai ai."* Come and eat!

◆◆◆

CREAMED ONIONS

Everyone knows about the shortages and rationing during World War II. But few have heard about the great Maui surplus. It seems that in May 1942, as local farmers were about to harvest a bumper crop of sweet Maui onions, a shipment of 900 tons of onions arrived on the island. The local populace responded with an innovative "Maui Onion Week," touting delights such as "creamed onions." Onion breath had become patriotic!

LANGUAGE   The language common to all Hawaii is English, but because of its diverse cultural heritage, the archipelago also supports several other tongues. Foremost among these are Hawaiian and pidgin.

Hawaiian, closely related to other Polynesian languages, is one of the most fluid and melodious languages in the world. It's composed of only 12 letters: five vowels—*a, e, i, o, u* and seven consonants—*h, k, l, m, n, p, w*. The glottal stop ('), when used, counts as a thirteenth letter.

At first glance, the language appears formidable: how the hell do you pronounce *humuhumunukunukuapuaa*? But actually it's quite simple. After you've mastered a few rules of pronunciation, you can take on any word in the language.

The first thing to remember is that every syllable ends with a vowel, and the next to last syllable usually receives the accent.

The next rule to keep in mind is that all the letters in Hawaiian are pronounced. Consonants are pronounced the same as in English (except for the *w*, which is pronounced as a *v* when it introduces the last syllable of a word—as in *ewa* or *awa*). Vowels are pronounced the same as in Latin or Spanish: *a* as in *among*, *e* as in *they*, *i* as in *machine*, *o* as in *no* and *u* as in *too*. Hawaiian has four vowel combinations or diphthongs: *au*, pronounced *ow*, *ae* and *ai*, which sound like *eye*, and *ei*, pronounced *ay*. As noted above, the glottal stop (') occasionally provides a thirteenth letter.

By now, you're probably wondering what I could possibly have meant when I said Hawaiian was simple. I think the glossary that follows will simplify everything while helping you pronounce common words and place names. Just go through the list, starting with words like *aloha* and *luau* that you already know. After you've practiced pronouncing familiar words, the rules will become second nature; you'll no longer be a *malihini*.

Just when you start to speak with a swagger, cocky about having learned a new language, some young Hawaiian will start

SOUNDS FISHY

What are all those strange-sounding fish dishes on the menu? A quick translation will help you when choosing a seafood platter from Hawaiian waters. Firm-textured with a light taste, the most popular fish is *mahimahi*, or dolphin fish (no, it's not one of those amazing creatures that do fancy tricks on the waves); its English equivalent is dorado. *Ahi* is yellowfin tuna and is especially delicious as sashimi (raw) or blackened. *Opakapaka* is pink snapper and is a staple of Pacific Rim cuisine. Other snappers include *uku* (gray snapper), *onaga* (ruby snapper) and *ehu* (red snapper). *Ono* (which means "delicious" in Hawaiian) is king mackerel, a white fish that lives up to its name.

talking at you in a tongue that breaks all the rules you've so carefully mastered. That's pidgin. It started in the 19th century as a lingua franca among Hawaii's many races. Pidgin speakers mix English and Hawaiian with several other tongues to produce a spicy creole. It's a fascinating language with its own vocabulary, a unique syntax and a rising inflection that's hard to mimic.

Pidgin is definitely the hip way to talk in Hawaii. A lot of young Hawaiians use it among themselves as a private language. At times they may start talking pidgin to you, acting as though they don't speak English; then if they decide you're okay, they'll break into English. When that happens, you be one *da kine brah*.

So *brah*, I take *da kine* pidgin words, put 'em together with Hawaiian, make one big list. Savvy?

aa (ah-**ah**)—a type of rough lava
ae (eye)—yes
aikane (eye-**kah**-nay)—friend, close companion
akamai (ah-kah-**my**)—wise
alii (ah-**lee**-ee)—chief
aloha (ah-**lo**-ha)—hello; greetings; love
aole (ah-**oh**-lay)—no
auwe (ow-**way**)—ouch!
brah (bra)—friend; brother; bro'
bumby (**bum**-bye)—after a while; by and by
da kine (da kyne)—whatdyacallit; thingamajig; that way
dah makule guys (da mah-**kuh**-lay guys)—senior citizens
diamondhead—in an easterly direction (Oahu only)
duh uddah time (duh **uh**-duh time)—once before
ewa (**eh**-vah)—in a westerly direction (Oahu only)
hale (**hah**-lay)—house
haole (**how**-lee)—Caucasian; white person
hapa (**hah**-pa)—half
hapa-haole (**hah**-pa **how**-lee)—half-Caucasian
heiau (hey-**yow**)—temple
hele on (**hey**-lay own)—hip; with it
hoaloha (ho-ah-**lo**-ha)—friend
holo holo (**ho**-low **ho**-low)—to visit
howzit? (hows-it)—how you doing? what's happening?
huhu (who-who)—angry
hukilau (**who**-key-lau)—community fishing party
hula (**who**-la)—Hawaiian dance
imu (ee-moo)—underground oven
ipo (ee-po)—sweetheart
kahuna (kah-**who**-nah)—priest; specialist or expert in any field
kai (kye)—ocean
kaka-roach (**kah**-kah roach)—ripoff; theft

kamaaina (kah-mah-**eye**-nah)—one born and raised in
  Hawaii; a longtime island resident
kane (**kah**-nay)—man
kapu (**kah**-poo)—taboo; forbidden
kapuna (**kah**-poo-nah)—elder
kaukau (cow-cow)—food
keiki (**kay**-key)—child
kiawe (key-**ah**-vay)—mesquite tree
kokua (ko-**coo**-ah)—help
kona winds (**ko**-nah winds)—winds that blow against the
  trades
lanai (lah-**nye**)—porch; also island name
lauhala (lau-**hah**-lah) or *hala* (**hah**-lah)—a pandanus tree
  whose leaves are used in weaving
lei (lay)—flower garland
lolo (low-low)—stupid
lomilomi (**low**-me-**low**-me)—massage; also raw salmon
luau (**loo**-ow)—feast
mahalo (mah-**hah**-low)—thank you
mahalo nui loa (mah-**ha**-low **new**-ee **low**-ah)—thank you
  very much
mahu (**mah**-who)—gay; homosexual
makai (mah-**kye**)—toward the sea
malihini (mah-lee-**hee**-nee)—newcomer; stranger
mana (**mah**-nah)—spiritual or divine power
mauka (**mau**-kah)—toward the mountains
nani (**nah**-nee)—beautiful
ohana (oh-**hah**-nah)—family
okole (oh-**ko**-lay)—rear; ass
okolemaluna (oh-ko-lay-mah-**loo**-nah)—a toast: bottoms up!
ono (**oh**-no)—tastes good
pahoehoe (pah-**hoy**-hoy)—smooth or ropy lava
pakalolo (pah-kah-**low**-low)—marijuana
pakiki head (pah-**key**-key head)—stubborn
pali (**pah**-lee)—cliff
paniolo (pah-nee-**oh**-low)—cowboy
pau (pow)—finished; done
pilikia (pee-lee-**key**-ah)—trouble
puka (**poo**-kah)—hole
pupus (**poo**-poos)—hors d'oeuvres
shaka (**shah**-kah)—great; perfect
swell head—"big" head; egotistical
tapa (**tah**-pah) also **kapa**—fabric made from the beaten
  bark of mulberry shrubs
wahine (wah-**hee**-nay)—woman
wikiwiki (**wee**-key-**wee**-key)—quickly; in a hurry
you get stink ear—you don't listen well

Music has long been an integral part of Hawaiian life. Most families keep musical instruments in their homes, gathering to play at impromptu living room or backyard jam sessions. Hawaiian folk tunes are passed down from generation to generation. In the earliest days, it was the sound of rhythm instruments and chants that filled the air. Drums, including the *pahu hula*, were fashioned from hollowed-out gourds, coconut shells or hollowed sections of coconut palm trunks, then covered with sharkskin. Gourds and coconuts, *uliuli*, adorned with tapa cloth and feathers, were also filled with shells or pebbles to produce a rattling sound. Other instruments included the nose flute, or *ohe*, a piece of bamboo similar to a mouth flute, but played by exhaling through the nostril; the bamboo organ; and *puili*, sections of bamboo split into strips, which were struck rhythmically against the body. Stone castanets, *illili*, and *ke laau* sticks are also used as hula musical instruments.

Western musical scales and instruments were introduced by explorers and missionaries. As ancient Hawaiian music involved a radically different musical system, Hawaiians had to completely re-adapt. Actually, western music caught on quickly, and the hymns brought by missionaries fostered a popular musical style— the *himeni*, or Hawaiian church music.

Tune in to KPOA-FM 93.5 and 102.7 for island sounds and Hawaiian music.

Strangely enough, a Prussian bandmaster named Henry Berger had a major influence on contemporary Hawaiian music. Brought over by King Kalakaua to lead the Royal Hawaiian Band, Berger helped Hawaiians make the transition to Western instruments.

Hawaii has been the birthplace of several different musical instruments and styles. The ukulele, modeled on a Portuguese guitar, quickly became the most popular Hawaiian instrument. Its small size made it easy to carry, and with just four strings, it was simple to play. During the early 1900s, the steel guitar was exported to the mainland. Common in country-and-western music today, it was invented by a young man who experimented by sliding a steel bar across guitar strings.

The slack-key style of guitar playing also comes from Hawaii, where it's called *ki ho'alu*. When the guitar was first brought to Hawaii in the 1830s by Mexican and Spanish cowboys, the Hawaiians adapted the instrument to their own special breed of music. In tuning, the six (or twelve) strings are loosened so that they sound a chord when strummed and match the vocal range of the singer. Slack-key is played in a variety of ways, from plucking or slapping the strings to sliding along them. A number of different tunings exist, and many have been passed down orally through families for generations. Some of the more renowned guitarists playing today include Keola Beamer, Raymond Kana and Cyril Pahinui.

During the late 19th century, "*hapa*-haole" songs became the rage. The ukulele was instrumental in contributing to this Hawaiian fad. Written primarily in English with pseudo-Hawaiian themes, songs like "Tiny Bubbles" and "Lovely Hula Hands" were later introduced to the world via Hollywood.

The Hawaiian craze continued on the mainland with radio and television shows such as "Hawaii Calls" and "The Harry Owens Show." In the 1950s, little mainland girls donned plastic hula skirts and danced along with Hilo Hattie and Ray Kinney.

It was not until the 1970s that both the hula and music of old Hawaii made a comeback. Groups such as the Sons of Hawaii and the Makaha Sons of Niihau, along with Auntie Genoa Keawe and the late Gabby Pahinui, became popular. Before long, a new form of Hawaiian music was being heard, a combination of ancient chants and contemporary sounds, performed by such islanders as Henry Kapono, Kalapana, Olomana, the Beamer Brothers, the Peter Moon Band and the Brothers Cazimero.

Hula *halaus*, or schools, are serious business even on the mainland. Competitions bring together *halaus* throughout the islands. On Maui, check out the Annual Festival of Hula held in January.

Today many of these groups, along with other notables such as Hapa, the Kaau Crater Boys, Brother Noland, Willie K., Butch Helemano and Obrien Eselu, bring both innovation to the Hawaiian music scene and contribute to the preservation of an ancient tradition. The trend continues with hybrid infusions of reggae and rock, while performers like Kealii Reichel and groups like Kapena maintain the soft-edged sounds so well-suited to the islands.

An entire new category of music has become established in Hawaii: dubbed "Jawaiian," the sound incorporates Jamaican reggae and contemporary Hawaiian music, and is especially popular amongst the state's younger population. In addition, now-deceased masters of Hawaiian song like Gabby Pahinui and Israel Kamakawiwoole have gained renewed popularity and respect for the links they created between old and contemporary Hawaiian music.

HULA

Along with palm trees, the hula—swaying hips, grass skirts, colorful leis—is linked forever in people's minds with the Hawaiian Islands. This western idea of hula is very different from what the dance has traditionally meant to native Hawaiians.

Hula is an old dance form, its origin shrouded in mystery. The ancient hula, *hula kahiko*, was more concerned with religion and spirituality than entertainment. Originally performed only by men, it was used in rituals to communicate with a deity—a connection to nature and the gods. Accompanied by drums and chants, *hula kahiko* expressed the islands' culture, mythology and history in hand and body movements. It later evolved from a strictly religious rite to a method of communicating stories and legends. Over the years, women were allowed to study the rituals and eventually became the primary dancers.

When westerners arrived, *hula kahiko* began another transformation. Explorers and sailors were more interested in its erotic element, ignoring the cultural significance. Missionaries simply found it scandalous and set out to destroy the tradition. They dressed Hawaiians in western garb and outlawed *hula kahiko*.

The hula tradition was resurrected by King David Kalakaua. Known by the moniker "Merrie Monarch," Kalakaua loved music and dance. For his coronation in 1883, he called together the kingdom's best dancers to perform the chants and hulas once again. He was also instrumental in the development of the contemporary hula, the *hula auwana*, which added new steps and movements and was accompanied by ukuleles and guitars rather than drums.

By the 1920s, modern hula had been popularized by Hollywood, westernized and introduced as kitschy tropicana. Real grass skirts gave way to cellophane versions, plastic leis replaced fragrant island garlands, and exaggerated gyrations supplanted the hypnotic movements of the traditional dance.

Fortunately, with the resurgence of Hawaiian pride in recent decades, Polynesian culture has been reclaimed and *hula kahiko* and traditional chants have made a welcome comeback.

FOUR

Lahaina

Maui's top tourist destination is a waterfront enclave that stretches for over two miles along a natural harbor, but measures only a couple of blocks deep. Simultaneously chic and funky, Lahaina has gained an international reputation for its art galleries, falsefront stores and waterfront restaurants.

It also happens to be one of Hawaii's most historic towns. A royal seat since the 16th century, Lahaina was long a playground for the *alii*. The royal surfing grounds lay just south of today's town center, and in 1802, Kamehameha I established his headquarters here, taking up residence in the Brick Palace, the first Western-style building in Hawaii.

It was in Lahaina that the first high school and first printing press west of the Rockies were established in 1831. From Lahaina, Kamehameha III promulgated Hawaii's first constitution in 1840, and established a legislative body that met in town until the capital was eventually moved to Honolulu.

During the 1820s, this quaint port also became a vital watering place for whaling ships and evolved into the whaling capital of the world. At its peak in the mid-1840s, the whaling trade brought over 400 ships a year into the harbor.

To the raffish sailors who favored it for its superb anchorage, grog shops and uninhibited women, Lahaina was heaven itself. To the stiff-collared missionaries who arrived in 1823, the town was a hellhole—a place of sin, abomination and vile degradation. Some of Lahaina's most colorful history was written when the Congregationalists prevented naked women from swimming out to meet the whalers. Their belligerent brethren anchored in the harbor replied by cannon-balling mission homes and rioting along the waterfront.

The town declined with the loss of the whaling trade in the 1860s, and was transformed into a quiet sugar plantation town, serving the Pioneer Sugar Mill that opened during the same decade. Not until developers began building resorts in nearby Kaanapali a century later did it fully revive. During the 1960s, Lahaina was designated a national historic landmark and restoration of many important sites was begun. By the 1970s, the place was a gathering spot not only for the jet set but the ultra hip as well. Clubs like the Blue Max made Lahaina a hot nightspot where famous musicians came to vacation and jam.

Today, Lahaina retains a gentrified charm with shops, galleries, clubs and restaurants lining Front Street, an oceanside "Main Street." Most points of interest lie within a half-mile of the old sea wall that protects this narrow thoroughfare from the ocean, so the best way to explore the town is on foot.

Start at **Lahaina Harbor**, located on Wharf Street, and take a stroll along the docks. In addition to tour boats, pleasure craft from around the world put in here or cast anchor in the Lahaina Roads just offshore. During the heyday of the whaling industry in the 1840s, the Auau Channel between Lahaina and Lanai was a forest of masts.

Carthaginian II, the steel-hulled brig at dock's end, preserves those days in a shipboard museum. Actually a turn-of-the-20th-century brig that was converted into a replica of an old square-rigged sailing ship, this floating display case features videotapes on whales and intriguing artifacts from days of yore. Admission. ~ 808-661-8527.

Across Wharf Street sits the **Pioneer Inn**, a rambling hostelry built in 1901. With its second-story veranda and landscaped garden, this aging woodframe hotel is a great place to bend an elbow and breathe in the salt air. ~ 658 Wharf Street; 808-661-3636, fax 808-667-9366; www.pioneerinnmaui.com, e-mail info@pioneerinnmaui.com.

Just north of here a Hawaii Visitors Bureau sign points out the chair-shaped **Hauola Stone**, a source of healing power for ancient Hawaiians, who sat in the natural formation and let the waves wash over them.

There is nothing left of the **Brick Palace**, the two-story structure commissioned in 1798 by Kamehameha I. Located just inshore from the Hauola Stone and built by an English convict, the palace was used by the king in 1802 and 1803 (although some say he preferred to stay in his grass shack next door). Today the original foundation has been outlined with brick paving.

To the south, a **banyan tree**, among the oldest and largest in the islands, extends its rooting branches across almost an entire acre. Planted in 1873 to mark the advent of Protestant missionaries in Maui 50 years earlier, this shady canopy is a resting place for tourists and mynah birds alike. ~ Front and Hotel streets.

The sprawling giant presses up against the **Old Courthouse**, constructed in 1859 from coral blocks taken from the home built for King Kamehameha III. The historic building is home to the **Lahaina Visitors Center** (808-667-9193), where you can pick up maps and brochures, including one that provides all the details needed for a self-guided walking tour of Lahaina. The **Lahaina Art**

Society (808-661-0111), a non-profit association of local artists, is also located in the courthouse. Art shows are presented under the banyan tree by the Art Society every other weekend. On alternate weekends Hawaiian crafts are the theme.

Those stone ruins on either side of the courthouse are the remains of the **Old Fort**, built during the 1830s to protect Lahaina from the sins and cannonballs of lawless sailors. The original structure was torn down two decades later to build a jail, but during its heyday the fortress guarded the waterfront with 47 cannons.

Across Front Street is the **Baldwin Home**, Lahaina's oldest building. Constructed of coral and stone in the early 1830s, the place sheltered the family of Reverend Dwight Baldwin, a medical missionary. Today the house contains period pieces and family heirlooms, including some of the good doctor's rather fiendish-looking medical implements. Beneath the hand-hewn ceiling beams rests the Baldwin's Steinway piano; the dining room includes the family's china, a fragile cargo that made the voyage around Cape Horn; and in the master bedroom stands a four-poster bed fashioned from native *koa*. Admission. ~ 808-661-3362, fax 808-661-9309; www.lahainarestoration.org, e-mail info@maui.net.

The **Master's Reading Room** next door, an 1834 storehouse and library, is home to the Lahaina Restoration Foundation and not open to the public.

A Chinese gathering place that dates to 1912, the **Wo Hing Museum** has been lovingly restored. While the temple has been converted into a small museum, the old cookhouse adjacent is used to show films of the islands made by Thomas Edison in 1898 and 1903 during the early days of motion pictures. ~ 858 Front Street; 808-661-5553, fax 808-661-9309.

The **Holy Innocents' Episcopal Church** is a small structure dating from 1927. Very simple in design, the sanctuary is filled with beautiful paintings. The Hawaiian madonna on the altar and the tropical themes of the paintings are noteworthy features. Services are Sunday at 7 a.m. and 10 a.m. ~ 561 Front Street; 808-661-4202, fax 808-661-8667; e-mail ccannon@aloha.net.

Several other historic spots lie along Wainee Street, which parallels Front Street. **Waiola Cemetery**, with its overgrown lawn and eroded tombstones, contains graves dating to 1829. Queen Keopuolani, the wife of Kamehameha I and the mother of Hawaii's next two kings, is buried here. So is her daughter, Princess Nahienaena, and Governor Hoapali, who ruled Hawaii from 1823 to 1840. Surrounded by blossoming plumeria trees, there are also the graves of early missionaries and Hawaiian commoners.

Maui's first Christian services were performed in 1823 on the grounds of **Waiola Church** next door. Today's chapel, built in 1953, occupies the spot where the Wainee church was constructed in 1832. The earlier structure, Hawaii's first stone church, seated 3000 parishioners and played a vital role in the conversion of the local population to Christianity and Western ways. ~ 535 Wainee Street; 808-661-4349, fax 808-661-1734.

A little farther north on Wainee Street sits the **Lahaina Hongwanji Temple** with its three distinctive turrets. The building dates from 1927, but the Buddhist Hongwanji sect has been meeting at this site since 1910.

On the corner of Prison and Wainee streets rise the menacing walls of old **Hale Paahao**, a prison built by convicts in 1854 and used to house rowdy sailors as well as more hardened types. The coral blocks used to build this local hoosegow were taken from the Old Fort on Front Street.

Just north of the jail along Wainee Street sits the **Episcopal Cemetery** and **Hale Aloha**. Walter Murray Gibson, a controversial figure in 19th-century Hawaiian politics who eventually became an adviser to King David Kalakaua, is buried here. Hale Aloha, completed in 1858 and restored several years ago, served as a church meetinghouse.

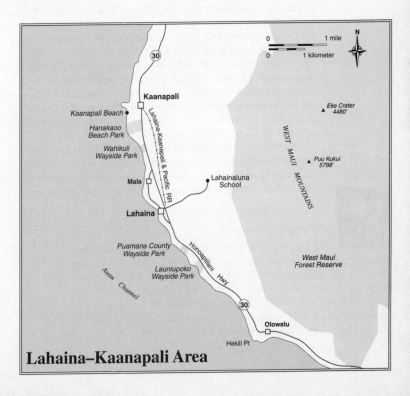

Lahaina–Kaanapali Area

Nearby is **Maria Lanakila Church**, a lovely white-washed building with interior pillars that was built in 1928 to replace a 19th-century chapel. Adjacent is the **Seamen's Cemetery**, a poorly maintained ground where early sailors were laid to rest. ~ Wainee and Dickenson streets.

The **Lahaina Shingon Mission**, a simple plantation-era structure with an ornately gilded altar, was built in 1902 by a Japanese monk and his followers. It now represents another gathering place for Maui's Buddhists. ~ 682 Luakini Street between Hale and Dickenson streets; phone/fax 808-661-0466.

The proverbial kids-from-eight-to-eighty set will love the **Sugar Cane Train**, a reconstructed 1890-era steam train. Operating near the West Maui resort area, the Lahaina–Kaanapali & Pacific Railroad engine and passenger cars chug along a six-mile route midway between the mountains and ocean. Various package tours are available with the train rides, including a ride on a semisubmersible vessel in Lahaina, helicopter tours, bicycle trips down the slopes of a volcano, and a viewing of the film *Hawaii: Islands of the Gods*, shown on the 180-degree screen at the Omni Theatre. Admission. ~ The main station is off Hinau Street in Lahaina; 808-661-0089, 800-499-2307, fax 808-661-8389; www.sugarcanetrain.com.

Oceanic adventurers might want to take an opportunity to stop in at **Atlantis Submarines** and reserve an underwater tour. The voyage takes you aboard a 48-passenger submersible down to depths of 150 feet. En route you may see close-up views of technicolor coral reefs and outlandish lava formations. A trip to the depths requires deep pockets; these two-hour excursions aren't cheap. ~ 665 Front Street, in the Pioneer Inn; 808-667-2224, fax 808-667-5747; www.goatlantis.com.

And for a splendid view of Lahaina, turn off Route 30 onto Lahainaluna Road, pass the now-closed, century-old Pioneer Mill, and head *mauka* (toward the mountains) to **Lahainaluna School**. Established by missionaries in 1831, it is one of the country's old-

sights

AUTHOR FAVORITE

For a journey of a spiritual nature, don't miss **Lahaina Jodo Mission**, a Buddhist enclave one-half mile north of Lahaina on Ala Moana Street. There's a temple and a three-tiered pagoda here, as well as the largest ceremonial bell in Hawaii. The giant bronze Buddha, with the West Maui Mountains in the background, is a sight to behold. It rests amid stone walkways and flowering oleander bushes in a park-like setting. ~ 12 Ala Moana Street; 808-661-4304, fax 808-661-0939.

est high schools. Today this historic facility serves as a public high school for the Lahaina area. ~ 808-662-3997, fax 808-662-3997.

Hale Pai, its printing house dating to 1837, printed Hawaii's first money and many of the first bibles, religious tracts and primers produced in the islands. Hale Pai is open as a museum and research library. It houses a working reproduction of the original printing press. Closed Saturday and Sunday. ~ Phone/fax 808-667-7040; e-mail halepai@maui.net.

To fully capture the spirit of Lahaina, there's only one place to stay—the **Best Western Pioneer Inn**. Located smack on Lahaina's waterfront, this wooden hostelry is the center of the area's action. On one side, sloops, ketches and glass-bottom boats are berthed; on the other side lies bustling Front Street with its falsefront shops. The Inn is noisy, vibrant and crowded with tenants and tourists. On the ground floor, you can hunker down over a glass of grog at the saloon, or stroll through the Inn's lushly planted courtyard. Accommodations are located in the section overlooking the courtyard. These are small and plainly decorated, with telephones, overhead fans, air conditioning and lanais. A swimming pool completes the picture. ~ 658 Wharf Street; 808-661-3636, 800-457-5457, fax 808-667-5708; www.pioneerinnmaui.com, e-mail info@pioneerinnmaui.com. DELUXE.

LODGING

While the building is actually quite modern, the **Plantation Inn** possesses the look and ambience of an early-20th-century hostelry. Modeled after the plantation architecture of an earlier era, it features 19 rooms individually decorated in period furniture. Most are adorned with either poster, brass or canopy bed, stained-glass windows and tile bathrooms. Combining the atmosphere of the past with the amenities of the present, guest rooms also feature televisions, refrigerators and air conditioning, as well as VCRs on request. There's a pool with a shaded pavilion and jacuzzi on the premises. Continental breakfast. ~ 174 Lahainaluna Road; 808-667-9225, 800-433-6815, fax 808-667-9293; www.theplantationinn.com, e-mail info@theplantation inn.com. DELUXE TO ULTRA-DELUXE.

The Oscar for most original inn goes to the **Lahaina Inn**. Constructed in the early 20th century, this 12-room beauty was fully restored and appointed in Gay Nineties finery. Each room is wall to ceiling with gorgeous antiques—leaded glass lamps, mirrored armoires, original oil paintings, cast-iron beds and brass locks. Attention to detail is a way of life: the place simply exudes the aura of another era. If you don't stay here, stop by and visit. ~ 127 Lahainaluna Road; 808-661-0577, 800-808-669-3444, fax 808-667-9480; www.lahainainn.com, e-mail inntown@lahainainn.com. MODERATE TO DELUXE.

The **Aston Maui Islander Hotel** is a warren of woodframe buildings spread across lushly landscaped grounds. The ambience is an odd combination of tropical retreat and motel atmosphere. It features 360 trimly decorated rooms, some of which are small studios (with kitchens) and one-bedroom efficiencies. Amenities include a swimming pool, laundry, tennis court and picnic area. ~ 660 Wainee Street; 808-667-9766, 800-367-5226, fax 808-661-3733; www.astonhotels.com. MODERATE TO ULTRA-DELUXE.

CONDOS

Though it's more expensive than many others, **Lahaina Shores Hotel** has the advantage of a beachfront location in Lahaina. This sprawling condominium complex offers studio apartments beginning at $160, while one-bedroom units start at $225. With a swimming pool, jacuzzi and the nearby beach, it's quite convenient. ~ 475 Front Street; 808-661-4835, 800-628-6699, fax 808-667-1145; www.lahaina-shores.com, e-mail info@classicresorts.com. DELUXE TO ULTRA-DELUXE.

HIDDEN ▶

Perhaps the nicest complex to stay on this side of the island is **Puamana**, a 28-acre retreat about a mile southeast of Lahaina. This townhouse complex, a 1920s-era sugar plantation, rests along a rock-strewn beach. The oceanfront clubhouse, open to guests, was once the plantation manager's house, and the landscaped grounds are still given over to mango, plumeria and torch ginger trees. Guests stay in low-slung plantation-style buildings that sport shake-shingle roofs and house from two to six units. Prices begin in the deluxe range for one-bedroom facilities that contain kitchens and sleep up to four people, and end in the ultra-deluxe range for two- and three-bedroom efficiencies that sleep up to six and eight, respectively. To round out the amenities there are three pools and a tennis court. There's a three-night minimum that increases to seven nights during the Christmas season. ~ 34 Pualima Place; 808-667-2551. Reservations through Klahani Resorts: 800-628-6731, fax 808-661-5875; www.klahani.com, e-mail klahani @hotmail.com. DELUXE TO ULTRA-DELUXE.

DINING

The **Pioneer Inn Restaurant** brings back the Lahaina of old. The main dining room is a cozy anchorage dotted with nautical fixtures and specializing in regional fare. The emphasis is on the "bounty of Hawaii"; in other words, fresh fish, upcountry produce and local herbs. Select one of the day's fresh fish specials and you can't go wrong. Breakfast begins at 6 a.m. ~ 658 Wharf Street; 808-661-3636, fax 808-667-5708. DELUXE.

Across the lobby from the Pioneer Inn Restaurant, the **Pioneer Grill and Bar** offers similar but less formal fare and boasts a view of Lahaina Harbor. Portuguese bean soup is a specialty of both eateries and both fire their dishes on a *kiawe* grill. No dinner served. ~ 658 Wharf Street; 808-661-3636, fax 808-667-9366. MODERATE TO DELUXE.

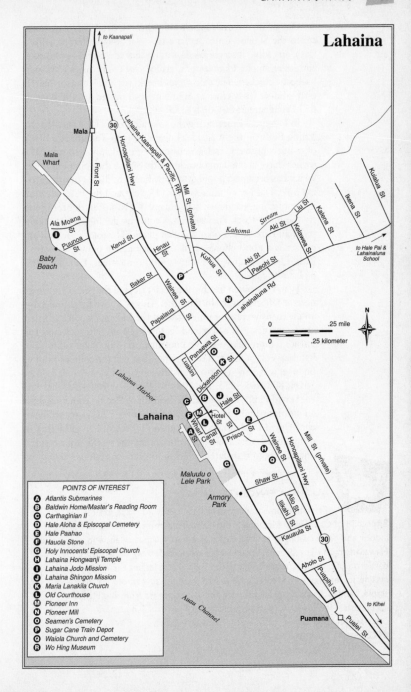

Lahaina

to Kaanapali

Mala

Mala Wharf

30

Lahaina-Kaanapali & Pacific RR

Honoapiilani Hwy

Front St

Mill St (private)

Kahoma Stream

Kulalua St

Ikena St

Kelena St

Liu St

Aki St

Kelawea St

to Hale Pai & Lahainaluna School

Ala Moana St

Puunoa St

Baby Beach

Kenui St

Hinau St

Kuhua St

Aki St

Paeohi St

Baker St

Wainee St

P

Lahainaluna Rd

N

0   .25 mile

0   .25 kilometer

N

Papalaua St

R

Liakini

Panaewa St

Dickenson St

K   St

Luakini

B

J

Hale St

O

D

E

C

F

M

Hotel St

L

Wharf

Prison St

Wainee St

Honoapiilani Hwy

Mill St (private)

A   Canal St

Lahaina

Lahaina Harbor

H

G

Maluulu o Lele Park

Armory Park

Shaw St

Alio St

Ilikahi St

Kauaula St

30

Aholo St

Puapihi St

Auau Channel

Puamana

Pualei St

to Kihei

POINTS OF INTEREST

- **A** Atlantis Submarines
- **B** Baldwin Home/Master's Reading Room
- **C** Carthaginian II
- **D** Hale Aloha & Episcopal Cemetery
- **E** Hale Paahao
- **F** Hauola Stone
- **G** Holy Innocents' Episcopal Church
- **H** Lahaina Hongwanji Temple
- **I** Lahaina Jodo Mission
- **J** Lahaina Shingon Mission
- **K** Maria Lanakila Church
- **L** Old Courthouse
- **M** Pioneer Inn
- **N** Pioneer Mill
- **O** Seamen's Cemetery
- **P** Sugar Cane Train Depot
- **Q** Waiola Church and Cemetery
- **R** Wo Hing Museum

One of my favorite light-food stops is a devil-may-care place called the **Sunrise Café**. Set in a tiny clapboard building with a fresh, airy look, it serves salads, sandwiches and espresso, plus such entrées as smoked *kalua* pork, grilled chicken breast and mango barbecue chicken. The café serves breakfast, lunch and an "early-bird" dinner (they close at 6:30 p.m.). ~ Located around back at 693 Front Street; 808-661-8558. BUDGET.

In Lahaina Center facing the seawall is one of the best family-dining finds on the westside. **Lucarelli's Hop Tomato** is a blend of a microbrewery and a reasonably priced Italian bistro. The owners have created an outdoor patio on the shopping-mall side, which has become a popular "hoppy hour" and after-hours watering hole. Did I say "microbrewery?" Yes! And the beer selection is outstanding, particularly if you enjoy a robust dark beer (gotta try the Black Rock Porter). Pizzas come by the foot, Neapolitan-style, and are served on a wooden plank. The toasted ravioli appetizer is a good choice, as is the spicy penne putanesca entrée. Kids' dishes are just $4 each. ~ 900 Front Street, Lahaina; 808-661-8580. MODERATE.

I can't say much for the nomenclature, but the prices are worth note at **Cheeseburger in Paradise**. This is a rare catch indeed—an inexpensive restaurant smack on the Lahaina waterfront that serves three meals a day and features live nightly rock-and-roll music. Granted, you won't find much on the menu other than hamburgers, salads and sandwiches. But if some couples can live on love, why can't the rest of us live on ocean views? ~ 811 Front Street; 808-661-4855, fax 808-661-9508. BUDGET TO MODERATE.

David Paul's Lahaina Grill, headlining Pacific Rim cuisine, is an intimate dining room with a personalized touch. According to chef David Paul Johnson, the menu represents "a gathering of technique, flavors and skills from around the world, utilizing local ingredients to translate each dish into an exceptional dining ex-

AUTHOR FAVORITE

I'o is the name and creative, delicious food is the game. Brainchild of Chef James McDonald, this beachfront restaurant offers both indoor and patio seating in an area that was a favored spot of ancient Hawaiian royalty. The decor is an undersea world of fantasy set against a backdrop of high-tech fixtures. This is the style that matches the chef's cuisine; for example, he creates a New Age salad utilizing an old Hawaii staple, hand-picked pohole fern shoots and sweet papaya from the Hana rainforests, served with a roasted garlic pesto. The local fish preparations are amazing. Dinner only. ~ 505 Front Street, Lahaina; 808-661-8422. DELUXE TO ULTRA-DELUXE.

perience." Currently you can order the tequila shrimp with fire-cracker rice, soft-shell crabs, Kona coffee–roasted rack of lamb or macadamia-smoked tenderloin, but the menu changes regularly. Decide for yourself whether he carries it off. Dinner only. ~ 127 Lahainaluna Road; 808-667-5117, 800-360-2606; www.lahaina grill.com, e-mail lahainagrill@aol.com. ULTRA-DELUXE.

A defining experience in Lahaina dining is **Gerard's Restaurant**. Here you'll encounter a French restaurant in a Victorian setting with tropical surroundings. Housed in the Plantation Inn, a bed and breakfast reminiscent of early New Orleans, Gerard's provides a chandelier-and-pattern-wallpaper dining room as well as a veranda complete with overhead fans and whitewashed balustrade. The chef prepares fresh fish, rack of lamb, *confit* of duck and puff pastry with shiitake mushrooms. Of course, that is after having started off with ahi steak tartar or crab bisque. Dinner only. ~ 174 Lahainaluna Road; 808-661-8939; e-mail gerard@maui.net. ULTRA-DELUXE.

The surf-and-turf menu at **Woody's Oceanfront Grill** features blackened ahi, barbecued ribs, grilled *ono* and New York strip. Familiar appetizers are prepared with an island twist such as onion rings with mango ketchup and grilled tiger shrimp served with a fresh mint and papaya relish. Dining is on two decks overlooking the water. ~ 839 Front Street; 808-661-8788; e-mail woodys@ mauigateway.com. MODERATE TO DELUXE.

The preferred style of dining in Lahaina is steak and seafood at one of the waterfront restaurants along Front Street. And the common denominator is the ever-popular, usually crowded **Kimo's**, where you can enjoy all the tropical amenities while dining on seafood fettuccine, lobster or prime rib. Most days a week they have live Hawaiian music. ~ 845 Front Street; 808-661-4811; www.hulapie.com, e-mail tskimos@aol.com. MODERATE TO DELUXE.

At **Longhi's**, a European-style café that specializes in Mediterranean dishes, informality is the password. The menu changes daily and is never written down; the waiter simply tells you the day's offerings. Usually there'll be several pasta dishes, sautéed vegetables, salads, a shellfish creation, steak, a wine-soaked chicken or veal dish and perhaps eggplant parmigiana. Longhi's prepares all of its own bread and pasta, buys Maui-grown produce and imports many cheeses from New York. The dinners reflect this diligence. Breakfasts and lunches are cooked with the same care. Definitely recommended, especially for vegetarians, who can choose from many of the dishes offered. ~ 888 Front Street; 808-667-2288; e-mail longhi@maui.net. DELUXE TO ULTRA-DELUXE.

The **Bubba Gump Shrimp Co.** pays homage to the movie *Forrest Gump*. Featuring "shrimp any way you can think of eating it," and other American-style food, it is also filled with *Gump* memorabilia. ~ 889 Front Street; 808-661-3111, fax 808-667-6650; www.bubbagump.com. MODERATE TO DELUXE.

In the Lahaina Shopping Center, the **Thai Chef Restaurant** is a cozy place with an inviting assortment of Southeast Asian dishes. Try the Korean papaya salad, sautéed chili chicken or seafood with red curry sauce. ~ 843 Wainee Street; 808-667-2814; thaichef maui.aol.com. MODERATE.

Local Food is a takeout stand that sells plate lunches, juices and fruits. No dinner. Closed Saturday and Sunday. ~ 222 Papalaua Street; 808-667-2882, fax 808-669-1137. BUDGET.

If you've seen one **Hard Rock Café**, you know about the line for the T-shirt window, the line for a table and the line for the bar. What a formula: just get yourself a show car from the '50s, a few surfboards, guitars and Buddy Holly posters, throw in an exposed-beam ceiling and circular bar and you've got the Maui branch of this popular empire. The menu runs from beef and veggie burgers to lime barbecue chicken, marinated T-bones and fajitas. ~ Lahaina Center, 900 Front Street; 808-667-7400, fax 808-667-5929; www.hardrock.com. MODERATE.

Light, bright and airy, **Compadres** is a great place to sip a margarita or enjoy a Mexican meal with an island flair. The tropical ambience is as appealing as the steaming dishes served here. Especially popular are the fajitas and pork carnitas, but the menu also offers burgers, salads and vegetarian dishes. Breakfast, lunch and dinner—they open at 8 a.m. ~ Lahaina Cannery Mall, 1221 Honoapiilani Highway; 808-661-7189; e-mail compadresmaui@ hi.freei.net. MODERATE TO DELUXE.

If you like Greek food, you'll enjoy **Athens Greek Restaurant**, a fast-food stand at the Lahaina Cannery Mall where the gyros are generously stuffed with fresh ingredients and the shish kebabs come in chicken, fish and beef varieties (go for the fish). Take your meal to a nearby table and catch the passing scene. ~ Lahaina Cannery Mall, 1221 Honoapiilani Highway; 808-661-4300. BUDGET.

MOKUULU, A ROYAL AND SACRED SANCTUARY

Beneath a county park in Lahaina, archaeologists have uncovered one of the islands' most historical sites—**Mokuulu**. It is thought to have once been the political and spiritual center of Maui, with royal residences and a royal mausoleum there, as well as Mokuhinia, a natural wetland and fishpond. Carbon dating shows it to be one of the earliest signs of human existence in the islands. **Friends of Mokuulu** is an organization created to try and restore the site. ~ Friends of Mokuula, 505 Front Street, Lahaina; www.mokuula.com.

Slightly (I said *slightly*) off the tourist track is the **Old Lahaina Luau**. Dinner here is based on the traditional luau—from the grass hut buildings to the menu of roast pork, kalua pig, sweet potato, mahimahi and poi. Reserve early, show up on time and be prepared to make an evening of it. ~ 1251 Front Street, behind the Lahaina Cannery Mall; 808-667-1998, 800-248-5828; www.old lahainaluau.com, e-mail kim@oldlahainaluau.com. DELUXE.

Aloha Mixed Plate, on the edge of town, is a beach shack by day serving saimin, udon, burgers and plate lunches. ~ 1285 Front Street; 808-661-3322, fax 808-661-3087. BUDGET.　◀ *HIDDEN*

Near the top of the cognoscenti's list of gourmet establishments is an unlikely looking French restaurant in Olowalu called **Chez Paul**. The place is several miles outside Lahaina in a reno-　◀ *HIDDEN* vated building that also houses Olowalu's funky general store. But for years this little hideaway has had a reputation far transcending its surroundings. You'll probably drive right past the place at first, but when you do find it, you'll discover a menu featuring such delicacies as homemade duck pâté with mustard seed, grilled rack of lamb with mango chutney, island fish poached in champagne and several other tempting entrées. While the tab is ethereal, the rave reviews this prim dining room receives make it worth every franc. Closed Sunday in summer. ~ Honoapiilani Highway, Olowalu; 808-661-3843, fax 808-667-5692; e-mail lucien@aloha.net. ULTRA-DELUXE.

Foodland is open daily from 6 a.m. to midnight. ~ Old Lahaina　**GROCERIES** Center, Wainee Street; 808-661-0975.

For health-food items, stop by **Westside Natural Food**. Open from 7:30 a.m. to 9 p.m. Monday to Saturday and 8:30 a.m. to 8 p.m. on Sunday. ~ 193 Lahainaluna Road; 808-667-2855.

South of Lahaina, the **Olowalu General Store** has a limited supply of grocery items. ~ Honoapiilani Highway, Olowalu; 808-661-3774.

Lahaina's a great place to combine shopping with sightseeing.　**SHOPPING** Most shops are right on Front Street in the historic wooden buildings facing the water. For a walking tour of the stores and waterfront, start from the Pioneer Inn at the south end of the strip and walk north on the *makai* or ocean side. Then come back along the *mauka*, or mountain, side of the street.

One of the first shops you will encounter on this consumer's tour of Lahaina will be **The Gecko Store**. The only shop I've seen with a sand floor, it stocks inexpensive beachwear as well as T-shirts and toys. ~ 703 Front Street; 808-661-1078.

The **Endangered Species Store**, which features a multitude of conservation-minded items, is a worthy stop. Among other things, you will find chimes, statues and a healthy supply of T-shirts and stuffed animals. ~ 707 Front Street; 808-661-0208.

Lahaina Galleries is of special note not only for the contemporary artworks but also because of the imaginative ways in which they're displayed. Even if you're not just dying to write that five-figure check, stop by for a viewing. ~ 728 Front Street; 808-667-2152, 800-228-2006; www.lahainagalleries.com.

Célébrités is a trendy showcase for the artistic work of several musicians and actors, including John Lennon, Miles Davis, the Rolling Stones' Ronnie Wood, Anthony Quinn and Charles Bronson. They also have album cover art and pieces signed by the Beatles and the Stones. ~ 764 Front Street; 808-667-0727.

There are just a few more street numbers before this shopper's promenade ends. Then if you cross the road and walk back in the opposite direction, with the sea to your right, you'll pass **South Seas Trading Post**, where you can barter greenbacks for Nepali wedding necklaces, Chinese porcelain opium pillows or New Guinea masks. ~ 780 Front Street; 808-661-3168.

Past the sea wall, in an overgrown cottage set back from the street, lie several shops including **Pacific Vision**, with its hand-etched glass, hand-painted clothing, and bedding. ~ 819 Front Street; 808-661-0188.

Sgt. Leisure Resort Patrol has an array of imaginative T-shirts. ~ 855B Front Street; 808-667-0661.

The **Wharf Cinema Center** is a multilevel complex of shops and restaurants. Most interesting is **Island Coin & Stamps** (808-667-6155), where all sorts of Hawaiiana and other collectibles make tempting souvenirs. The theater is small, but the movies are first run if you're in the mood for a film while you're on Maui.

If you have children in tow, take a break and head to the **Fun Factory** (808-667-1922). There's enough video games and other electronic attractions to keep them busy for hours. While they're being entertained, you can enjoy a drink at the **Blue Lagoon Tropical Bar and Grill** (808-661-8141) in the adjacent courtyard. ~ 658 Front Street; 808-661-8748.

Contemporary Village Gallery features paintings by modern Hawaiian artists. Amid the tourist schlock is some brilliant artwork. ~ 180 Dickenson Street; 808-661-5559.

Also stop in at the Lahaina Art Society's **Banyan Tree Gallery**. This is a great place if you're in the market for local artwork; on display are pieces by a number of Maui artists. ~ 648 Wharf Street, first floor of the Old Courthouse; 808-661-0111.

The **Lahaina Cannery Mall**, a massive complex of stores housed in an old canning factory, is the area's most ambitious project. **Hawaiian Island Gems** (808-661-1731) is where you can pick up Hawaiian heirlooms, jewelry, Tahitian and Akoya pearls or designs by Kabana and Steven Douglas. **Kite Fantasy** (808-661-

4766; www.kitefantasy.com) is the place to pick up stunt and sport kites including diamond, box and bird designs. Here you'll also find wind socks, kaleidoscopes, games and a wide array of toys. Complete flying instructions, including tips on where to launch your kite, are provided by the helpful staff. ~ 1221 Honoapiilani Highway.

> If you're on Maui for Halloween, don't miss Lahaina's uninhibited celebration. The costumes are wild and everyone's out for a good time. It's the closest Hawaii gets to Mardi Gras.

Those are just a couple ideas to provide you with a jump start. Propel yourself through this place and you'll find a dozen more reasons that make it a favorite among Lahaina residents.

On the corner of Front and Papalana streets, **Lahaina Center** is another shopping mall, a sprawling complex of theaters, stores and restaurants. Among the shops here is **Just Mauied**, which caters to honeymooners, featuring frames made of *tapa*, a local tree bark, mugs and other cutesy items (808-661-5883). **Hilo Hattie Fashion Center** (808-667-7911) specializes in the tackiest alohawear imaginable. ~ 900 Front Street.

NIGHTLIFE

Front Street's the strip in Lahaina—a dilapidated row of buildings from which stream some of the freshest sounds around.

At the **Pioneer Grill and Bar**, there is no music, but it's worth a drop-in anyway. Tucked into a corner of the Best Western Pioneer Inn, this spot features a seagoing motif complete with harpoons, figureheads and other historical nautical decor. Usually packed to the bulkheads with a lively crew, it's a great place to enjoy a tall cold one. ~ 658 Wharf Street; 808-661-3636.

Moose McGillycuddy's is a hot club offering a large dancefloor and a variety of live music acts. The house is congenial and the drinks imaginatively mixed; for contemporary sounds with dinner, arrive before 9 p.m. Cover on Wednesday. ~ 844 Front Street; 808-667-7758.

Since it's named after Jimmy Buffett's famous lyric, it's only appropriate that **Cheeseburger in Paradise** should have live music. With a variety of performers, they have "fun" tunes from 4:30 'til close—around 10 p.m. every night. There is no dancefloor, however. ~ 811 Front Street; 808-661-4855.

Lahaina's favorite pastime is watching the sun set over the ocean while sipping a tropical concoction at a waterfront watering place. A prime place for this very rewarding activity is **Kimo's**, which features traditional Hawaiian music Monday through Thursday, and rock-and-roll on Friday and Saturday. ~ 845 Front Street; 808-661-4811.

The Bubba Gump Shrimp Co. hosts musicians nightly who play music that is—you guessed it—the sort featured in *Forrest Gump*. For those who didn't see the movie, that means classic '60s and '70s tunes. ~ 889 Front Street; 808-661-3111.

If you want to sample Maui and Hawaii microbrews, head to **Maui Brews**. With over 16 micros on tap, a full bistro menu and live music (cover), who could not enjoy themselves? Sit under the thatch at the bar or hang out at the ocean-view lanai. ~ Lahaina Center, 900 Front Street; 808-667-7794.

If it's Friday in Lahaina, you can also browse the town's art galleries, which sponsor a special **Art Night** every week. This is a great opportunity to meet some of the artists who have made Lahaina an international art scene. The artists, who welcome visitors at galleries where their work is displayed, talk story and add a unique personal touch to a night on the town.

For an awe-inspiring glimpse into Hawaii's past, watch the 40-minute film at the **Omni Theatre/Hawaii Experience**. Offering a three-dimensional perspective of the state's cultural and natural history, this film is shown on a huge domed 180-degree screen. Admission. ~ 824 Front Street; 808-661-8314.

When **Maui Myth & Magic Theatre** debuted, most people weren't sure what it really was, judging by its name. Now, just mention the theater's name or the name of its award-winning production, 'Ulalena, and chances are you'll hear that it's fantastic and not to be missed. Both high-tech and culturally beautiful, it's constantly evolving. The mix is one part live theater with two parts musical à la Broadway and one part Cirque du Soleil. What makes 'Ulalena unique is the story—it is a manifestation of the ancient Hawaiian *kumulipo* (creation chant) combined with Hawaii's mythology and history through the ages. Performances run twice nightly, Tuesday through Saturday. Admission. ~ Old Lahaina Center, 878 Front Street; 808-661-9913, 877-688-4800; www.mauitheatre.com.

Magic seems to pervade LahainaTown these days, and another entertainment experience is **Warren & Annabelle's**. "Warren" is Warren Gibson, a master at sleight-of-hand magic and owner of this theater. "Annabelle" is the ghost of a woman who lived in Lahaina during the whaling era and lost her sweetheart to the sea. She can still be seen (or rather, heard) at her piano, playing tunes for the return of her lost love. Elegantly appointed in turn-of-the-20th-century splendor, Annabelle's Parlor is also a restaurant/lounge. The waitstaff sings while helping guests call out song requests to Annabelle. After the preliminaries, doors open to the theater for an entertaining magic show. Unlocking the secret passage to enter the parlor is also part of the fun. The show runs Monday through Saturday. Admission. ~ 900 Front Street; 808-667-6244; www.warrenandannabelles.com.

BEACHES & PARKS
PAPALAUA WAYSIDE PARK 🛶 🛥 🏊 *Kiawe* trees and scrub vegetation spread right to the shoreline along Papalaua Wayside

Park. There are sandy patches between the trees large enough to spread a towel, but I prefer sunbathing at beaches closer to Lahaina. Bounded on one side by Honoapiilani Highway, this narrow beach extends for a mile to join a nicer, lawn-fringed park; then it stretches on toward Olowalu for several more miles. If you want to be alone, just head down the shore. Swimming is good, snorkeling is okay out past the surf break and surfing is excellent at Thousand Peaks breaks and also very good several miles east in Maalaea Bay. There's an outhouse and picnic area at the county wayside. ~ Located about ten miles south of Lahaina on Honoapiilani Highway.

OLOWALU BEACHES 🏖 🤿 🏄 🐟 To the north and south of Olowalu General Store lie narrow corridors of white sand. This is an excellent area to hunt for Maui diamonds. Swimming is very good, and south of the general store, where road and water meet, you'll find an excellent coral reef for snorkeling. There is also a growing green sea turtle population that can be seen by snorkelers at the 14-mile marker. Surfers will find good breaks with right and left slides about a half-mile north of the general store. *Ulua* are often caught from Olowalu landing. There are no facilities, but there is a market nearby. ~ Go south from Lahaina on Honoapiilani Highway for about six miles.

LAUNIUPOKO WAYSIDE PARK 🏖 🤿 🏄 There is a seaside lawn shaded by palm trees and a sandy beach. A rock seawall slopes gently for entering swimmers, but offers little to sunbathers. It's located near the West Maui Mountains, with great views of Kahoolawe and Lanai. When the tide is high, it's a good place to take children to swim safely and comfortably in the tidal pool on the other side of the seawall. Otherwise, swimming and snorkeling are mediocre. There is good surf-casting from the seawall and south for three miles. The park has a picnic area, restrooms and showers. ~ Located three miles south of Lahaina on Honoapiilani Highway.

PUAMANA COUNTY WAYSIDE PARK 🏖 🤿 🏄 🐟 A narrow beach and grass-covered strip wedged between Honoapiilani Highway and the ocean, Puamana Park is dotted with iron-

---

ROYAL HAWAIIAN HOLIDAYS

Although the Hawaiian capital moved to Honolulu in 1850, Lahaina remained a favorite vacation spot for several kings, including Kamehameha III, IV and V, and Queen Liliuokalani. All had second homes in the area and returned often to indulge in those favorite Hawaiian pastimes—rest and relaxation.

wood trees. The excellent views make this a choice spot for an enjoyable picnic. Facilities include restrooms and showers. ~ Located about two miles south of Lahaina on Honoapiilani Highway.

ARMORY PARK ⚓ 🦅 🏊 🚤 The one thing going for this park is its convenient location in Lahaina. Otherwise, it's heavily littered, shadowed by a mall and sometimes crowded. If you do stop by, try to forget all that and concentrate on the sandy beach, lawn and truly startling view of Lanai directly across the Auau Channel. Swimming is okay, snorkeling good past the reef and, for surfing, there are breaks in the summer near the seawall in Lahaina Harbor. This surfing spot is not for beginners! Threadfin and *ulua* are common catches here. Restrooms and tennis courts are across the street at Maluulu o Lele Park near the playing field. ~ Located on Front Street next to the 505 Front Street mall.

BABY BEACH ⚓ 🦅 🚤 This curving stretch of white sand is the best beach in Lahaina. It lacks privacy but certainly not beauty. From here you can look back to Lahaina town and the West Maui Mountains or out over the ocean to Kahoolawe, Lanai and Molokai. Or just close your eyes and soak up the sun. Swimming is good and well protected, if shallow. Snorkeling is only fair. In summer there are breaks nearby at Mala Wharf; left slide. Threadfin is often caught. ~ Take Front Street north from Lahaina for about a half-mile. Turn left on Puunoa Place and follow it to the beach.

WAHIKULI WAYSIDE PARK ⚓ 🦅 🚤 This narrow stretch of beach and lawn, just off the road between Lahaina and Kaanapali, faces Lanai and Molokai. There are facilities aplenty, which might be why this pretty spot is so popular and crowded. Swimming is very good, but snorkeling is only fair. (There's a better spot just north of here near the Lahaina Canoe Club.) The most common catches here are *ulua* and threadfin. Facilities include picnic areas and restrooms; there are tennis courts up the street

SEA WORLD AT SEA

Take an early-morning voyage on a boat out of Lahaina and you might just encounter one of the ocean's friendliest and most acrobatic creatures. Cruising between Maui and Lanai, you'll suddenly find yourself in the midst of over 100 sea mammals—a pod of spinner dolphins who will play tag with your craft and dance above the waves like a troupe of whirling dervishes. There's nothing quite like it. Other dolphins that may be sighted in Hawaiian waters are the bottlenose, Risso's, melon-headed, rough-toothed, pygmy killers, and spotted or striped dolphins.

at the Civic Center. ~ Located between Lahaina and Kaanapali on Honoapiilani Highway.

HANAKAOO BEACH PARK Conveniently located beside Kaanapali Beach Resort, this long and narrow park features a white-sand beach and grassy picnic ground, and is referred to by locals as Canoe Beach. On Saturday during summer season, this is the place to watch Hawaiian canoe racing. The road is nearby, but the views of Lanai are outstanding. Swimming is good, snorkeling fair, but surfing poor. Common catches include *ulua* and threadfin. There are picnic areas, restrooms and showers. ~ Located between Lahaina and Kaanapali on Honoapiilani Highway.

FIVE

Kaanapali–Kapalua Area

Even in the case of Maui's notorious land developers, there is method to the madness. The stretch of coastline extending for six miles along Maui's western shore, crowded to the extreme with hotels and condominiums, is anchored by two planned resorts. Like handsome bookends supporting an uneven array of dog-eared paperbacks, Kaanapali and Kapalua add class to the arrangement.

Supporting the south end, **Kaanapali** is a 500-acre enclave that extends along three miles of sandy beach and includes six hotels, a half-dozen condominiums, two golf courses and an attractive shopping mall. Back in the 19th century it was a dry and barren segment of the sugar plantation that operated from Lahaina. Raw sugar was hauled by train from the mill out to Black Rock, a dramatic outcropping along Kaanapali Beach, where the produce was loaded onto waiting ships.

In 1963, Kaanapali's first resort opened near Black Rock and development soon spread in both directions. Important to developers, who built the Sheraton Maui hotel around it, **Black Rock** (Puu Kekaa) is a volcanic cinder cone from which ancient Hawaiians believed that the dead departed the earth in their journey to the spirit world. According to legend, the great 18th-century Maui chief Kahekili proved his bravery by leaping from the rock to the ocean below.

Kaanapali's modern-day contribution to Pacific culture is the **Whalers Village Museum**. This facility comprises an outdoor pavilion and a museum that details Lahaina's history of whaling. Outdoors, you'll find a 30-foot-long whale skeleton and a whaling longboat on display. The "golden era of whaling" is also portrayed in scrimshaw exhibits, a scale-model whaling ship, harpoons and other artifacts from the days when Lahaina was one of the world's great whaling ports. Self-guided tours are available. There's a wonderful shop on site, with a selection of fossilized whale ivory scrimshaw in addition to Victorian-era antiques. ~ Whalers Village, 2435 Kaanapali Parkway, Kaanapali; 808-661-5992, fax 808-661-8584.

An earlier chief, Piilani, built a road through the area in the 16th century and gave his name to modern-day Route 30, the Honoapiilani Highway. Translated as "the bays of Piilani," the road passes several inlets located north of Kaanapali that have been developed in haphazard fashion. Honokowai, Kahana and Napili form a continuous wall of condominiums that sprawls north to Kapalua Bay and offers West Maui's best lodging bargains.

Kapalua, the bookend holding the north side in place, is a former pineapple plantation that was converted into a luxurious 1500-acre resort. Here two major hotels, three golf courses and several villa-style communities blanket the hillside from the white sands of Kapalua Bay to the deep green foothills of the West Maui Mountains. Like the entire strip along Maui's western flank, Kapalua enjoys otherworldly sunsets and dramatic views of Lanai and Molokai.

In the Kaanapali area the modestly priced hotel is not an endangered species, it's totally extinct! So prepare yourself for steep tariffs.

LODGING

In the realm of luxury hotels, the **Hyatt Regency Maui** is one of the better addresses in Hawaii. Built in 1980, its atrium lobby, Asian artwork and freeform swimming pool set the standard for resorts ever since. Unlike more recent hotels, in which the size of guest rooms is sacrificed for the sake of lavish grounds, the Hyatt Regency maintains an ideal balance between public and private areas. If you're seeking beautiful surroundings, friendly service and beachfront location, this 815-room extravaganza is the ticket. ~ 200 Nohea Kai Drive, Kaanapali; 808-661-1234, 800-233-1234, fax 808-667-4499; www.maui.hyatt.com, e-mail hrmsales @maui.net. ULTRA-DELUXE.

The first plantation laborers on Maui began to arrive from China in 1852.

Westin Maui plays to the senses in a resort that was the ultimate fantasy of its well-known developer. A waterfall cascades through the lobby. Bronze statues of soldiers and the Buddha stand guard in the hallways. The 758 rooms are large and comfortable with oversized beds for luxurious slumber and tiny balconies where you can sit and relax when the sun is low. Lush tropical gardens laced with swan-filled lagoons create an escape from that other world of work and responsibility that seems so far away. ~ 2365 Kaanapali Parkway, Kaanapali; 808-667-2525, 888-625-4949, fax 808-661-5764; www.westin.com. ULTRA-DELUXE.

The 430-room **Kaanapali Beach Hotel** sits right on the beach and sports four restaurants and a large lobby. Guest rooms enjoy private lanais and guests lounge around a grassy courtyard and a swimming pool. ~ 2525 Kaanapali Parkway, Kaanapali; 808-661-0011, 800-262-8450, fax 808-667-5978; www.kbhmaui.com, e-mail res@kbhmaui.com. DELUXE TO ULTRA-DELUXE.

At Black Rock, the sacred lava promontory where cliff divers plunged into the Pacific, the ancient tradition is reenacted as part of a nightly torch-lighting ceremony at the **Sheraton Maui Hotel**. Here 510 rooms and suites are spread across spacious grounds that hold three six-story towers and a five-story Halemoana wing. The hotel's distinctive architecture—it is partially built atop the rock—places some rooms near the water's edge. Views of the neighbor islands and the West Maui Mountains are breathtaking. Decorated with rattan furniture, tropical prints and seashell-patterned bedspreads, all the rooms are trim and comfortable. You can watch the sunset from several restaurants and lounges, swim in a 140-yard pool or enjoy snorkeling along Black Rock. ~ 2605 Kaanapali Parkway, Kaanapali; 808-661-0031, 800-325-3535, fax 808-661-0458; www.sheraton-maui.com. ULTRA-DELUXE.

Or check out, and check in to, the **Royal Lahaina Resort**. Spreading across 27 acres, it encompasses 542 guest rooms, 11 tennis courts, 3 swimming pools, 3 restaurants, a coffee shop and a white-sand beach that extends for a half-mile. Rooms in the highrise hotel price in the ultra-deluxe category, while the prices for the nicest accommodations, the multiplex cottages that dot the landscaped grounds, head for the sky. ~ 2780 Kekaa Drive, Kaanapali; 808-661-3611, 800-447-6925, fax 808-494-3960; www.2maui.com. ULTRA-DELUXE.

A waterfall splashes near the bottom of one of the three atrium towers at **Embassy Suites Resort**. Hop aboard a glass-walled elevator at this all-suite hotel and luxuriate in one of the 413 units. Each one is spacious, attractive and equipped with sofas and oak cabinets. You'll have a lanai and large bath of your own, and to share with other guests there is a 24-foot waterslide and gazebo pavilion, koi ponds and waterways galore. Besides that, breakfast is free and you're invited to a daily cocktail reception. ~ 104 Kaanapali Shores Place, Kaanapali; 808-661-2000, 800-669-3155, fax 808-667-1353; www.embassy-maui.com. ULTRA-DELUXE.

A subtle architectural style gives the **Kapalua Bay Hotel** a low profile. But don't be misled. Part of a 23,000-acre plantation, this relatively small hotel, with 196 rooms and suites, is the hub of one of Maui's most appealing and romantic resorts. A hillside setting overlooking a white-sand crescent beach means that nearly all the rooms have spectacular ocean views. The accommodations are luxurious and tasteful and include rattan- and wicker-furnished sitting areas, baths with sunken tubs, a jacuzzi and vanity areas. Floor-to-ceiling french doors open onto spacious lanais. Rock-lined ponds, tropical gardens, three golf courses, restaurants, shops and two tennis facilities add to Kapalua's charm. ~ 1 Bay Drive, Kapalua; 808-669-5656, 800-325-3589, fax 808-669-4690; www.kapaluabayhotel.com. ULTRA-DELUXE.

The **Ritz-Carlton, Kapalua**, unique among Ritz-Carltons, is a haven for local culture. The hotel sits above the ocean on grounds that overlook not only the formal gardens and manicured lawns associated with this chain, but a sacred resting place for ancient Hawaiian spirits. It was this burial ground that initially put the hotel at odds with Hawaiian culture but then led it to become one of the strongest supporters of the Hawaiian people in the islands. Responding to an uproar in the community in the early 1990s over where the hotel should be built, the Ritz-Carlton moved the location away from the sacred ground. In the ensuing years, the hotel continued to show its good faith by hiring a Hawaiian liaison and sponsoring an annual celebration of Hawaiian culture (see "Five-star Culture" feature in this chapter), becoming a luxury accommodation with a soul. Its 548 guest rooms are spacious and well-appointed with plantation-era furnishings and private lanais; the grounds are as beautiful as they are sacred. The usual five-star hotel amenities include an outstanding restaurant, The Anuenue Room, a fitness center, a golf course, and 24-hour room service. Kapalua Bay, one of three beaches here, has been desig-

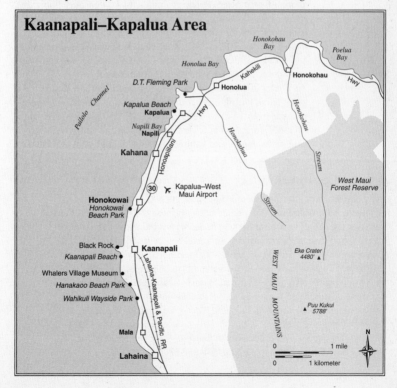

Kaanapali–Kapalua Area

nated among the best beaches in America. ~ 1 Ritz-Carlton Drive, Kapalua; 808-669-6200, fax 808-669-2028; www.ritzcarlton. com. ULTRA-DELUXE.

CONDOS   Most condominiums in this area are on the beach or just across the road from it. They are ideally situated for swimming or sunbathing; the major drawback, ironically, is that there are so many other condos around.

Kaanapali Alii ranks as one of Maui's better buys. Here the immense 1500- to 1900-square-foot suites can easily be shared by two couples or a family. All 264 condo units have large living and dining rooms, full kitchens, sitting areas and two baths. Fully carpeted and furnished with rattan, contemporary artwork and potted palms, these units start at $325 and top out at $750. The contemporary highrise facility rests along the beach and has a pool and tennis court. ~ 50 Nohea Kai Drive, Kaanapali; 808-667-1400, 800-642-6284, fax 808-667-1145; www.kaanapali alii.com, e-mail info@classicresorts.com.

Adjacent to the shops of Whalers Village, **The Whaler on Kaanapali Beach** offers spacious units with *koa* parquet floors and some rattan furniture. With its twin 12-story towers, this oceanfront condominium boasts marble baths and has 145 units priced from $235 to $700. ~ 2481 Kaanapali Parkway, Kaanapali; 808-661-4861, 800-922-7866, fax 808-661-8315; www.whaler-maui.com, e-mail res.wha@aston.hotels.com.

For its 204 condominium units, **Maui Eldorado Resort** has a golf-course setting a short distance from the beach. The rooms, ranging from $195 to $395 per day, are decorated with a tropical motif, furnished in wicker and bamboo and equipped with private baths, lanais and vanities. Lowrise buildings in the complex

PUEONE O HONOKAHUA

The Kapalua area includes one of Maui's most important cultural zones, **Pueone o Honokahua**. This 14-acre preserve, near the Ritz-Carlton, Kapalua, was the site of fishing shrines and *heiaus* where the ancient Hawaiians worshipped their gods and made astronomical observations. Today you can see a burial ground dating back to A.D. 950 and portions of the King's Highway, a 16th-century stone road around Maui. Also extant are the outlines of terraced taro patches farmed by early inhabitants. Although this land has been claimed in turn by King Kamehameha III, the sugar king H. P. Baldwin, and lastly the Maui Land and Pineapple Company, the state now protects and preserves it as a native Hawaiian sanctuary. The Ritz-Carlton conducts a free tour called "A Sense of Place" at the preserve every Friday from 10 a.m. to 12 p.m. (808-669-6200).

offer a peaceful alternative to the busy hotel scene. Residents enjoy three swimming pools and a private beach club on the sands of Kaanapali. ~ 2661 Kekaa Drive, Kaanapali; 808-661-0021, 800-688-7444, fax 808-667-7039; www.outrigger.com.

Aston Kaanapali Shores has hotel room–style accommodations for $195 including a refrigerator; studios from $255 double with a balcony and full kitchen; and one-bedroom units with a garden view and full kitchen for $365. ~ 3445 Lower Honoapiilani Road, Kaanapali; 808-667-2211, 800-922-7866, fax 808-661-0836; www.astonhotels.com.

The lava rock–walled units at **Papakea Resort** provide a pleasant retreat. Ranging from $170 studios to $270 two-bedroom units, all 130 condominiums come with spacious lanais. ~ 3543 Lower Honoapiilani Road, Honokowai; 808-669-4848, 800-922-7866, fax 808-665-0662; www.astonhotels.com.

One-bedroom apartments at the beachfront **Maui Sands** begin at $105 single or double; two bedrooms run from $154 for one to four people. There is a seven-night minimum. ~ 3600 Lower Honoapiilani Road, Honokowai; 808-669-1902, 800-367-5037, fax 808-669-8790; www.mauigetaway.com, e-mail getaway@maui.net.

One-bedroom apartments at the oceanfront **Aston Paki Maui** start at $200, depending on the view, and sleep one to four people; two-bedroom units start at $330, accommodating up to six people. Swimming pool with jet spa. ~ 3615 Lower Honoapiilani Road, Honokowai; 808-669-8235, 800-535-0085, fax 808-669-7987; www.astonhotels.com.

The one-bedroom apartments at **Honokowai Palms** have a lanai; they run $80 double and sleep up to four people. A two-bedroom unit without lanai is $85 for one to six people. It's located right across the street from the ocean. ~ 3666 Lower Honoapiilani Road, Honokowai; 808-667-2712, 800-669-6284, fax 808-661-5875; www.klahani.com, e-mail klahani@hotmail.com.

On the waterfront, **Hale Maui** has one-bedroom condos from $85 double. The drawback to this budget rate is that there is no pool—but you won't miss it with the beach in your backyard. ~ 3711 Lower Honoapiilani Road, Honokowai; 808-669-6312, fax 808-669-1302; www.maui.net/~halemaui, e-mail halemaui@maui.net.

The one-bedroom apartments at the oceanfront **Kaleialoha** start at $115 double; $10 each additional person. ~ 3785 Lower Honoapiilani Road, Honokowai; 808-669-8197, 800-222-8688, fax 808-669-2502; www.mauicondosoceanfront.com, e-mail kal@maui.net.

Hale Ono Loa offers two one-bedroom units ($80–$100) for up to four people. The condos are oceanfront but there's no beach access. ~ 3823 Lower Honoapiilani Road, Honokowai;

808-667-2712, 800-669-6284, fax 808-661-5875; www.kla-hani.com, e-mail klahani@hotmail.com.

Polynesian Shores has one-bedroom apartments that start at $135 double; two-bedroom units, $175 double; three-bedroom apartments, $225 double. All units have ocean views. ~ 3975 Lower Honoapiilani Road, Honokowai; 808-669-6065, 800-433-6284, fax 808-669-0909; www.polynesianshores.com.

Mahina Surf features one-bedroom units that start at $125 double ($110–$145 from April 15 to December 14); two-bedroom accommodations range from $155 to $190. There are oceanfront views with a lava-rock beach. There's a three-night minimum stay. ~ 4057 Lower Honoapiilani Road, Kahana; 808-669-6068, 800-367-6086, fax 808-669-4534; www.mahinasurf.com, e-mail mahainasf@maui.net.

Kahana Reef All Oceanfront has studio and one-bedroom apartments for $135–$155 single or double. As the name suggests, all units are oceanfront; they require a four-night minimum stay. ~ 4471 Lower Honoapiilani Road, Kahana; 808-669-6491, 800-822-4409, fax 808-669-2192; www.mauicondo.com.

One-bedroom condos at **Napili Point Resort** are $229–$269 for up to four people (reduced rates in low season). Two-bedroom units start at $329. Here sliding doors lead out to ocean-view patios. Located on a lava rock coastline, the resort is a short walk from sandy Napili Bay beach. ~ 5295 Lower Honoapiilani Road, Napili; 808-669-9222, 800-669-6252, fax 808-669-7984; www.napili.com.

Outrigger Napili Shores Resort is a beautifully landscaped low-rise resort with studios and one-bedrooms running from $177 to $239. The units are appointed with rattan and oak pieces and the complex is graced by gardens of plumeria and hibiscus.

AUTHOR FAVORITE

Face it: there are few words in the English language more romantic than "villa." And there are few condominiums on Maui more alluring than **Kapalua Villas**. Situated on a 1650-acre resort and surrounded by three golf courses and an ocean, they offer views that sweep past the mountains and out to the neighbor islands. The units are lowrise structures with sunken tubs, large lanais, and rattan and wicker furniture. Individually owned and decorated, the accommodations provide direct access to swimming, golf and tennis. One-bedroom units range from $195 to $255; two-bedroom units run from $275 to $425. ~ 500 Office Road, Kapalua; 808-669-8088, 800-545-0018, fax 808-669-5234; www.kapalua villas.com.

The pool and beach areas are idyllic. ~ 5315 Lower Honoapiilani Road, Napili; 808-669-8061, 800-688-7444, fax 808-669-5407; www.outrigger.com, e-mail napilishores@outrigger.com.

Studio apartments at **The Napili Bay** are $105 double for oceanfront views. ~ 33 Hui Drive, Napili; 808-661-5200, 888-661-7200, fax 808-661-2649; www.mauibeachfront.com, e-mail beach front@maui.net.

The **Napili Kai Beach Resort** has 162 units—studios, one-bedroom and two-bedroom affairs—that range in price from $205 to $695. Most come with kitchens. All are fully carpeted and have private lanais, rattan furniture, picture windows and direct access to an impressive beach. ~ 5900 Honoapiilani Road, Napili; 808-669-6271, 800-367-5030, fax 808-669-0086; www.napilikai.com, e-mail stay@napilikai.com.

DINING

Spats Trattoria is an elegant Italian restaurant featuring regional cuisine. Candlelit tables, antique armchairs and brass chandeliers are augmented by a menu of decadent dishes such as lobster on ribbon pasta covered with an herb cream sauce. Dinner only. ~ Hyatt Regency Maui, 200 Nohea Kai Drive, Kaanapali; 808-661-1234. DELUXE TO ULTRA-DELUXE.

Overlooking serene Japanese gardens, the open-air **Swan Court** defines the ultimate Maui experience. Guests enter this upscale restaurant in the Hyatt Regency Maui via a grand staircase to the classical strains of the resident pianist. With a waterfall and gliding swans in the background, you can choose from a variety of daily-changing entrées such as Hunan marinated lamb chops, grilled lobster satay with coconut and lemongrass, island-style bouillabaisse with macadamia sambal and sautéed *ono* with marinated shrimp won tons. For dessert, there's a daily soufflé selection and dessert sampler. ~ 200 Nohea Kai Drive, Kaanapali; 808-661-1234. ULTRA-DELUXE.

For an elegant dining experience at a reasonable price, try **Tropica** restaurant in the Westin Maui. Feast on fare prepared on rotisseries, grills and in wood ovens, as well as fresh seafood, while watching swans swim in the lagoon. ~ 2365 Kaanapali Parkway, Kaanapali; 808-667-2525. DELUXE.

One way to eat at a reasonable price is by stopping at the take-out stands on the lower level of Whalers Village. There are tables inside or out in the courtyard. **Village Korean Barbeque** has Korean dishes. ~ 808-661-9798. **Pizza Paradiso** serves an assortment of pies (including by the slice) plus spaghetti and meatballs and salads. For breakfast you can order a "breakfast pizza," bagel or coffee. ~ 808-667-0333. **Kawara Sobe Takase Restaurant** has noodle dishes, *onigiri* (rice balls wrapped with seaweed) and tempura. ~ 2435 Kaanapali Parkway, Kaanapali; 808-667-0815. BUDGET.

The sunsets are otherworldly at **Leilani's On The Beach**, a breezy veranda-style dining room. Trimmed in dark woods and lava rock, the upstairs dining room is dominated by an outrigger canoe that hangs suspended from the ceiling. On the menu you'll find Malaysian shrimp, Cajun-style fresh fish, ginger chicken and teriyaki steak. At the end of the day this is sunset territory, a place to relax and take in the scene from the umbrella shade of the downstairs **Beachside Grill**, where cocktails accompany burgers, sandwiches and salads. Frequently there is live rock-and-roll in the afternoon. Touristy but appealing. ~ Whalers Village, 2435 Kaanapali Parkway, Kaanapali; 808-661-4495, fax 808-667-9027. MODERATE TO DELUXE.

Peter Merriman, the chef extraordinaire who earned his reputation with a restaurant on the Big Island, transported his brand of Hawaii regional cuisine across the Alenuihaha Channel to open **Hula Grill** on the beach in Kaanapali. Specializing in seafood, this 1930s-era beach house has wok-charred ahi, seafood dim sum dishes and an array of entrées that includes Hawaiian seafood gumbo, *opakapaka* in parchment, firecracker mahimahi and teriyaki ahi. For landlubbers there's New York steak, Thai beef curry and goat cheese pizza. ~ Whalers Village, Kaanapali; 808-667-6636, fax 808-661-1148. DELUXE.

The **Kaanapali Mixed Plate Restaurant** serves an all-you-can-eat buffet at a price that is surprisingly out of place for this expensive hotel. A complete breakfast is offered; lunch and dinner include a few entrées, a salad bar, soup and dessert buffets. Meat-eaters will revel in the dinner buffets all-you-can-eat prime rib. ~ Kaanapali Beach Hotel, 2525 Kaanapali Parkway, Kaanapali; 808-661-0011, fax 808-667-5978. BUDGET TO MODERATE.

Located on the scenic Kaanapali North Course, **Basil Tomatoes Italian Grille** is a cozy eatery featuring northern Italian versions of veal chop, fresh fish, lasagna and a variety of pastas. Flavorful food and an intimate setting make this a top choice for dinner. ~ At the entrance to the Royal Lahaina Resort, 2780 Kekaa Drive, Kaanapali; 808-662-3210, fax 808-661-5254. DELUXE.

ABOVE MAUI

High atop the Hyatt Regency Maui's Lahaina Tower, a 16-inch reflecting telescope probes deep space seven nights a week, taking tourists on a trip through the planets and galaxies. **The Tour of the Stars** is a one-hour program managed by the hotel's director of astronomy and designed for the public. It allows guests to look through stationary eyepieces while the computer-driven telescope searches the heavens. Reservations are required. Admission. ~ 200 Nohea Kai Drive, Kaanapali; 808-661-1234.

From the ship's rigging, captain's chairs and marlin trophies, you could never guess what they serve at **Erik's Seafood Grotto**. What a surprise to discover a menu filled with crabmeat-stuffed prawns, lobster-stuffed chicken breast, salmon and wahoo. Early-bird specials. ~ 4242 Lower Honoapiilani Road, Kahana; 808-669-4806, fax 808-669-3997. MODERATE TO DELUXE.

Terrace Restaurant at Sands of Kahana is one of those rare finds that you count yourself lucky to have discovered. Here's the scene: it's set between two swimming pools in a large, covered patio, with an unbelievable view. A wide expanse of the Pacific facing the island of Molokai is what you can usually expect, and in winter and spring, the humpback whales provide an unparalleled show of nature. Now for the food: whether you choose breakfast or dinner, the menu is sure to please. "Great American food" accurately describes it—prime rib, meatloaf, steak and lobster are dinner choices, and just plain bacon and eggs, waffles and omelettes are some breakfast items. Try the Sunday beachside barbecue for a good family value. ~ 4299 Lower Honoapiilani Road, Kahana; 808-669-5399. MODERATE.

Dollie's Pub and Café offers fettuccine alfredo, pizza and sandwiches. This is a sports-on-the-television bar with a small kitchen and adjacent dining room. ~ 4310 Lower Honoapiilani Road, Kahana; 808-669-0266, fax 808-665-0614. BUDGET TO MODERATE.

One of Maui's leading restaurants, **Roy's Kahana Bar and Grill** eschews the waterfalls, swans, tinkling pianists and other accoutrements of the island's top dining rooms. Instead, this spacious second-story establishment looks like a gallery with its exposed-beam ceiling, track lighting and paintings. The open kitchen serves up such creations as fresh seared lemongrass *shutome* with Thai basil peanut sauce, kiawe-grilled filet mignon with garlic mashed potatoes and Chinese barbecue cabernet, grilled ginger chicken with shoyu glaze and garlic chive rice and blackened ahi with soy-mustard butter. Reservations are a must! ~ Kahana Gateway Shopping Center, 4405 Honoapiilani Highway, Kahana; 808-669-5000, fax 808-669-6909. DELUXE TO ULTRA-DELUXE.

A good choice for food, libations and conversation is **Fish & Game Brewing Company & Rotisserie**. It's quite a mouthful, but this establishment boasts three dining rooms as well as a microbrewery. The open-hearth rotisserie oven, along with the gleaming copper vats, dominate the first room. The main dining room contains an exhibition kitchen and live lobster tank, while the private dining room showcases a fireplace, cigar humidors and leather wingback chairs. Fresh fish and seafood are island-caught; for the carnivorous, there's roasted meats and the tastiest rack of lamb on the island. Sports fans will also enjoy the large-screen TVs in the bar. ~ Kahana Gateway Shopping Center, 4405 Lower Honoapiilani Road, Kahana; 808-669-3474. DELUXE.

For Mongolian beef, Peking duck or hot Szechuan bean curd, try **China Boat**. At this family-style restaurant, you can ease into a lacquered seat and take in the Japanese *ukiyoe* prints that adorn the place. Adding to the ambience are lava walls that showcase beautiful Chinese ceramic pieces. Patio dining is also available. ~ 4474 Lower Honoapiilani Road, Kahana; 808-669-5089, fax 808-669-6132. MODERATE.

In addition to its namesake, **Maui Tacos** has chimichangas, tostadas, burritos, quesadillas and enchiladas. Nothing fancy, just a few formica booths and tables with molded plastic chairs. But the salsa's fresh daily, the beans are prepared without lard and the chips are made with cholesterol-free vegetable oil. Egg burritos and huevos rancheros are served for breakfast. Frozen yogurt and fruit smoothies are also available. ~ Napili Plaza, 5095 Napilihau Street, Napili; 808-665-0222, 888-628-4822; www.mauitacos. com, e-mail eatmaui@maui.net. BUDGET.

The **Orient Express** features a variety of Thai and Chinese dishes including shrimp saté, clay-pot seafood dishes, sour shrimp soup, red-curry beef and Thai noodles stir-fried with pork, egg and crushed peanuts. Part of the Napili Shores Resort, this lava-walled restaurant has a shocking-pink-and-purple color scheme. Dinner only. ~ 5315 Lower Honoapiilani Road, Napili; 808-669-8077. MODERATE.

Perched on the white sandy beach along one of the most beautiful bays on Maui is **Sea House Restaurant at Napili Kai Beach Resort**. The restaurant and its Whale Watcher's Bar have been ensconced there since the early 1960s, but it's only since Chef Michael Gallagher took over in the kitchen that this restaurant has made a name among the culinary elite of Maui. His signature ancho-chili free-range chicken breast melts in your mouth. Steaks, seafood pasta, and fresh island fish are also available, and the *pupus* menu offers a wonderful selection of island specialties. A Friday-night institution is the Napili Kai Foundation Children's Hula and Dinner Show. Open daily for breakfast, lunch and dinner. ~ 5900 Lower Honoapiilani Road, Napili; 808-669-1500. DELUXE.

Maui aficionados agree that **The Plantation House Restaurant** is among the island's best. Capturing their accolades is a spacious establishment with panoramic views of the Kapalua region and a decor that mixes mahogany and wicker with orchids and a roaring fire. Not to be upstaged by the surroundings, the chef prepares fresh island fish seven different ways. The most popular is the "taste of the rich forest"—the fish is pressed with wild mushrooms and roasted, then served on spinach with garlic mashed potatoes and Maui onion meunière sauce. For lighter appetites there are salads, pastas, honey guava scallops, and for lunch a wide range of soups and sandwiches. Breakfast is also served. ~ 2000 Plantation Club Drive, Kapalua; 808-669-6299,

Five-star Culture

Step into the lobby of the Ritz-Carlton, Kapalua during the opening ceremonies of the hotel's "Celebration of the Arts" and you'll experience something unique among five-star hotels. Sacred chants fill the air, the vibrations mingling with the scent of plumeria in an electric atmosphere. An annual festival honoring the hotel's commitment to Hawaiian culture, it's a time when native Hawaiians from all the islands (many flown in and housed free by the hotel) come together for three days of workshops, films, concerts, artist demonstrations and Hawaiian feasts. Best of all, it's an event filled with an overwhelming spirit of *aloha* and open not only to hotel guests but the general public as well.

Samples from past celebrations include: "A Sense of Place," a workshop led by chanter and hula teacher Charles Ka'upu explaining the plight of the Hawaiian people and the challenges they face; "The Steel Guitar—Sweet Melodies," a gathering of Hawaii's finest steel guitar performers; a hike to the Kapunakea Preserve, a mountain enclave teeming with an astonishing variety of indigenous plants; and "Goddesses of Hawaii," a lively discussion of past and present Hawaiian women and their spiritual mentors.

In the evenings, the Ritz-Carlton rolls out the *lauhala* mat and brings in a bevy of local entertainers to perform during *hukilaus* and *luaus*. The final night of this three-day event is highlighted with a concert featuring big-name Hawaiian musicians and entertainers.

Ironically, the festival was the result of a land dispute. In order to accommodate the local Hawaiian community, the hotel promised when it was originally built to locate the building away from a Hawaiian burial site and vowed to work in the future to help preserve Hawaiian culture. Today, in addition to supporting numerous community programs, the Ritz-Carlton renews its commitment with this annual celebration.

All weekend the grounds are filled with artists and crafts people showcasing their wares and helping visitors learn to string Niihau shell necklaces, carve *'ohe hano ihos* (nose flutes), and create tapa wall hangings. Most important of all, the festival is an opportunity for hotel guests and the public to "talk story" with the Hawaiian community and share in an ancient and vibrant culture. The event is held each year over Easter weekend. Most workshops, panel, movies and other events are free; there's an admission charge for concerts and meals. ~ Ritz-Carlton, Kapalua; 1 Ritz-Carlton Drive, Kapalua; 808-669-6200, fax 808-669-2028.

fax 808-669-1222; www.theplantationhouse.com. DELUXE TO
ULTRA-DELUXE.

There's little doubt that Hawaii's finest sunsets occur off the
southwest coast of Maui. One of the best spots to catch the spec-
tacle is **The Bay Club** at the Kapalua Bay Hotel, an oceanfront
dining room that looks out on Molokai and Lanai. More than
just a feast for the eyes, this open-air restaurant offers a gourmet
menu at lunch and dinner. You can watch the sky melt from deep
blue to flaming red while dining on fresh fish, seared sea scallops, Brazilian lobster tail, rack of lamb or New York steak. A
rough life indeed. Evening dress code: no shorts, jeans, open-toed
shoes or T-shirts. Dinner only. ~ 1 Bay Drive, Kapalua; 808-669-
5656, fax 808-669-4694. ULTRA-DELUXE.

Sansei Restaurant & Sushi Bar has developed a cult following among both locals and tourists alike for its Pacific Rim sushi.
One version incorporates spicy crab, cilantro and various vegetables with Thai sweet chili sauce for dipping instead of the usual
soy and wasabi. In another, smoked salmon, Maui onions and
cream cheese combine to create the "bagel roll." The tuna sashimi
is cut thin and covered with Thai fish sauce and peanuts. It's sushi
quite unlike any you've ever tasted. And there's also a selection
of entrées, including roasted duck breast with foie-gras glaze. ~
115 Bay Drive in the Kapalua Shops, Kapalua; 808-669-6286, fax
808-669-0667; www.sanseihawaii.com. DELUXE.

GROCERIES   Out in the Kaanapali area, the best place to shop is **Star Market**,
a good-sized supermarket that's open from 5 a.m. to 2 a.m. every
day. ~ 3350 Lower Honoapiilani Road, Kaanapali; 808-667-9590.

Toward Kapalua, try the **Napili Market**, a well-stocked supermarket that's open from 6:30 a.m. to 11 p.m. every day. ~ Napili
Plaza, 5095 Napilihau Street, Napili; 808-669-1600.

SHOPPING   Worthy of mention is **Whalers Village** in the Kaanapali Beach
Resort. This sprawling complex combines a shopping mall with
a museum. Numbered among the stores you'll find gift emporia
featuring coral and shells, a shirt store with wild island designs,
other stores offering fine men's and women's fashions.

Several shops in this split-level complex should not be missed.
Lahaina Printsellers Ltd. (808-667-7617) purveys "fine antique
maps and prints." **Sgt. Leisure** (808-667-9433) sells brightly colored resort ware and T-shirts with original designs unlike those
seen elsewhere. At **Blue Ginger Designs** (808-667-5793) original
styles in women's and children's clothing are featured. For women's
and children's swimwear and sportswear, head to **Maui Waterwear**
(808-661-3916). Another store worth visiting here is **Endangered
Species** (808-661-1139), a preservationist shop selling photos,
sculptures and paintings of sharks, whales and rainforests. Through

the sales of these products it also helps support many environmental causes. The **Ka Honu Gift Gallery** (808-661-0173) showcases locally produced goods including ornaments, dolls, lotions, soaps and jewelry. Handcrafted Hawaiian coral jewelry is the specialty of **Maui Divers of Hawaii** (808-661-1097). The **Dolphin Gallery** (808-661-5115) is a place to look for sculpture, art and jewelry. ~ 2435 Kaanapali Parkway.

Perhaps the best place in Whalers Village to discover the whaling tradition is **Lahaina Scrimshaw**. During their long journeys, sailors once whiled away the hours by etching and engraving on ivory, creating beautiful articles of scrimshaw. The sale of ivory from animals taken by hunters is banned, but the fossilized remains of ancient mammoths and walruses have kept this art alive. Using ivory that is thousands of years old, artists create a wide array of functional and decorative pieces, many of which are traded by aficionados of this art form. ~ 808-661-4034.

With the continuing influx of wealthy tourists, the upper tier of Whalers Village has gone stratospheric with several high-fashion boutiques. Among the shops representing this shift to the chic is **Chanel Boutique**, which displays fine jewelry, cosmetics and designer threads. Chanel also has a line of handbags and other fashion accoutrements guaranteed to put a hole in your wallet. ~ 2435 Kaanapali Parkway; 808-661-1555.

And then, to make shopping the grand adventure it should be, there are the displays. Within this mazework mall you'll discover blunderbusses, intricate scrimshaw pieces, the skeletal remains of leviathans and whaling boats with iron harpoons splayed from the bow. Practically everything, in fact, that a whaler (or a cruising shopper) could desire.

HEALING, HAWAIIAN-STYLE

Lokahi, the Hawaiian concept of unity and accord, is addressed in "Hawaiian Health & Healing," a monthly program presented by the Hyatt Regency Maui's **Spa Moana**. Native Hawaiian healers focus on non-Western methods of healing, such as the manifestation of spiritual power, cultivating belief and behavioral energy, and utilizing medicinal plants. "Welcome to Wellness" with Dr. Elaine Willis is also part of this on-going program, which addresses health of the body, mind and spirit. These complimentary classes are held the first Wednesday of every month from 9 to 10 a.m. It's a treat to combine them with one of the Spa's specialty therapies—try a *limu* (seaweed) body-firming and detox masque or *lomi lomi* massage, the ancient Hawaiian-style of body manipulations and strokes. ~ For reservations, call **808-667-4725**; www.maui.hyatt.com.

For serious shoppers, ready to spend money or be damned, there is nothing to compare with the neighboring hotels. Set like gems within this tourist cluster are several world-class hotels, each hosting numerous elegant shops.

Foremost is the **Hyatt Regency Maui**, along whose wood-paneled lobby are stores that might well be deemed mini-museums. One, called **Elephant Walk**, displays *koa* wood products, baskets and Niihau shell ornaments. There are art galleries, a fabric shop, clothing stores, jewelry stores and more—set in an open-air lobby that is filled with rare statuary and exotic birds. ~ 210 Nohea Kai Drive, Kaanapali; 808-667-2848.

Another favorite Hyatt Regency shop is **Hawaii Quilt Company**, where you'll find wallhangings, Thai silk pillows and needle-point supplies as well as an array of quilts. Many of the quilts are designed by local artists. ~ 210 Nohea Kai Drive, Kaanapali; 808-661-1234.

La Bareda is an excellent place to find inexpensive Hawaiian souvenirs such as sarongs, straw hats, jewelry and T-shirts. This shop in the Maui Marriott hotel is also knee-deep in key chains, pennants and ceramic pineapples. ~ 100 Nohea Kai Drive, Kaanapali; 808-667-5082.

The **Kapalua Bay Hotel** sports another upscale shopping annex. Among the temptations is **Mandalay** (808-669-6170), specializing in silks and cottons from Asia. There are blouses and jackets for women as well as a small collection of artfully crafted jewelry. Also stop by **South Seas of Kapalua** (808-669-1249), which carries native masks from New Guinea and other artwork from Oceania. If you're traveling with young ones or looking for a souvenir for those you left behind, stop by **Kapalua Kids** (808-669-0033). Here you can buy children's books on Hawaii as well as soft toys and an array of clothing. ~ 1 Bay Drive.

At the **Plantation Course Golf Shop** you'll find an impressive collection of jackets, shirts, sweaters, sweatshirts and shorts, many with a tropical flair. This is also a good place to look for the work of signature designers. ~ 2000 Plantation Club Drive, Kapalua; 808-669-8877.

NIGHTLIFE   Possibly the prettiest place in these parts to enjoy a drink 'neath the tropic moon is the bar at **Hula Grill**. Located in the Whalers Village mall, this beach house–style gathering place is decorated with original Hawaiian outrigger canoes. It features live Hawaiian music and hula nightly until nine o'clock. The place is located right on the water, so you can listen to a slow set, then stroll the beach. ~ 2435 Kaanapali Parkway; 808-667-6636; www.hulapie.com.

Hawaiian musicians perform nightly at the Hyatt Regency Maui in the elegant waterfront **Swan Court**. For contemporary music, head over to the **Weeping Banyan**, an open-air lounge. **Spats**

Trattoria (cover) also offers entertainment nightly. ~ 200 Nohea Kai Drive; 808-661-1234, 800-233-1234, fax 808-667-4498.

There's music and Hawaiian entertainment at the Westin Maui in the **'Ono Surf Bar & Grill** and **Koala Seafood and Barbeque Buffet**. ~ 2365 Kaanapali Parkway; 808-667-2525.

At the Maui Marriott, the **Makai Bar** cooks every night with a solo or duo performing Hawaiian and pop numbers. ~ 100 Nohea Kai Drive; 808-667-1200.

The Sheraton Maui is a prime nightspot both early and later in the evening. Just before sunset you can watch the torchlighting and cliff-diving ceremony from the **Lagoon Bar**. ~ 2605 Kaanapali Parkway, Kaanapali; 808-661-0031.

There's occasional Hawaiian-style entertainment at the **Royal Ocean Terrace Lounge**, a beachfront watering hole on the grounds of the Royal Lahaina Resort. Arrive early and you can watch the sunset between Lanai and Molokai, followed by the ubiquitous torch-lighting ceremony. ~ 2780 Kekaa Drive; 808-661-3611.

For soft entertainment in a relaxed setting, try the **Bay Club** at the Kapalua Bay Hotel. This open-air lounge with nightly pianist is set in a lovely restaurant overlooking the water. The melodies are as serene and relaxing as the views of neighboring Molokai. ~ 1 Bay Drive; 808-669-8008.

At **The Lehua**, in the lobby of the Kapalua Bay Hotel, you can enjoy piano music nightly over cocktails and great views of the Pacific. ~ 1 Bay Drive; 808-669-5656.

A Hawaiian duo plays in the evenings at **The Lobby Lounge and Library** at the Ritz-Carlton, Kapalua. At the **Anuenue Lounge** you can enjoy a pianist. ~ 1 Ritz-Carlton Drive, Kapalua; 808-669-6200.

KAANAPALI RESORT BEACHES The sprawling complex of Kaanapali hotels sits astride a beautiful white-sand beach that extends for three miles. Looking out on Lanai and Molokai, this is a classic palm-fringed strand. The entire area is heavily developed and crowded with tourists glistening in coconut oil. But it is an extraordinarily fine beach where the swimming is very good and the skindiving excellent around Black Rock at the

BEACHES & PARKS

NEED A BREAK FROM THE KIDDIES?

Tired of building sandcastles? If you're staying in a condo or hotel without children's programs (and you're tearing your hair out) you can check your kids into day camps at the Ritz-Carlton, Kapalua's **Ritz Kids** (808-669-6200) or the **Keiki Kamp** (808-667-2525) at the Westin Maui Resort in Kaanapali, even if you're not a guest.

Sheraton Maui. The beach has no facilities, but most of the resorts have public restrooms and there are restaurants nearby. ~ Take the public right-of-way to the beach from any of the Kaanapali resort hotels.

HONOKOWAI BEACH PARK Compared to the beaches fronting Kaanapali's nearby resorts, this is a bit disappointing. The large lawn is pleasant enough, but the beach itself is small, with a reef that projects right to the shoreline. On the other hand, the view of Molokai is awesome. In the shallow reef waters the swimming and snorkeling are fair; surfing is nonexistent. *Ulua* and threadfin are among the most frequent catches. Picnic tables, restrooms and showers are available. ~ Located north of Kaanapali in Honokowai on Lower Honoapiilani Road (which is the oceanfront section of Route 30).

NAPILI BAY You'll find wall-to-wall condominiums along the small cove. There's a crowded but beautiful white-sand beach studded with palm trees and looking out on Molokai. Swimming and snorkeling are delightful and the surfing here is particularly good for beginners. ~ Located several miles north of Kaanapali, with rights-of-way to the beach from Lower Honoapiilani Road via Napili Place or Hui Drive.

KAPALUA BEACH This is the next cove over from Napili Bay. It's equally beautiful, but not as heavily developed. The crescent of white sand that lines Kapalua Bay is bounded on either end by rocky points and backdropped by a line of coconut trees and the Kapalua Bay Hotel. Swimming and snorkeling are excellent. ~ There's a right-of-way to the beach from Lower Honoapiilani Road near the Napili Kai Beach Club.

D. T. FLEMING PARK One of Maui's nicest beach parks, D. T. Fleming has a spacious white-sand beach and a rolling lawn shaded with palm and ironwood trees. There's a nice view of Molokai's rugged East End. Unfortunately, a major resort resides just uphill from the beach. Sometimes windy, the park is plagued by rough and dangerous surf during the winter. Use caution! You'll find good swimming and bodysurfing and fair snorkeling during the summer. There are also good breaks nearby at Little Makaha, named after the famous Oahu beach. For anglers the prime catches are *ulua* and *papio*. There are restrooms, a picnic area and showers. ~ Located about seven miles north of Kaanapali just off Honoapiilani Highway.

Northwest Maui

To escape from the crowds and commotion of the Kaanapali–Kapalua area and travel north on the Honoapiilani Highway is to journey from the ridiculous to the sublime. As you curve along the edge of the West Maui Mountains, en route around the side of the island to Kahului and

Wailuku, you'll pass several hidden beaches that lie along an exotic and undeveloped shore. This is a region of the Valley Isle not frequented by the tourist crowd.

Near the rocky beach and lush valley at **Honokohau Bay**, the Honoapiilani Highway (Route 30) becomes the Kahekili Highway (Route 340). This macadam track snakes high above the ocean, hugging the coastline. From the highway rises a series of multi-hued **sandstone cliffs** that seems alien to this volcanic region and creates a picturesque backdrop to the rocky shore.

SIGHTS

As the road continues, the scenery is some of the most magnificent on Maui. Down a dirt side road sits the rustic village of **Kahakuloa**. Nestled in an overgrown valley beside a deep blue bay, the community is protected by a solitary headland rising directly from the sea. Woodframe houses and churches, which appear ready to fall to the next gusting wind, are spotted throughout this enchanting area. Kahakuloa is cattle country, and you'll

◀ HIDDEN

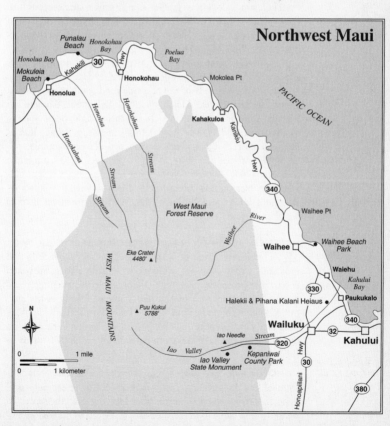

find that the villagers live and farm much as their forefathers did back when most of Maui was unclaimed terrain. It was from the shoreline near Kahakuloa that the Polynesian canoe *Hokulea* left on its famous voyage.

The road ascends again outside Kahakuloa. Opening below you, one valley after another falls seaward in a series of spine-backed ridges. Above the road, the mountain range rises toward its 5788-foot summit at Puu Kukui.

HIDDEN ▶

Six miles beyond Kahakuloa, you'll stumble upon **Aina Anuhea Tropical Gardens**, which in this heavenly environment represents a further ascent into the ethereal. Its six acres of curving paths lead along a mountain stream, through a Japanese garden, past a waterfall and up to a solitary gazebo perched high above the world. Along the way you can take in the ginger and heliconia, the maile and lokelani. A new volcano area is embraced by indigenous Hawaiian flora. Admission. ~ Kahekili Highway, between Kahakuloa and Waihee; 808-242-4592; e-mail ainanuhea@aol.com.

There are lush gulches farther along as the road descends into the plantation town of **Waihee**. Here rolling countryside, dotted with small farm houses, slopes from the roadside up to the foothills of the West Maui Mountains.

You're still on the Kahekili Highway, but now once again it really is a highway, a well-traveled road that leads toward Kahului. Located just northwest of town, a side road leads to two sacred spots. The first, **Halekii Heiau**, overlooking Kahului Bay and Iao Stream, dates from the 1700s. Today this temple, once as large as a football field, is little more than a stone heap. **Pihana Kalani Heiau**, a short distance away, was once a sacrificial temple.

Before driving this route, as well as the back road from Hana to Ulupalakua, remember that the car rental agencies will not insure you over these winding tracks. Many cover the roads anyway, and I highly recommend that you explore them both if weather permits.

BEACHES & PARKS

MOKULEIA BEACH OR SLAUGHTERHOUSE BEACH 🐋

🏊 This lovely patch of white sand is bounded by cliffs and looks out on Molokai. Set at the end of a shallow cove, the beach is partially protected. Swimming, snorkeling and surfing are all good. This is part of a marine sanctuary so fishing is not permitted. There are no facilities here. ~ Take Honoapiilani Highway for exactly eight-tenths of a mile past D. T. Fleming Park. Park on the highway and take the steep path down about 100 yards to the beach.

HIDDEN ▶

HIDDEN ▶

HONOLUA BAY 🐋🏊 A rocky beach makes this cliff-rimmed bay unappealing for sunbathers, but there are rich coral deposits offshore and beautiful trees growing near the water. In winter you're likely to find crowds along the top of the cliff watching surfers work some of the finest breaks in all Hawaii: perfect tubes up to 15 feet. Swimming is good, but the bottom is rocky. Snorkeling is excellent, particularly on the west side of the bay. No fishing is allowed; this is part of a marine sanctuary. There are no facilities (and usually very few people) here. ~ Located about one-and-a-third miles north of D. T. Fleming Park on Honoapiilani Highway. The dirt road to the beach is open only to cars with boats in tow. Park with the other cars along the highway and follow the paths to the beach.

PUNALAU OR WINDMILL BEACH 🏊 🐟 🏄 ⛵ A very se- ◄ *HIDDEN*
cluded white-sand beach studded with rocks, Punalau is surrounded by cliffs and intriguing rock formations. The swimming is okay and when the water is calm snorkeling is excellent. A fascinating reef extends along the coast all through this area. Surfing is fine, peaking in winter; there are left and right slides. Leatherback, *papio*, milkfish, *moano* and big-eyed scad are the primary catches for anglers. No facilities. Day-use fee, $5. ~ Located three-and-a-half miles north of D. T. Fleming Park on Honoapiilani Highway. Turn left onto the dirt road and follow it a short distance to the beach.

▲ A permit is required from Maui Pineapple Co., Honolua Division, 4900 Honoapiilani Highway, Lahaina (808-669-6201, fax 808-669-7089; www.pineapplehawaii.com) and must be obtained in person. There is a three-day maximum stay.

HONOKOHAU BAY 🏊 🐟 🏄 ⛵ This rocky beach is surrounded by cliffs. To the interior, a lush valley rises steadily into the folds of the West Maui Mountains. When the water is calm, swimming and snorkeling are good. The surf offers rugged, two-to twelve-foot breaks. Keep in mind the changeable nature of this wave action, since it can vary quickly from the gentle to the dangerous. Milkfish, *papio*, leatherback, *moano* and big-eyed scad are the principal species caught in these waters. ~ Located about six miles north of D. T. Fleming Park on Honoapiilani Highway.

▲ Camping is allowed here, but the place is very rocky, and there are no facilities.

SIX

Kihei–Wailea–Makena Area

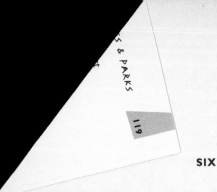

Stretching from Maalaea Bay to Makena is a near continuous succession of beautiful beaches that make Kihei and Wailea favored resort destinations. Second only to the Lahaina–Kaanapali area in popularity, this seaside enclave rests in the rainshadow of Haleakala, which looms in the background. Maui's southeastern shore receives only ten inches of rain a year, making it the driest, sunniest spot on the island. It also experiences heavy winds, particularly in the afternoon, which sweep across the island's isthmus.

Since the 1970s, this long, lean stretch of coast has become a developer's playground. Kihei in particular, lacking a master plan, has grown by accretion from a small local community into a haphazard collection of condominiums and mini-malls. It's an unattractive, six-mile strip lined by a golden beach.

Situated strategically along this beachfront are cement **pillboxes**, reminders of World War II's threatened Japanese invasion. Placed along Kihei Road just north of town, they are not far from **Kealia Pond Bird Sanctuary**, a 300-acre reserve frequented by migratory waterfowl as well as Hawaiian stilts and Hawaiian coots. You can take a nature walk here on an elevated boardwalk.

To the south lies **Wailea**, an urbane answer to the random growth patterns of its scruffy neighbor. Wailea is a planned resort, all 1450 manicured acres of it. Here scrubland has been transformed into a flowering oasis that is home to five top-class hotels and six condos, as well as the required retinue of golf courses, tennis courts and overpriced shops. Like Kihei, it is blessed with beautiful beaches.

Home to some of Maui's most luxurious resorts, Wailea is the place to find Picasso originals, 50,000-square-foot spas and villas designed to keep a smile on the face of a high roller. Plantation- and Mediterranean-style architecture, accented by polished limestone tile and granite boulders imported from Mount Fuji, make this swank resort area an international retreat.

Connected by a mile-and-a-half-long ocean walk, and lining five crescent beaches, the resort's luxury properties comprise a self-contained retreat. Covering an area three times the size of Waikiki, Wailea has matured from a series of five crescent beaches separated by lava rock promontories into an elegant mix of hotels, condominiums, golf courses (there are three 18-hole championship links and two clubhouses), tennis court and water sports facilities. The Shops of Wailea is the latest addition to the resort's upscale infrastructure.

Adjacent to Wailea, the **Makena** area is a quiet, low-density destination resort with a single hotel (the Maui Prince) and several small condominiums sharing a full range of resort facilities, including two 18-hole golf courses. The setting, dominated by the upcountry slopes of Haleakala and the dry mix of *kiawe* and cactus that provide ground cover, is highlighted by the wide and luxurious sands of **Makena Beach**, which I highly recommend visiting. Makena remains one of Maui's finest strands. A hippie hangout in the 1960s and early 1970s, it still retains a freewheeling atmosphere, especially at nearby **Little Beach** (also known as Baby Beach), Maui's most famous nude beach. ~ Located along Makena Alanui about four miles beyond Wailea

Past here the road gets rough as it presses south to **Ahihi–Kinau Natural Area Reserve**. Encompassing over 2000 acres of land and ocean bottom, this preserve harbors an amazing array of marine life and contains the remains of an early Hawaiian fishing village. Almost 100 larval fish species and about two dozen species of stony coral have been found in this ecologically rich reserve. You can hike on a restored portion of the stone-lined Royal Road that in pre-contact times circled the island. The landscape of lava-scarred lowlands is dominated by the green upcountry pastures of Haleakala's mid-level slopes. This was the route of the annual Makahiki procession, when chiefs and their tax collectors made the rounds of the royal dominions, collecting praise and tribute.

◄ HIDDEN

The road continues on, bisecting the **1790 lava flow**, which resulted from Haleakala's last eruption. The flow created Cape Kinau, a thumb-shaped peninsula dividing Ahihi Bay and **La Perouse Bay**. When I drove this route in a compact rental car, I reached La Perouse Bay before being forced by poor road conditions to turn back. The bay is named for the ill-starred French navigator, Jean-François de la Pérouse, who anchored here in 1786, the first Westerner to visit Maui. After a brief sojourn in this enchanting spot, he sailed off and was later lost at sea.

◄ HIDDEN

Anywhere along this coastline you can gaze out at **Molokini**, a crescent-shaped islet that is a favorite spot among snorkelers. Resting in the Alalakeihi Channel three miles west of Maui, it measures a scant 19 acres in area and rises 165 feet above sea level. The island is actually a tuff cone created by volcanic eruptions deep underwater that solidified into a hard substance called tuff. Black coral divers harvested the surrounding waters until the 1970s. According to Hawaiian legend, Molokini was created when the volcano goddess Pele cut a rival lover—a lizard—in two, turning the tail into Molokini and the head into the cinder cone near Makena Beach.

LODGING   Hotels are rare in Kihei. And in Wailea, a hotel in anything less than an ultra-deluxe price range is a contradiction in terms. The **Nona Lani Cottages**, with eight wooden cottages, provides a little relief. They're situated across busy Kihei Road from a white-sand beach. Each is a one-bedroom unit with lanai, all-electric kitchen and a living room capable of housing one or two extra sleepers. There's wall-to-wall carpeting and a shower-tub combination, plus television and air conditioners in all bedrooms, but no phone. (Be forewarned: we've had complaints, so you might want to check it out first.) There is a four-night minimum from April 16 to December 15; seven-night minimum from December 16 to April 15. Rooms without kitchens also available for $63, all seasons, two-night minimum. ~ 455 South Kihei Road, Kihei; 808-879-2497, 800-733-2688, fax 808-891-0273. MODERATE.

Spread across 28 acres, the **Aston Maui Lu Resort** is tropically landscaped with palm trees and flowering plants. Within the grounds, which are across the street from a beach, you'll find a pool and two tennis courts. The guest rooms are furnished in standard fashion and located in a series of interconnecting buildings with some accommodations on the beach. ~ 575 South Kihei Road, Kihei; 808-879-5881, 800-922-7866, fax 808-879-4627; www.astonhotels.com. MODERATE TO DELUXE.

The **Maui Coast Hotel** is a 265-room facility across the street from the beach. It's light, airy, modern and has a pool, outdoor jacuzzis, tennis courts and a cluster of nearby restaurants. There's poolside Hawaiian entertainment nightly. ~ 2259 South Kihei Road, Kihei; 808-874-6284, 800-426-0670, fax 808-875-4731; www.westcoasthotels.com, e-mail mch@maui.net. DELUXE TO ULTRA-DELUXE.

Down the road at the **Maui Oceanfront Inn** you'll find a series of six buildings designed in mock-Hawaiian style and sandwiched between the highway and a white-sand beach. The rooms are tiny but attractively decorated with carpeting, air conditioning, television and refrigerator. ~ 2980 South Kihei Road, Kihei; 808-879-7744, 800-537-8483, fax 808-874-0145; www.mauiocean frontinn.com. DELUXE TO ULTRA-DELUXE.

The all-suite **Kea Lani Hotel** is a 22-acre resort done in southern Mediterranean style. Turning its back on Hawaiian royalty, the Eurocentric lobby would look familiar to Louis XIV. Seven waterfalls, four fountains and a swim-up bar create attractions decadent enough for the Sun King himself. Among the accommodations are 413 suites and 37 oceanfront villas, each appointed with oak fixtures, floral prints and mirrored doors. The Roman-style baths feature Italian marble (of course) and all the two-story villas come with their own plunge pool. ~ 4100 Wailea Alanui, Wailea; 808-875-4100, 800-659-4100, fax 808-875-1200; www.kealani. com. ULTRA-DELUXE.

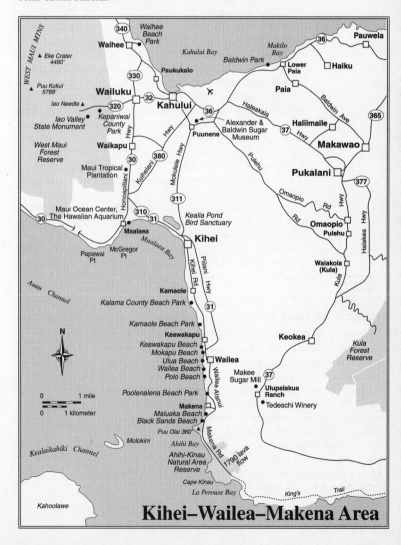

Kihei–Wailea–Makena Area

Although right in the heart of Wailea, the **Renaissance Wailea Beach Resort** is hidden among luxurious landscaping, giving the resort an aura of secluded elegance. It is far from the madding crowds that populate other parts of Maui and, at 345 rooms, smaller than many other major resorts. Guests who stay in the two-story Mokapu Beach Club get continental breakfast served to them on their lanai each morning. A real retreat. ~ 3550 Wailea Alanui, Wailea; 808-879-4900, 800-992-4532, fax 808-874-5370; www.marriotthotels.com. ULTRA-DELUXE.

Nestled against Wailea Beach is the **Grand Wailea Resort Hotel & Spa.** Its attention to grandiosity is immediately revealed in the lobby's larger-than-life Botero sculptures, only part of the hotel's $30 million art collection. The peach-colored building horseshoes around a network of pools, a waterslide and meticulously manicured landscaping; most of the 700 lavish rooms offer balconies and ocean views. The beach is great for swimming, and snorkelers often see sea turtles in the coral reefs that bookend the cove. A spa, shops and fine restaurants complement the resort. Unlike some resorts of this size and ambition, the service is good and the experience enjoyable, even for people attuned to the subtler pleasures in life. ~ 3850 Wailea Alanui, Wailea; 808-875-1234, 800-888-6100; www.grandwailea.com, e-mail info@grand wailea.com. ULTRA-DELUXE.

The lushly landscaped **Four Seasons Resort Maui at Wailea** is the ultimate among ultimate destinations. The only Maui resort we know to feature a trompe l'oeil artwork in the lobby, it's a windswept, Hawaiian palace–style complex set on a luxurious beach. Furnished with wicker and rattan, most of the 380 plantation-style guest rooms offer ocean views. Casablanca fans, trop-

AUTHOR FAVORITE

For a special retreat, check in to **PollyMakena**, a pair of oceanfront villas just a hop, skip and a jump from Makena Beach. Ideal for families or small groups, the larger villa has three bedrooms and a loft; the smaller unit has two bedrooms and sleeps up to five people. Beautifully appointed, they're filled with a fascinating assortment of treasures collected by the charming owner, Parks Hay. A hot tub and hammock surrounded by tiki torches adorn the front yard and create a small island of relaxation; a teeming tidepool fronts one of the complexes. PollyMakena is set on "Wedding Cove," so you're bound to witness at least one ceremony during your stay, adding to the romance of this special place. ~ For reservations contact Tropical Villa Vacations, 2050 Kanoe Street, Suite 208, Kihei; 888-875-2818, fax 877-875-8828. DELUXE TO ULTRA-DELUXE.

ical plants and marbletop vanities add to the comfort. Louvered doors open onto spacious lanais. Reflecting pools, waterfalls and fountains give the public areas an elegant tropical air. ~ 3900 Wailea Alanui, Wailea; 808-874-8000, 800-334-6284, fax 808-874-2244; www.fourseasons.com. ULTRA-DELUXE.

Its remote location makes the **Maui Prince Hotel** an unusual find. Built around a courtyard adorned with lush tropical gardens and lily ponds, the 310-room establishment rewards those willing to drive a few extra minutes to Maui's southernmost retreat. Here you're likely to be lulled to sleep by the sound of the surf. Decorated with heliconia and bougainvillea, the rooms and suites open onto lanais. This V-shaped hotel is next door to two of Maui's top golf courses. ~ 5400 Makena Alanui, Makena; 808-874-1111, 800-321-6284, fax 808-879-8763; www.princehawaii.com. ULTRA-DELUXE.

The combination of seclusion and prime location near Kihei's beaches are part of the appeal at **Hale Makaleka Women's B&B**. This home offers a single guest room with its own bath and entrance. Brilliant tropical birds in the garden, a luscious breakfast of tropical fruits and bagels, and a personable owner are included in the price of admission. Women only. Call for directions. ~ 808-879-2971. MODERATE.

Leilani Kai is a cozy eight-unit apartment hotel located right on the beach. Studio apartments are $73 double; one-bedroom units are $84 or $95 double; two bedrooms will run you $106 for one to four people. ~ 1226 Uluniu Street, Kihei; 808-879-2606, fax 808-879-0241; e-mail lkresort@msn.com.

CONDOS

Oceanside one-bedroom apartments at **Kihei Kai** are $100 to $125 double ($90 to $115 from mid-April to mid-December). Each has television, phone, full kitchen and lanai. ~ 61 North Kihei Road, Kihei; 808-879-2357, 800-735-2357; www.kiheikai maui.com, e-mail kiheikai@maui.net.

Sunseeker Resort is a small, personalized place where studios with kitchenettes go for $60 double and one-bedrooms for $80 double. Add $6 for each additional person. Two-bedrooms with full kitchens go for $125. ~ 551 South Kihei Road, Kihei; 808-879-1261, 800-532-6284; www.mauisunseeker.com, e-mail sun seeker@mymauiparadise.com.

A highrise condo, **Mana Kai Maui Resort** has "hotel units" that consist of the extra bedroom and bath from a two-bedroom apartment, renting from $283 to $303 in peak season. One-bedroom units with kitchens are $226–$247. The condo has a beachfront location, as well as an adjoining restaurant and bar. ~ 2960 South Kihei Road, Kihei; 808-879-1561, 800-367-5242, fax 808-879-7825; www.crhmaui.com, e-mail res@crhmaui.com.

Lihi Kai has nine beach cottages with full kitchens, all renting for $69 single or double. Rates are lower for a seven-night stay. To be sure of getting a cottage, it's best to make reservations far in advance. There is a three-night minimum. ~ 2121 Iliili Road, Kihei; 808-879-2335, 800-544-4524.

Across the street from a beach park, **Kamaole Beach Royale** is a seven-story condo with one-bedroom apartments for $105 double; two-bedroom units, $120 to $135 double. Add $10 for each additional person. No credit cards. ~ 2385 South Kihei Road, Kihei; 808-879-3131, 800-421-3661, fax 808-879-9163; www.mauikbr.com.

Kapulanikai can be described as a cozy place with only 12 apartments, all of which overlook the ocean and a grassy, park-like setting. One-bedroom apartments are $80 single or double ($65 from April to mid-December). ~ 73 Kapu Place, Kihei; phone/fax 808-879-1607; www.bellomaui.com/html/kapulani_kai.html.

For gay-friendly accommodations, you can either stay at **Jack & Tom's Condos or Cottage** or they can direct you to any of the other facilities they manage. Most condos have air conditioning; all have cable TV, ceiling fans and kitchen and laundry facilities. Prices range roughly from $50 to $175. ~ Maui Suncoast Realty, 3134 Hoomua, Kihei, HI 96753; 808-874-1048, 800-800-8608, fax 808-879-6932; www.mauisuncoast.com, e-mail mauijack@aol.com.

Another booking agency with both a straight and gay clientele, **Andrea's Maui Oceanfront Condos** has one- and two-bedroom oceanfront condos surrounded by lush gardens. Amenities include tennis courts, pool, jacuzzi, sauna and putting green. ~ P.O. Box 424, Puunene, HI 96784; 310-399-1223, 800-289-1522, fax 310-399-0407; www.mauicondos.com. DELUXE TO ULTRA-DELUXE.

DINING

Margarita's Beach Cantina is one of those big brassy Mexican restaurants that are ever more present along the beaches—the kind that have live sports on big-screen television and a buzzing night scene. What sells this place is the oceanside dining and happy-hour margarita specials. The menu covers lunch and dinner, featuring carnitas, tacos and chimichangas, as well as hamburgers, chicken sandwiches and a Tuesday- and Saturday-night lobster special. ~ 101 North Kihei Road, Kihei; 808-879-5311. MODERATE.

Ever since condominiums mushroomed from its white sands, Kihei has no longer qualified as a poor person's paradise. Yet there are still several short-order griddles like **Suda's Store and Snack Shop**, whose griddle is only open from 6 a.m. to 12:30 p.m. The "famous" chow-fun is $2.75 a bowl. Closed Sunday. ~ 61 South Kihei Road, Kihei; 808-879-2668. BUDGET.

Owner-chef Jacques Pauvert (of Jacques Bistro fame) has a second winner with **Jacques on the Beach** at the Menehune Shores condominium. Recommended are the flavorful catch-of-the-day specialties, which are tastefully prepared with European style and island flair. The upbeat atmosphere adds high energy to dining out. This is one of the best dining options in the Maalaea end of Kihei. ~ 760 South Kihei Road, Kihei; 808-875-7791, fax 808-875-7786. DELUXE.

For inexpensive Korean and local food, there's **The Kal Bi**   ◄ HIDDEN
House. Squeezed into a corner of Kihei Center (next to Longs Drugs) and furnished with plastic seats, it's not much on atmosphere. But it's hard to beat their cheap barbecued ribs, grilled chicken and beef marinated in Korean sauce, *katsu* chicken or Korean soups. A good place for a takeout meal. ~ Kihei Center, 1215 South Kihei Road, Kihei; 808-874-8454. BUDGET.

Parked in the same complex is **Stella Blues Café & Delicatessen,** where you can dine indoors or outside beneath a sidewalk umbrella. The bill of fare includes vegetarian dishes, pastas and sandwiches. Breakfast, lunch and dinner. ~ Kihei Center, 1215 South Kihei Road, Kihei; 808-874-3779. MODERATE.

If you'd like something from Southeast Asia, **Royal Thai Cuisine** sits across the street in the original Azeka Place. Here the chairs are wood and the menu includes *dozens* of selections such as crab legs, chili shrimp, cashew chicken or seafood combinations. No lunch on weekends. ~ Azeka Place Shopping Center, 1280 South Kihei Road, Kihei; 808-874-0813. BUDGET TO MODERATE.

Azeka's Market Snack Shop runs a take-out window. For atmosphere there's a parking lot, but for food there's a fair choice, with hamburgers and plate lunches priced low. Breakfast and lunch only. ~ Azeka Place Shopping Center, 1280 South Kihei Road, Kihei; 808-879-0611. BUDGET.

Hapa's Restaurant features four house-brewed lagers, Italian food, a sushi bar, and nightly entertainment. ~ Lipoa Center, 41 East Lipoa Street, Kihei; 808-879-9001. MODERATE.

My vote for the best Thai restaurant on the island (and there are quite a few) is **Thailand Cuisine**, discreetly set in the Kukui Mall. What makes this one a standout is the ambience, which is

MAKENA LANDING

Now a peaceful cove, **Makena Landing**, located on Makena Road, was once a port as busy as Lahaina. During the California gold rush, prevailing winds prompted many San Francisco–bound ships coming up from Cape Horn to resupply here. Fresh fruits and vegetables, badly needed by the would-be miners, were traded in abundance. Later local ranchers delivered their cattle to market by tethering them to longboats and swimming the animals out to steamers waiting just offshore from Makena Landing.

punctuated by the graciousness of its hostess-owner. Lush green plants, hand-woven textiles and hand-embroidered silks are everywhere. The dishes are an enticing combination of traditional Thai favorites with island produce. The chef uses an imaginative blend of spices, herbs, roots and leaves to enhance the natural flavors of the key ingredients, like chicken, beef or shrimp. The Vegetarian Lovers selections are truly vegan. No lunch on Sunday; dinner is served nightly. ~ 1819 South Kihei Road, Kihei; 808-875-0839. MODERATE TO DELUXE.

A perennial favorite that keeps folks coming back because the food is so *ono* is **Alexander's Fish, Chicken & Chips**, which faces Kihei Road in Kalama Village. It's a casual, open-air café that serves fresh-sliced, fried potatoes and savory, lightly battered island fish. Choose from ahi, ono or mahimahi, which are brought in from fishing boats daily. Seafood, chicken and ribs are also on the menu. Take-out is a plus for condo vacationers. ~ 1913 South Kihei Road, Kihei; 808-874-0788. BUDGET TO MODERATE.

Bada-boom, bada-bing, it's a beautiful thing! (Or so Brooklynites say.) Any way you say it, **Bada Bing Restaurant & Rat Pack Lounge** is a great find. Tucked into the colorful ramshackle buildings of Kihei's Kalama Village, this establishment's interior is spacious, with an outdoor lanai under huge shade trees. Anything Italian is hot on Maui these days, and their menu reflects this trend. House specialties like chicken marsala or piccata are good choices, as is the shrimp scampi. Antipasti offerings include spinach, artichoke and roasted garlic dip with croutons. For a hearty lunch, the Calzonetta sandwiches really satisfy. After dinner, swing into the Rat Pack Lounge. ~ 1945 South Kihei Road, Kihei; 808-875-0188. MODERATE.

Surfside Spirits and Deli has a takeout delicatessen serving sandwiches, salads and slaw. Breakfast too! ~ 1993 South Kihei Road, Kihei; 808-879-1385. BUDGET.

The Sports Page Grill & Bar serves salads and sandwiches. The hot dogs—like the Boston Red Sox version topped with baked beans and cheese—pay tribute to baseball teams. The sandwiches

HOCKEY IN HAWAII?

Those balmy 80°F island afternoons are a bit much for an outdoor ice arena, so Maui has built the state's first in-line skating rink. Beautifully situated on the beach at Kalama Park in Kihei, this facility is regulation size. The Maui In-line Hockey Association is working to create a complete hockey program open to visitors and residents alike. ~ South Kihei Road, across from Kihei Town Center.

immortalize famous sports stars. There's the Bonnie Blair ham, Yogi Berra corned beef and cheese and Fred Couples Par 3 club. ~ 2411 South Kihei Road, Kihei; 808-879-0602, fax 808-874-9078. BUDGET.

For genuine local-style tastes in a clean, inviting diner, stop by **Da Kitchen Express** in the Rainbow Mall. They offer a variety of dishes that represent the different ethnicities that make up the population of Hawaii. Plate lunches, which are composed of a hot entrée, two scoops of white rice and macaroni or potato salad, are the way to go. Teriyaki beef and chicken katsu are favorites, as are the traditionally Hawaiian dishes *laulau* and *kalua* pork. Breakfast, lunch and dinner. ~ 2439 South Kihei Road, Kihei; 808-875-7782. BUDGET.

Upstairs in the Rainbow Mall you'll find **Maui Pizza Café**. Its menu is telling: Chef Deano's pizzas match up to New York standards (try the "Sweet & Spicy Tri-Sausage" one), and the pasta dishes will match any palate (they're offered in a small or large size). Appetizers and salads run the gamut from Asia to the Mediterranean. This is also a great late-night spot. ~ 2439 South Kihei Road, Kihei; 808-891-2200. MODERATE.

Bentwood chairs, brass fixtures and plastic tablecloths create a comfortable although uncreative atmosphere at **Sandcastle Restaurant and Lounge**. The menu consists of middle-of-the-road American entrées with pizzas, pastas and fresh fish to round things off. ~ Kamaole Shopping Center, 2463 South Kihei Road, Kihei; 808-879-0606; www.sandcastlemaui.com, e-mail trg@maui.net. MODERATE.

At **Canton Chef** the cuisine ranges from roast duck to beef with oyster sauce. This traditional Chinese restaurant offers almost 100 different choices including a selection of spicy Szechuan dishes. ~ Kamaole Shopping Center, 2463 South Kihei Road, Kihei; 808-879-1988. BUDGET TO MODERATE.

Did you say Greek? No problem. Located nearby is the **Greek Bistro** with a full selection of Mediterranean dishes such as moussaka, souvlaki, lamb kebabs and dolmas. Dinner only. ~ Kai Nani Village, 2511 South Kihei Road, Kihei; 808-879-9330. MODERATE.

Or forget the ethnic food and head next door to the **Kihei Prime Rib and Seafood House**. A reliable if undistinguished dining room, it offers a good salad bar, early-bird specials and numerous beef and fresh fish dishes. There are views across the road overlooking the ocean. Dinner only. ~ Kai Nani Village, 2511 South Kihei Road, Kihei; 808-879-1954. DELUXE TO ULTRA-DELUXE.

The **Five Palms Beach Grill**'s open-air views of the coast combined with a Hawaii Regional–style menu draw a lively crowd that toasts and dines its way through sunset. The casual atmosphere belies the sophisticated cuisine, which includes dishes such as wok-fried *opakapaka* with curry sauce and jasmine rice and Pulehu rack of lamb. There's Hawaiian music on Sunday evening. Five Palms is also open for breakfast and lunch. ~ Mana Kai Maui Resort, 2960 South Kihei Road, Kihei; 808-879-2607, fax 808-875-4803. DELUXE TO ULTRA-DELUXE.

Why do celebrities such as Richard Dreyfuss, Cuba Gooding, Jr., Halle Berry and Debra Winger book reservations at **Carelli's On The Beach**? Perhaps it's the imaginative Italian menu at this Keawakapu Beach establishment. Specialties include steamed clams in garlic, interesting pastas and fire-roasted rack of lamb. The open-air dining room, with its murals of Venice and Naples, adds to the allure. Dinner only. ~ 2980 South Kihei Road, Kihei; 808-875-0001, fax 808-874-7571. DELUXE.

At **Hana Gion** you can choose between tableside *teppanyaki* cooking or a private booth. Built in Japan, broken down and shipped to Maui for reassembly, this beautiful restaurant in the Renaissance Wailea Beach Resort was created with the guidance of one of Kyoto's leading restaurant-owning families. Specialties such as tempura, *shabu-shabu* and sukiyaki are served by kimono-clad waitresses. There's also a popular sushi bar on the premises. It's a good idea to call before going. Dinner only. Closed Thursday. ~ 3550 Wailea Alanui, Wailea; 808-879-4900, fax 808-874-5370. ULTRA-DELUXE.

From the day his ship docked in 1924 until his death four decades later, the writer Don Blanding lured visitors to the islands with more than a dozen books. An exhibition of this haole poet laureate's work is found at the Outrigger Wailea Resort restaurant named for one of his best-known volumes, **Hula Moons**. The establishment is like a small museum appointed with art pieces, ceramic plates and aloha shirts that Blanding designed, as well as his books, poems and sheet music. The menu includes Australian lamb chops, macadamia nut–crusted mahimahi and vegetarian entrées. Berry cheesecake tart highlights the dessert list. ~ 3700 Wailea Alanui, Wailea; 808-879-1922, fax 808-891-0324. DELUXE TO ULTRA-DELUXE.

With a prime oceanview at The Shops at Wailea, **Tommy Bahama's Tropical Café** is like walking into a 1940s movie set on a South Seas island—soft green wainscoting, bold tropical fabrics and fresh tropical flowers beneath gently rotating ceiling fans. An open-air lanai invites relaxation, especially with a cocktail from the Bungalow Bar. The menu is more of a tribute to the restaurant's Florida roots. There are Caribbean-style names for the dishes, such as Rum Runners' Fruit Salad, Mama Bahama's Jerk Chicken Sandwich and Salmon St. Croix. But the quality of the cuisine is excellent, and the desserts are to die for. ~ 3750 Wailea Alanui, Wailea; 808-875-9983. DELUXE.

The other fun and casual restaurant at The Shops at Wailea is **Cheeseburger, Mai Tais & Rock-n-Roll**. It's a sister restaurant to Lahaina's wildly popular Cheeseburgers in Paradise. Along with a familiar decor of tropical prints, bamboo and coconut wood, this Cheeseburger also sports a Hawaiian memorabilia and logo shop. The owners think they provide the best cheeseburger on the island and I have to agree—it's juicy and delectable, and comes with sautéed onions on a whole-wheat bun. The "Beef-Less in Wailea" veggie burgers are worth a try, too. Stay for the live music, beginning every day at 4 p.m. ~ 3750 Wailea Alanui, Wailea; 808-874-8990. BUDGET TO MODERATE.

Café Kula at the Grand Wailea Resort has a terrace dining area that offers light, healthy breakfast and lunch choices. Start the day with a breakfast burrito, vegetable quiche, muesli or pastries. For lunch try the garden burger or garden salad served with chicken and a pineapple vinaigrette. ~ 3850 Wailea Alanui, Wailea; 808-875-1234, fax 808-874-2478. BUDGET TO MODERATE.

Seasons, the signature restaurant at the Four Seasons Resort Wailea, gained a vaunted reputation soon after it opened in 1990. Marble trim and knockout ocean views create the suitable ambience. But the cuisine is what the dining room is particularly known for. Specializing in fresh fish and locally grown produce prepared in a contemporary American style, it's one of Maui's top restaurants. Dinner only. Closed Sunday and Monday. ~ 3900 Wailea Alanui, Wailea; 808-874-8000, fax 808-874-5370. ULTRA-DELUXE.

The menu's not-so-subtle distinction between "seafood" and "not seafood" entrées should tip you off on what the specialties are at **Nick's Fishmarket Maui**. With a menu that ranges from Kona abalone to Maine lobster to Australian tiger prawns, you may never

AUTHOR FAVORITE

The tab at **A Pacific Café Maui** will fluctuate dramatically depending on whether you order an inexpensive pizza or one of the dishes specially prepared on the wood-burning grill. A sister to the famous gourmet restaurant on Kauai, the Maui sibling is beautifully designed with a bolted-beam ceiling, bright pastel walls and a heart-shaped bar. From that smoky grill they serve up ahi steak, Chilean sea bass and Mongolian rack of lamb. Or how about roast duck with garlic mashed potatoes or scallops in polenta crust? Highly recommended. Dinner only. ~ Azeka Place II, 1279 South Kihei Road, Kihei; 808-879-0069, fax 808-879-0325. DELUXE TO ULTRA-DELUXE.

eat meat again. But if you want turf over surf, there's lamb chops, filet mignon and free-range chicken. There's alfresco seating. I thought it was overpriced and resting on the laurels of its Oahu facility. Dinner only. ~ Kea Lani Hotel, 4100 Wailea Alanui, Wailea; 808-879-7224; www.tri-star-restaurants.com. ULTRA-DELUXE.

Consider the *kiawe*-grilled hamburgers, the giant onion rings, the *pupus* or the salads at the Kea Lani Hotel's **Polo Beach Grille and Bar**. This poolside dining spot is also a great place for a cool drink. ~ 4100 Wailea Alanui, Wailea; 808-875-4100, fax 808-875-1200. MODERATE TO DELUXE.

A tranquil oceanfront setting makes the **Prince Court** the place to enjoy Hawaiian regional cuisine. At this signature restaurant in the Maui Prince Hotel, you can choose from a menu that begins with rock shrimp potstickers, kona lobster cakes and Maui onion bisque. The bill of fare continues with such dishes as Hawaiian catch *laulau*. Wicker furniture and tropical foliage add to the elegance. Dinner only except for Sunday brunch. ~ 5400 Makena Alanui, Makena; 808-874-1111. DELUXE TO ULTRA-DELUXE.

Hakone is the kind of restaurant you'd expect to find at any self-respecting Japanese-owned resort. The shoji screens, Japanese fans and a sushi bar are authentic; the ocean views are entirely Hawaiian. Start with tempura or miso soup. Entrées include sashimi, *sukiyaki* and New York steak. Better yet, go on Monday night when they have the Japanese buffet and try a little bit of everything. Outstanding. Reservations are required. Dinner only. Closed Sunday. ~ Maui Prince Hotel, 5400 Makena Alanui, Makena; 808-874-1111, fax 808-879-8763. DELUXE TO ULTRA-DELUXE.

GROCERIES Foodland is a large supermarket open 24 hours a day. ~ Kihei Town Center, South Kihei Road, Kihei; 808-879-9350.

Star Market, open all day except between 2 a.m. and 5 a.m., has a large selection of groceries. ~ 1310 South Kihei Road, Kihei; 808-879-5871.

Azeka's Market up the road is often price-competitive. Open from 7:30 a.m. to 5 p.m. ~ Azeka Place Shopping Center, 1280 South Kihei Road, Kihei; 808-879-0611.

For healthful items, try **Hawaiian Moons Natural Foods**, which also has a salad bar. Open 8 a.m. to 9 p.m. Monday through Saturday and 8 a.m. to 7 p.m. on Sunday. ~ 2411 South Kihei Road, Kihei; 808-875-4356.

SHOPPING Shopping in Kihei is centered in the malls and doesn't hold a lot of promise. You'll find swimwear shops and an assortment of other clothing outlets, but nothing with style and panache. Foremost among the malls is **Azeka Place Shopping Center**, which stretches along the 1200 South block of Kihei Road.

Kukui Mall just down the road has that most wonderful of inventions—a bookstore: a **Waldenbooks** bookstore to be exact. ~ 1819 South Kihei Road, Kihei; 808-874-3688.

You're likely to find a bargain or two at the **Maui Clothing Company's Outlet Store** if resortwear and Maui logowear are your thing. There's plenty to choose from. ~ Kihei Gateway Plaza, 362 Huku Li'i Place #106, Kihei; 808-879-0374.

Kalama Village Shopping Center, an open-air market with about 20 vendors, is a funky counterpoint to Kihei's other shopping spots. Here you'll find T-shirts, shells, jewelry and souvenirs sold at cut-rate prices by local people. If you're a Kona coffee fan, check out the **Bad Ass Coffee Company** (808-879-1950). There are flavorful blends, pure mild Kona and hearty roasts. ~ 1941 South Kihei Road, Kihei.

If you don't find what you're searching for at any of these addresses, there are countless other strip malls along Kihei Road.

Centrally located off North Kihei Road on the connector road, Piikea Avenue, **Piilani Village Shopping Center** is where locals flock to shop. The complex features a selection of stores, services and restaurants. Anchored by two flagship stores, **Safeway** market and **Hilo Hatties** (808-875-4545) Hawaiian clothing and gifts, Piilani also includes Roy's Kihei Bar & Grill. **Tropical Disc** (808-874-3000; www.tropicaldisc.com) is a Maui-owned and -operated record and music store, boasting over 3000 Hawaiian music titles to choose from, including hard-to-come-by older recordings and the state's hottest hits. Favorite island-style eateries offered are Asia Express, with a traditional Hong Kong noodle stand, and Cold Stone Creamery, hand-mixed ice cream and yogurt treats. Sporting enthusiasts will appreciate **Lightning Bolt Maui** (808-875-4554), and **Duke's Surf Shop** and **Hawaiian Riders Harley-Davidson and Exotic Car Rentals** (808-891-0889). ~ 225 Piikea Avenue, Kihei; 808-874-8900.

WARHOL, PICASSO AND THE PACIFIC OCEAN

Much of the $30 million art collection in the Grand Wailea Resort and Spa comes from the personal holdings of the owner, Takeshi Sekiguchi. At the hotel's **Napua Gallery**, you can see his original Warhol paintings and some of his best Picasso lithographs, including *Les Deux Femmes Nues*. This series focuses on Picasso's longtime companion, Françoise Gilot, and demonstrates the artist's personal evolution. Available for purchase are paintings, mixed-media works and sculpture by leading contemporary artists. ~ 3850 Wailea Alanui, Wailea; 808-875-1234.

The Shops at Wailea is a center of elegance in the already posh Wailea resort. With the look of a Mediterranean seaside village, complete with water fountains, the center is home to several dining options as well as shop-'til-you-drop possibilities. The Shops are comprised of two wings at two levels, and the storefronts lining the East Wing parallel the likes of Rodeo Drive and 5th Avenue. Notable jewelry stores include the Maui-based Sacco Designs, where master jeweler David Sacco creates his fine-art pieces. Speaking of art, Wailea now boasts galleries galore—Lahaina Galleries, Dolphin Galleries, Ki'i Gallery, Lassen Galerie, Elan Vital Galleries and Celebrités. Signature island shops include Martin & MacArthur, with their koa furniture, 1930-'40s Hawaiian-style aloha shirts and dresses, and made-in-Hawaii gifts; Endangered Species, offering conservation-oriented gifts; and Noa Noa, featuring batik clothing and island textiles, jewelry and antiques. Complimentary shuttles run from Wailea hotels to The Shops every 30 minutes. ~ 3750 Wailea Alanui, Wailea; 808-891-6770.

Poised to make itself the premier art center of Maui, The Shops at Wailea also hosts WOW! Wailea Wednesday art nights, which include art showings, entertainment, fashion events and dining specials from 6:30 to 9:30 p.m.

A wonderful place to buy high quality handicrafts is Hana Ka Lima, a market held on the grounds of the Aston Wailea hotel every Friday from 9 a.m. to 2 p.m. Artists and craftspeople from around the island sell traditional Hawaiian and Polynesian creations, including wood carvings, paintings, bead jewelry, bone necklaces and tapa cloth. Some artists even demonstrate their skills. ~ 3700 Wailea Alanui, Wailea; 808-879-1922.

At Mandalay Imports you'll find Thai silk, designer dresses, lacquer chests, Chinese opera coats, beaded belts and Balinese art. This shop in the Four Seasons Resort at Wailea also sells innovative necklaces and ceramic vases. ~ 3900 Wailea Alanui, Wailea; 808-874-5111.

NIGHTLIFE A Pacific Café Maui is the hot spot for live music and a lively crowd. ~ Azeka Place II, 1279 South Kihei Road; 808-879-0069.

At night, Hapa's Restaurant hosts an upbeat and occasionally flamboyant gay scene with risque revues and music. Cover on Monday and Wednesday through Saturday. ~ Lipoa Center, 41 East Lipoa Street, Kihei; 808-879-9001.

When you get the munchies, check out Maui Pizza Café. It's also a happenin' late-night spot with a comfortable lounge and live music. ~ 2439 South Kihei Road, Kihei; 808-891-2200.

The Rat Pack Lounge swings into action any night of the week with themed music nights, and live bands on Saturday. ~ 1945 South Kihei Road, Kihei; 808-875-0188.

The **Sunset Terrace Lounge** is a pleasant spot to see live Hawaiian entertainment when day turns to night. It's located at the Renaissance Wailea Beach Resort. ~ 3550 Wailea Alanui, Wailea; 808-879-4900.

Live Hawaiian entertainment is a nightly feature at the Aston Wailea Resort in **Kumu Bar and Grill**. Come for dinner or have a drink poolside as you enjoy an appealing island show. ~ 3700 Wailea Alanui, Wailea; 808-879-1922.

Leave it to the Grand Wailea Resort Hotel & Spa—the accent's on Grand—to have Maui's most elaborate high-tech nightclub. **Tsunami** cost $4 million to build and has 20 video monitors and a 14-foot-wide karaoke screen. Cover. ~ 3850 Wailea Alanui, Wailea; 808-875-1234.

A venue at the Four Seasons Resort at Wailea is **Ferraros**, where live Italian music is perfectly timed for enjoying a sunset drink. ~ 3900 Wailea Alanui, Wailea; 808-874-8000.

There is Hawaiian entertainment nightly at the **Molokini Lounge**. ~ Maui Prince Hotel, 5400 Makena Alanui, Makena; 808-874-1111.

BEACHES & PARKS

KIHEI BEACH This narrow, palm-fringed beach that runs from Maalaea Bay to Kihei can be seen from several points along Kihei Road and is accessible from the highway. The entire stretch is dotted with small parks and picnic areas and doesn't actually go by a specific name. There are buildings and numerous condominiums along this strip, but few large crowds on the beach. Beach joggers take note: You can run for miles along this unbroken strand, but watch for heavy winds in the afternoon. Shallow weed-ridden waters make for poor swimming and only fair snorkeling (you'll find better at Kamaole beaches). For those anglers in the crowd, bonefish, *papio*, mullet, goatfish, *ulua*, *moano* and mountain bass are all caught here. There are picnic tables and restrooms at Kihei Memorial Park, which is midway along the beach.

KALAMA COUNTY BEACH PARK This is a long, broad park (36 acres) that has an ample lawn but very little beach. Rather than lapping along the sand, waves wash up against a stone seawall. Backdropped by Haleakala, Kalama has stunning views of West Maui, Lanai and Kahoolawe. A new attraction is the in-line skating rink, which features a view so compelling you could easily lose concentration and run into a fellow skater. This park is an excellent place for a picnic but, before you pack your lunch, remember that it, like all Kihei's beaches, is swept by afternoon winds. For surfers there are summer breaks over a coral reef; left and right slides. Snorkeling and fishing are fair; swimming is poor. There are picnic areas, restrooms, a shower and tennis courts. ~ Located on South Kihei Road, across from Kihei Town Center.

KAMAOLE BEACH PARKS (I, II AND III) 🏖 🏄 🚻 Strung like beads along the Kihei shore are these three beautiful beaches. Their white sands are fringed with grass and studded with trees. With Haleakala in the background, they all offer magnificent views of the West Maui Mountains, Lanai and Kahoolawe—and all are windswept in the afternoon. Each has picnic areas, restrooms, lifeguard and showers. Kamaole III also has a playground. Swimming is very good on all three beaches. The best snorkeling is near the rocks ringing Kamaole III. Goatfish is the main catch. ~ Located on South Kihei Road near Kihei Town Center.

> Morning is the best time to go to the beach in Wailea and especially in Kihei. Later in the day, the wind picks up.

KEAWAKAPU BEACH 🏖 🏄 🚻 Ho hum, yet another beautiful white-sand beach . . . Like other nearby parks, Keawakapu has marvelous views of the West Maui Mountains and Lanai, but is plagued by afternoon winds. The half-mile-long beach is bordered on both ends by lava points. The swimming is good, but Keawakapu is not as well protected as the Kamaole beaches. Snorkelers explore the area around the rocks. The fishing is excellent. There are no facilities except showers. ~ Located on South Kihei Road between Kihei and Wailea.

MOKAPU AND ULUA 🏖 🏄 🚶 These are two crescent-shaped beaches fringed with palms and looking out toward Lanai and Kahoolawe. Much of their natural beauty has been spoiled by the nearby hotels and condominiums The beaches have landscaped miniparks and are popular with bodysurfers. Swimming and snorkeling are both good; restrooms and a shower are available. ~ Located in Wailea on Makena Alanui, adjacent to the Renaissance Wailea Beach Resort.

WAILEA BEACH 🏖 🏄 Another lovely white-sand strip, once fringed with *kiawe* trees, is now dominated by two very large, very upscale resorts, part of the ultramodern Wailea development here. Swimming is good (the beach is popular with bodysurfers) and so is snorkeling. Restrooms and showers are available. ~ Located on Makena Alanui in Wailea between the Grand Wailea Resort and the Four Seasons Resort at Wailea.

POLO BEACH 🏖 🏄 Though not quite as attractive as Wailea Beach, it still has a lot to offer. There's a bountiful stretch of white sand and great views of Kahoolawe and Molokini. The beach, popular with bodysurfers, has a landscaped minipark with picnic tables, restrooms and showers. Swimming is also good here and the snorkeling is excellent. ~ Located off Makena Alanui on Kaukahi Road in Wailea, adjacent to the Kea Lani Hotel.

POOLENALENA (OR PAIPU) BEACH PARK Once known by locals as Chang's Beach, this is a lovely white-sand beach that has been transformed into an attractive facility frequented by people from throughout the area. The beach has showers, restrooms, picnic tables and a wonderful shaded lawn; unfortunately it also has as its neighbor the Maui Prince Hotel. Swimming is good, snorkeling fair and fishing very good—many species are caught here. ~ Located on Makena Alanui about one-and-one-fifth mile before (north of) the Maui Prince Hotel.

BLACK SANDS BEACH OR ONEULI BEACH Black Sands is a long, narrow, salt-and-pepper beach located just north of Red Hill, a shoreline cinder cone. Fringed with *kiawe* trees, this stretch of beach is less attractive but more secluded than Makena. Facilities are nonexistent. Swimming and snorkeling are both fair, but the fishing is very good, many species being caught here. ~ Located on Makena Alanui, four-fifths mile past the Maui Prince Hotel. Turn right on the dirt road at the north end of Red Hill, then bear right and go one-third mile to the beach.

◄ HIDDEN

▲ There is unofficial camping but it's illegal and not recommended.

MAKENA STATE BEACH Much more than a beach, Makena is an institution. Over the years, it's been a countercultural gathering place. There are even stories about rock stars jamming here during Makena's heyday in the early 1970s. Once a hideaway for hippies, the beach today is increasingly popular with mainstream tourists. So far this long, wide corridor of white sand curving south from Red Hill is still the most beautiful beach on Maui. There are pit toilets. ~ From Wailea Shopping Village, go about four-and-one-half miles south on Makena Alanui. Turn right into the parking lot.

LITTLE BEACH (PUU OLAI BEACH OR "BABY BEACH") This pretty stretch of white sand next to Makena Beach, just across Red Hill, is a nude beach. It's also popular with the island's gay crowd. But if you go nude here or at Makena, watch out for police; they regularly bust nudists. Swimming is good (bodysurfing is especially good here) and you can snorkel near the rocks at the north end of the beach. The fishing is fair. There are no facilities. ~ Follow Makena Alanui for about four-and-one-half miles south from Wailea Shopping Village. Watch for Red Hill, the large cinder cone on your right. Just past Red Hill, turn right into the parking lot for Makena Beach. From here a path leads over Red Hill to Little Beach.

◄ HIDDEN

▲ Camping, though unofficial, is very popular here, but beware of thieves.

SEVEN

Kahului–Wailuku Area

The island's commercial, civic, and population centers are located in the adjoining towns of Kahului and Wailuku. With no clear dividing place, these two municipalities seem at first glance to be "twin towns." They drift into one another as you climb uphill from Kahului Harbor toward the mountains. Kahului is significantly younger than its neighbor, however, and focuses its daily life around commerce. Maui's main airport is here, together with a skein of shopping malls and a few hotels that line a blue-collar waterfront. Wailuku presents a more rolling terrain and is the seat of government for Maui County.

Kahului, with its bustling harbor and busy shopping complexes, offers little to the sightseer. The piers along the waterfront, lined with container-cargo ships and weekly cruise ships, are the embarkation point for Maui's sugar and pineapple crops. Established as a sugar town more than a century ago, Kahului has a commercial feel about it.

Coming from the airport along Kaahumanu Avenue (Route 32), you can wander through **Kanaha Pond Wildlife Sanctuary**. Once a royal fishpond, this is now an important bird refuge, especially for the rare Hawaiian stilt and Hawaiian coot.

The highway leads uphill to **Wailuku**, Maui's administrative center. Older and more interesting than Kahului, Wailuku sits astride the foothills of the West Maui Mountains at the entrance to Iao Valley. A mix of woodframe plantation houses and suburban homes, it even boasts a multi-story civic building. For a short tour of the aging woodfront quarter, take a right on Market Street and follow it several blocks to **Happy Valley**. This former red-light district still retains the charm, if not the action, of a bygone era. Here you'll discover narrow streets and tinroof houses framed by the sharply rising, deeply creased face of the West Maui Mountains.

The county government buildings reside along High Street. Just across the road rests picturesque **Kaahumanu Congregational Church**. Queen Kaahumanu attended services here in 1832 when the church was a grass shack, and requested that the first permanent church be named after her. Now Maui's oldest church, this grand stone-and-plaster structure was constructed in 1876, and has been kept in excellent condition for its many visitors. With a lofty white spire, it is the area's most dramatic manmade landmark. ~ 808-244-5189.

Nearby you'll find the **Bailey House Museum**, run by the Maui Historical Society. Lodged in the dwelling of a former missionary, the displays include 19th-century Hawaiian artifacts, remnants from the early sugar cane industry and period pieces from the missionary years. This stone-and-plaster house (completed in 1850) has walls 20 inches thick and beams fashioned from hand-hewn sandalwood. Together with an adjoining seminary building, it harkens back to Wailuku's days as an early center of western culture. Admission. ~ 2375-A Main Street; 808-244-3326; www.maui museum.org, e-mail baileyh@aloha.net.

Bounded on both sides by the sharp walls of Iao Valley, **Tropical Gardens of Maui** encompasses four densely planted acres of fruit trees, orchids and flowering plants. Iao Stream rushes through the property, which offers garden paths and a lily pond. Admission. ~ 200 Iao Road; 808-244-3085; www.tropicalgardens ofmaui.com, e-mail info@tropicalgardensofmaui.com.

Up the road at **Kepaniwai County Park and Heritage Gardens**, there's an outdoor cultural showcase to discover. Backdropped by Iao Valley's adze-like peaks, this adult playground features lovely Japanese and Chinese monuments as well as a taro patch. There are arched bridges, a swimming pool and an Oriental garden. The houses of Hawaii's many cultural groups are represented by a Hawaiian grass hut, New England saltbox (complete with white picket fence), Filipino bamboo house and a Portuguese villa. On this site in 1790 Kamehameha's forces overwhelmed the army of a Maui chief in a battle so terrible that the corpses blocking Iao Stream gave Kepaniwai ("damming of the waters") and Wailuku ("bloody river") their names.

After exploring Kepaniwai County Park and Heritage Center, continue up to the **Hawaii Nature Center**, situated on the edge of Iao Valley, off the gateway to Iao Valley State Park, features an Interactive Science Arcade designed for adults as well as children. The Nature Center also hosts hikes Monday through Friday into the Iao Valley, complete with environmental educators. Admission. ~ 875 Iao Valley Road; 808-244-6500.

◄ HIDDEN

Uphill at the **John F. Kennedy Profile** you'll see Hawaii's answer to Mt. Rushmore, chiseled by nature. Ironically, this geologic formation, which bears an uncanny resemblance to the former president, was never noticed until after his assassination.

◄ HIDDEN

Iao Valley State Monument, surrounded by those same moss-mantled cliffs, provides an excellent view of **Iao Needle**, a single spire that rises to a point 1200 feet above the valley (and 2250 feet above sea level). With the possible exception of Haleakala Crater, this awesome peak is Maui's most famous landmark. A basalt core that has withstood the ravages of erosion, the "Needle" and mist-filled valley have long been a place of pil-grimage for Hawaiians. In ancient times the area was set aside by the ruling chiefs as a sacred site, off limits to commoners. Kakae, the ruler of Maui in the late 1400s, declared the valley the sacred bur-ial place of Hawaiian royalty. It is said that the bones of many of the chiefs were concealed in caves to pre-vent their enemies from stealing them. In fact, it was *kapu* (prohibited) for anyone other than the *alii* to ven-ture up the valley, except during the Makahiki festival, when Iao Needle was used as an altar. Nowadays, you can join the spirits of the *alii* and enter the valley. If nothing else, be sure to explore the paths from the parking lot that lead across Iao Stream and up to a vista point.

The translation of Iao Valley is "Valley of Dawning Inspiration" or "Supreme Light." When you take a walk through the area you will understand why it is a sacred spot for Hawaiians.

LODGING   The hotel strip in the harbor town of Kahului lies along the beach on Kahului Bay.

The **Maui Seaside Hotel** consists of two separate complexes sitting beside each other along Kaahumanu Avenue (Route 32). There is a pool, restaurant and lounge. Rooms in the older pool-side wing are a bit less expensive: clean, but lacking in decorative flair, the surroundings are quite adequate. Just a few well-spent dollars more places you in a larger, more attractive room in the newer complex, which has more upscale appointments. Both fa-cilities feature phones, TVs, refrigerators and air conditioning. Some include kitchenettes. Ask about discounts. ~ 100 West Kaa-humanu Avenue, Kahului; 808-877-3311, 800-560-5552, fax 808-877-4618; www.sand-seaside.com. MODERATE TO DELUXE.

The nearby **Maui Beach Hotel** incorporates the old Maui Palms Hotel as its Palms wing, where rooms are about as inexpensive as things get on Maui. Rooms in the Palms wing are comfort-able, although decor and facilities are a bit dated; some units in-clude air conditioners and refrigerators. The main wing is more contemporary, with larger rooms that translate into higher rates. While conveniently located in Kahului, it is not your made-in-paradise setting, with "oceanfront" meaning the waters of Ka-hului Harbor. The grounds are appealingly studded with palms, and there is a pleasant pool area with a small adjacent beach, plus two restaurants and a sundries shop. The attitude is island-style friendly. ~ 170 Kaahumanu Avenue, Kahului; 808-877-0051, 888-649-3222, fax 808-871-5797. MODERATE TO DELUXE.

Northshore Inn is another clean, trim hostel-cum-hotel with shared rooms and private singles or doubles. The lobby/television room is decorated with surfboards, flags and modern art, and the

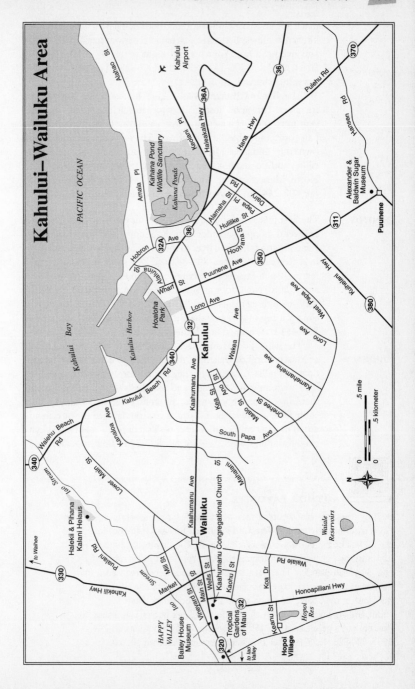

Kahului–Wailuku Area

place has an easy, windswept air about it. There are laundry and kitchen facilities; baths are shared. Every room has a refrigerator and overhead fan. Your seventh night is free. ~ 2080 Vineyard Street, Wailuku; 808-242-8999, 800-647-6284, fax 808-244-5004; www.hostelhawaii.com. BUDGET.

The **Banana Bungalow** is a kind of resort for low-budget travelers. This hotel/hostel caters to windsurfers, surfers and adventurers. It offers a jacuzzi, garden and fruit trees, a sand volleyball court and cable TV and movies. The folks here conduct their own tours and have a free airport drop-off. There are laundry facilities and a community kitchen and, of course, hammocks. ~ 310 North Market Street, Wailuku; 808-244-5090, 800-846-7835, fax 808-244-3678; www.mauihostel.com. BUDGET.

DINING

The best place in Kahului for a quick, inexpensive meal is at one of several shopping arcades along Kaahumanu Avenue (Route 32). For common fare, head over to the Maui Mall. Here you can drop in at **Restaurant Matsu** (808-871-0822), a short-order eatery that features such Japanese selections as tempura, bento plates, sushi and *saimin*. Next door at **Siu's Chinese Kitchen** (808-871-0828), they serve three meals a day. To round off the calorie count, you can try a cup of *guri guri* sherbet at **Tasaka Guri Guri Shop** (808-871-4513). ~ Maui Mall, Kahului. BUDGET.

HIDDEN ►

The white booths and black-tile tables are an appealing touch at **Marco's Grill & Deli.** So is the attention to detail at this family-operated Italian restaurant. They blend their own coffee and grind their own meat for sausages and meatballs. The result is a menu that ranges from chocolate cinnamon French toast at breakfast to submarine sandwiches and vodka rigatoni later in the day. In addition to pasta entrées, they serve seafood dishes. ~ 444 Hana Highway, Kahului; 808-877-4446, fax 808-874-7032. MODERATE.

AUTHOR FAVORITE

Built by a wealthy island banker as a wedding gift for his daughter-in-law, this "queen" of historic homes, **The Old Wailuku Inn at Ulupono**, reflects the Hawaii of the current owners' childhoods. The theme of Ulupono and its landscaped grounds are a tribute to Hawaii's poet laureate of the 1920s and '30s, Don Blanding. There are seven individually decorated bedrooms dedicated to an island flower or plant, each with a matching Hawaiian quilt and its own bath. Common areas are the breakfast room, living room, and library, which holds all of Don Blanding's books. The plantation era at its gentle best. ~ 2199 Kahookele Street, Wailuku; 808-244-5987, 800-305-4899, fax 808-242-9600; www.mauiinn.com. DELUXE.

If you're staying at one of Kahului's bayfront hotels, you might try **Vi's Restaurant** in the Maui Seaside Hotel. This open-air Polynesian-style establishment has steak with fish or shrimp and other assorted dinners. The ambience here is pleasant, and the staff congenial, but in the past the service has sometimes been slow. Vi doesn't serve lunch, but at breakfast (7 to 9 a.m.) the specials might include banana hot cakes. Dinner is from 6 to 8 p.m. ~ 100 West Kaahumanu Avenue, Kahului; 808-871-6494. MODERATE.

The **Rainbow Dining Room** lies along Kaahumanu Avenue in the Maui Beach Hotel. Overlooking the pool, this spacious open-air restaurant serves a Japanese buffet most of the week, and at lunch and breakfast features American cuisine. The former includes shrimp tempura, scallops, mixed vegetables, yakitori chicken, teriyaki steak, many different types of Japanese salad and a host of other dishes. ~ 170 Kaahumanu Avenue, Kahului; 808-877-0051, fax 808-871-5797. DELUXE.

Want something on the healthy side? **Down to Earth Deli & Cafe** serves veggie burgers, vegetarian subs and other heart-smart fare in the corner of a full-service natural foods supermarket. ~ 305 Dairy Road, Kahului; 808-877-2661, fax 808-877-7548. BUDGET.

Up the road apiece in Wailuku there are numerous ethnic restaurants guaranteed to please both the palate and the purse. **Sam Sato's** features local noodle dishes. Open for breakfast and lunch, it specializes in *manju* (a bean cake pastry), dry *mein* (a noodle dish) and the ubiquitous *saimin*. Closed Sunday. ~ 1750 Wili Pa Loop, Wailuku; 808-244-7124. BUDGET.   ◀ HIDDEN

The nearby **Fujiya** stirs up similar money belt–tightening Japanese meals. Well worth a visit. There's also a sushi bar. No lunch on Saturday. Closed Sunday. ~ 133 Market Street, Wailuku; 808-244-0206. BUDGET.

A local favorite, **Siam Thai Cuisine** is always a good choice for Southeast Asian fare. Attractively decorated with posters and artwork from Thailand, this restaurant features a complete menu that includes dozens of delicious dishes. Try the chicken-coconut soup, *tom-yum goong*, Siam chicken, or the *pod-pet,* beef or pork or chicken sautéed with ginger and bamboo shoots. No lunch on Saturday and Sunday. ~ 123 North Market Street, Wailuku; 808-244-3817. BUDGET.   ◀ HIDDEN

Saeng's Thai Cuisine sits in a beautifully designed building embellished with fine woodwork and adorned with Asian accoutrements. The menu, which lists three pages of dishes from Thailand, is like an encyclopedia of fine dining. Meals, which are served in the dining room or out on a windswept veranda, begin with *sateh* and spring rolls, venture on to dishes like the "evil prince" and "tofu delight," and end over tea and tapioca pudding. No lunch Saturday and Sunday. ~ 2119 Vineyard Street, Wailuku; 808-244-1567. BUDGET TO MODERATE.

A Saigon Café doesn't advertise itself with even a sign on the outside, but business still flourishes. You'll find a small space inside, but a big menu that includes vegetarian, clay pot, seafood and even steak entrées. ~ 1792 Main Street, Wailuku; 808-243-9560, fax 808-243-9566. BUDGET TO DELUXE.

Ramon's is the region's entry in the Mexican food category. This split-level eatery features entertainment and patio seating. The varied menu is spelled out with tacos, tamales, a sushi bar, local food items, seafood, fajitas and chile rellenos. ~ 2102 Vineyard Street, Wailuku; 808-244-7243. BUDGET TO MODERATE.

Tasty Crust is famous for its breakfasts, especially pancakes, which it serves in the morning, as well as at lunch and dinnertime. If you'd rather not have breakfast in the evening, try the hamburger steak plate. ~ 1770 Mill Street, Wailuku; 808-244-0845, fax 808-242-7170. BUDGET.

Wailuku's low-rent district lies along Lower Main Street, where ethnic restaurants cater almost exclusively to locals. These are informal, family-owned, formica-and-naugahyde-chair cafés that serve good food at down-to-earth prices. You'll find Japanese food at Tokyo Tei. No lunch on Sunday. ~ 1063-E Lower Main Street, Wailuku; 808-242-9630. BUDGET.

Southeast Asia is represented by Cali Café. Their menu features Vietnamese food like stir-fried vegetables, curried chicken rice plates, shrimp in clay pot and beef noodle dishes. Closed Sunday. ~ 1246 Lower Main Street, Wailuku; 808-244-2167. BUDGET.

GROCERIES Kahului features two sprawling supermarkets. Foodland is open daily from 6 a.m. to 11 p.m. ~ Kaahumanu Center, Kaahumanu Avenue, Kahului; 808-877-2808. Star Super Market is open daily from 6 a.m. to 10 p.m. ~ Maui Mall, Kaahumanu Avenue, Kahului; 808-877-3341.

Down to Earth Natural Foods has a complete line of health food items and fresh produce. Add to that a healthy stock of herbs and you have what amounts to a natural food supermarket. This gets my dollar for being the best place on Maui to shop for natural foods. ~ 305 Dairy Road, Wailuku; 808-877-2661.

There is also Ah Fook's Super Market in the Kahului Shopping Center. ~ Kaahumanu Avenue, Kahului; 808-877-3308.

Wakamatsu Fish Market has fresh fish every day but Sunday, when they are closed. ~ 145 Market Street, Wailuku; 808-244-4111.

Love's Bakery Thrift Shop sells day-old baked goods at old-fashioned prices. ~ 340 Ano Street, Kahului; 808-877-3160. The Holsum/Oroweat Thrift Shop is another place for baked goods. ~ 350 Hoohana Street, Kahului; 808-877-5445.

SHOPPING For everyday shopping needs, you should find the Kahului malls very convenient. Three sprawling centers are strung along Kaahumanu Avenue (Route 32).

Kaahumanu Center is Maui's finest and most contemporary shopping mall, with Liberty House (808-877-3361) and Sears (808-877-2221), a photo studio, Waldenbooks (808-871-6112), boutiques, shoe stores, candy stores, a sundries shop and a jeweler. For Japanese foods, try Shirokiya (808-877-5551). ~ 275 Kaahumanu Avenue.

Nearby Maui Mall has a smaller inventory of shops. Mom's (808-877-3711) stocks a connoisseur's selection of tobaccos and coffees, and even has a coffee bar and vegetarian deli. ~ 180 East Wakea Avenue.

You might also try Kahului Shopping Center, though I prefer the other, more convenient malls. ~ Kaahumanu Avenue.

Summerhouse Boutique might be called a chic dress shop. But they sell everything from jewelry to porcelain dolls and natural fiber garments. ~ 395 Dairy Road, Kahului; 808-871-1320.

The Gallery has jade and pearl pieces among its inventory of exotic jewelry. You'll also find Asian antiques and artwork. ~ Maui Mall, 70 East Kaahumanu Avenue, Kahului; 808-893-2216.

Up in Wailuku, a tumbledown town with a friendly face, you'll find the little shops and solicitous merchants that we have come to associate with small-town America. Along North Market Street are several imaginative shops operated by low-key entrepreneurs.

High-end oriental antiques, including a prized collection of Buddhas and estate pieces, are showcased at Gottling Ltd. Closed Sunday. ~ 34 North Market Street, Wailuku; 808-244-7779.

Bird of Paradise carries collectible Hawaiiana including old records, sheet music, bric-a-brac and plantation-style furnishings. ~ 56 North Market Street, Wailuku; 808-242-7699.

Brown & Kobayashi, another nearby antique store, specializes in rare pieces from the Orient. ~ 160-A North Market Street, Wailuku; 808-242-0804.

Some of the island's most reasonably priced souvenirs are found at the Maui Historical Society Museum Gift Shop, located in the

MAUI'S FAMOUS POTATO CHIPS

Always a favorite with locals, Maui potato chips have by now become a worldwide phenomenon. One of the most popular brands is "Kitch'n Cook'd," made at the family-owned and operated Maui Potato Chip Factory. This place has been around since the 1950s, annually increasing in popularity, and it now brings in orders from around the globe. These chips are hard to find in mainland stores, but you can stock up on them here where they're freshly made. No tours. Closed Saturday and Sunday. ~ 295 Lalo Place, off Route 360, Kahului; 808-877-3652.

Bailey House Museum. Here you'll find an outstanding collection of local history books and art prints. Quilts and *koa* bookmarks are also popular. ~ 2375-A Main Street, Wailuku; 808-244-3326.

NIGHTLIFE If you're in the mood for a movie, check out the offerings at the 12-screen **Megaplex.** ~ Maui Mall, 70 East Kaahumanu Avenue, Kahului; 808-244-8934, code 2004.

Nightly music and dancing attract a local crowd at **Sal's Place,** an Italian restaurant where the beat ranges from reggae to disco to Hawaiian. The music is live on select weekends. Otherwise it's deejay-selected. Cover. ~ 162 Alamaha Street, Kahului; 808-893-0609.

> Kahului, then Maui's largest town, was deliberately destroyed by fire in 1890 to kill rats that were spreading an epidemic of bubonic plague.

The crowd's also mostly local at the **Ale House,** which has karaoke Sunday through Wednesday, with live music and dancing until 2 a.m. from Thursday through Saturday. ~ 355 East Kamehameha Avenue, Kahului; 808-877-9001.

BEACHES & PARKS

HOALOHA PARK Located next to the Kahului hotels, this is Kahului's only beach, but unfortunately the nearby harbor facilities detract from the natural beauty of its white sands. What with heavy boat traffic on one side and several hotels on the other, the place is not recommended. There are much better beaches in other areas of the island. Swimming and snorkeling are poor; surfers will find good breaks (two to six feet, with a left slide) off the jetty mouth near the north shore of Kahului Harbor. It is, however, a good spot to beachcomb, particularly for Maui diamonds. Picnic tables are available. Goatfish, *papio* and triggerfish can be hooked from the pier; *ulua* and *papio* are often caught along the shore. ~ Located on Kaahumanu Avenue (Route 32), Kahului.

KEPANIWAI COUNTY PARK AND HERITAGE GARDENS This beautiful park is carefully landscaped and surrounded by sheer cliffs. You'll discover paths over arched bridges and through Japanese gardens, plus pagodas, a thatch-roofed hut, a taro patch and banana, papaya and coconut trees. An ideal and romantic spot for picnicking, it has picnic pavilions, restrooms and a swimming pool. ~ Located in Wailuku on the road to Iao Valley.

WAIHEE BEACH PARK This park is used almost exclusively by local residents. Bordered by a golf course and shaded with ironwood trees and *naupaka* bushes, it has a sandy beach and one of Maui's longest and widest reefs. There's a grassy area perfect for picnicking, established picnic areas and restrooms with showers. Beachcombing, *limu* gathering and fishing are all good. Swimming and snorkeling are okay, though the reef is rather shallow. ~ Located outside Wailuku on the rural road that circles the West Maui Mountains. To get there from Route 340 in Waiehu, turn right on Halewaiu Road and then take the beach access road from Waiehu Golf Course.

Central Maui is defined not by what it is but by what lies to the east and west of it. On one side Haleakala lifts

▼▼▼▼▼▼▼▼▼▼▼▼▼▼▼▼▼▼

Central Maui and Maalaea

into the clouds; on the other hand loom the West Maui mountains, a folded landscape over 5000 feet in elevation. Between them, at the center of the island, sits an isthmus, some areas planted in sugar cane and pineapple. Never rising more than a few hundred feet above sea level, it houses Kahului along its northern edge and serves as the gateway to both the Lahaina–Kaanapali and Kihei–Wailea areas.

Three highways cross the isthmus separating West Maui from the slopes of Haleakala. From Kahului, Mokulele Highway (Route 350) tracks south to Kihei through this rich agricultural area. The Kuihelani Highway (Route 380), running diagonally and through open stretches, joins the Honoapiilani Highway (Route 30) in its course from Wailuku along the West Maui Mountains. The low-lying area that supports this network of roadways was formed by lava flows from Haleakala and the West Maui Mountains.

The **Alexander & Baldwin Sugar Museum**, an award-winning nonprofit organization, is across from the largest operating sugar plantation in Hawaii. It provides a brief introduction to Hawaii's main crop. Tracing the history of sugar cultivation in the islands, its displays portray everything from early life in the cane fields, the multi-ethnic plantation life, to contemporary methods for producing refined sugar. Closed Sunday except in July and August. Admission. ~ Puunene Avenue and Hansen Road, Puunene; 808-871-8058.

SIGHTS

The **Maui Tropical Plantation** is a 60-acre enclave complete with orchards and groves displaying dozens of island fruit plants. Here you'll see avocados, papayas, bananas, pineapples, mangoes, coffee and macadamia nuts growing in lush profusion. There's a tropical nursery and a tram that will carry you through this ersatz plantation. Admission for the tram. ~ 1670 Honoapiilani Highway; 808-244-7643.

Truly both a learning center and a star attraction is **Maui Ocean Center, The Hawaiian Aquarium**. The first site to be constructed at Maalaea Harbor Village on Route 30, Maui Ocean Center is unlike any aquarium on the Mainland. It's a journey through the living ocean in both open-air and interior exhibits, each of which are interactive in touch, sight and sound. Showcasing not only Hawaii's unique marine life, from the coral reef to the open ocean, this aquarium also dedicates an exhibit to its host culture, showcasing the language, history and lore of Hawaii.

Locally trained marine naturalists are on hand to answer questions and give presentations. The Whale Discovery Center offers life-sized models of a Pacific humpback whale calf and spinner dolphins, but what's most interesting are the interactive exhibits of the whale's migration from Alaska to Hawaii. My favorite area, though, is Sting Ray Cove—an open pond with a glass wall on one side that allows you to be mesmerized by the variety of rays gliding by on undulating wings. Of course, the Open Ocean glass tunnel is usually a child's favorite, with a 240-degree view of reef sharks and hundreds of other marine animals in a constantly renewed saltwater aquarium. A gift store and two restaurants are located within the park. Admission. ~ 192 Maalaea Road, Maalaea; 808-270-7000, fax 808-270-7070; www.mauiocean center.com.

Past the small boat harbor at **Maalaea Bay**, the highway hugs the southwest coast. There are excellent lookout points along this elevated roadway, especially near the lighthouse at **McGregor Point**. During whale season you might spy a leviathan from this landlocked crow's nest. Just offshore there are prime whale breeding areas.

Down the road from McGregor Point, you'll see three islands anchored offshore. As you look seaward, the portside islet is **Molokini**, the crescent-shaped remains of a volcanic crater. **Kahoolawe**, a barren, desiccated island once used for naval target practice, sits in the center. Located seven miles off Maui's south coast, it is a bald, windblasted place, hot, arid and home to feral goats. Hawaiian activists long demanded an end to the bombing of this sacred isle by the U.S. Navy. After years of demonstrations, their demands were finally acknowledged in 1994 when the island was turned over to the state of Hawaii. The humpbacked island to starboard is **Lanai**. Lying eight miles across the Kealaikahiki Channel, it is a pear-shaped island boasting a 3370-foot peak and a population of about 3200 people. As you continue toward Kaanapali, **Molokai** sails into view. Known as the "Friendly Isle,"

A NEW ADDICTION

If you're not in the mood for a full meal, stop by the **Maui Popcorn Factory** for a new slant on an old-fashioned snack. The Volcano—popcorn mixed with rice crackers, doused with butter and sprinkled with *furikake*— explodes with flavor. After a few tastes of this special treat, you'll be like the Hawaiians, who carry a bag of rice crackers and a jar of *furikake* to the movie theaters to make their own. It's truly addicting. ~ 21 North Market Street, Wailuku; 808-242-9888.

it covers 260 square miles and contains the highest per capita concentration of native Hawaiians of any of the main islands. With a population of about 7000 people, it's a sleepy destination ideal for a Maui getaway excursion.

Overlooking scenic Maalaea Harbor's fishing fleet is the **Blue Marlin Harborfront Grill & Bar**, located on the lower level of the Maalaea Harbor Village complex. The fish is really fresh because it comes straight from the fishing boats, walked over by the fishermen themselves. À la carte favorites make for a good sampling: try the sashimi selection, fresh fish and chips, half-pounds of oysters on the half shell, or a local favorite, ahi *poke*. The ambiance is nautical and casual; diners have a choice of an open-air lanai or wide-view dining room. ~ 300 Maalaea Road, Maalaea; 808-244-8844. MODERATE TO DELUXE.

DINING

Capische?, also found in the Maalaea Harbor Village complex, is an intimate dining experience in a cosmopolitan setting. There are no outdoor views in this bistro, but the food more than makes up for it. Italian seafood is the cuisine speciality—a good example is *capellini alla Capische*—grilled-scallop-and-tiger-prawn skewers over squid-ink capellini pasta. The pasta is hand-made by the chef. Diners are serenaded on Sunday with light opera and show tunes. Dinner only. ~ 300 Maalaea Road, Maalaea; 808-243-9001. DELUXE.

Maalaea Harbor Village sits adjacent to the Maui Ocean Center and overlooks Maalaea Harbor. (A stoplight intersection on Route 30 now makes it safe for drivers to turn into and out of Maalaea.) This small complex is packed with unique stores, including **Island Soap & Candle Works** (808-986-8383), where fragrant, handmade vegetable-base soaps and beeswax candles are made and sold. **Shapers of Maalaea** (808-242-7873), a surf shop and surfing museum, overlooks the area's famous surf break, called "Freight Trains" by locals and "Maalaea Pipeline" by national surf publications. Other stores feature island wear and souvenirs; the **Pacific Whale Foundation Gift Store and Marine Resource Center** (808-879-8860) offers their marine-related T-shirts, hats and gifts, which add to the shopping mix. ~ 300 Maalaea Road, Maalaea.

SHOPPING

EIGHT

Hana Highway

The Hana Highway (Route 360), a smooth, narrow road running between Kahului and Hana, is one of the most beautiful drives in all Hawaii. Following the path of an ancient Hawaiian trail, it may in fact be one of the prettiest drives in the world. The road courses through a rainforest, a luxurious jungle crowded with ferns and African tulip trees, and leads to black sand beaches and rain-drenched hamlets. The vegetation is so thick it seems to be spilling out from the mountainside in a cascade of greenery. You'll be traveling the windward side of Haleakala, hugging its lower slopes en route to a small Hawaiian town that receives 70 inches of rain a year.

There are over 600 twists and turns and 56 one-lane bridges along this adequately maintained paved road. It'll take at least three hours to drive the 51 miles to Hana. To make the entire circuit around the south coast, plan to sleep in Hana or to leave very early and drive much of the day. If you can, take your time—there's a lot to see.

About seven miles east of Kahului, you'll pass the quaint, weather-beaten town of **Paia**. This old sugar plantation town, now a burgeoning artist colony and windsurfing mecca, has been painted in nursery colors. Along either of Paia's two streets, plantation-era buildings have been freshly refurbished.

On the eastern side of town is the **Mantokuji Buddhist Temple**, which celebrates sunset every day by sounding its huge gong.

Hookipa Beach Park, one of the world's premier windsurfing spots, lies about three miles east of town. Brilliantly colored sails race along the horizon as windsurfers perform amazing acrobatic stunts, cartwheeling across the waves. The latest craze is kite surfing. You can watch riders "kite the surfzone," jump, jibe or ride upwind.

Within the next ten miles the roadway is transformed, as your slow, winding adventure begins. You'll drive past sugar cane fields, across verdant gorges, through valleys dotted with tumbledown cottages and along fern-cloaked hillsides.

Route 36 becomes Route 360, beginning a new series of mileage markers that are helpful in locating sites along the way. Near the two-mile marker, a short trail leads to an idyllic swimming hole at **Twin Falls** (the path begins from the west side of the Hoolawa Stream bridge on the right side of the road).

Nearby **Huelo,** a tiny "rooster town" (so named because nothing ever seems to be stirring except the roosters), is known for the **Kaulanapueo Church.** A coral chapel built in 1853, this New England–style sanctuary strikes a dramatic pose with the sea as a backdrop.

Farther along, on **Waikamoi Ridge,** you'll see picnic areas and a nature trail. Here you can visit a bamboo forest, learn about native vegetation and explore the countryside. Remember to bring mosquito repellent, especially if you're planning a rainforest hike.

Another picnic area, at **Puohokamoa Falls** (11-mile marker), nestles beside a waterfall and large pool. If you packed a lunch, this is a perfect place to enjoy it. Trails above and below the main pool lead to other waterfalls.

A few zigzags farther, at **Kaumahina State Wayside** (12-mile marker), a tree-studded park overlooks Honomanu Gulch and Keanae Peninsula. From here the road descends the gulch, where a side road leads left to **Honomanu Bay** (14-mile marker) and its black sand beach.

Above Keanae Peninsula, you'll pass the **Keanae Arboretum** (16-mile marker). You can stroll freely through paved trails in these splendid tropical gardens, which feature many native Hawaiian plants including several dozen varieties of taro. Another section of the gardens is devoted to exotic tropical plants and there is a mile-long trail that leads into a natural rainforest.

Just past the arboretum, turn left onto the road to the **Keanae Peninsula** (17-mile marker). This rocky, windswept point offers stunning views of Haleakala. You'll pass rustic houses, a patchwork of garden plots and a coral-and-stone church built around 1860. A picture of serenity and rural perfection, **Keanae** is inhabited by native Hawaiians who still grow taro and pound poi. Their home is a lush rainforest—a quiltwork of taro plots, banana trees, palms —that runs to the rim of a ragged coastline.

Another side road descends to **Wailua** (18-mile marker), a Hawaiian agricultural and fishing village. Here is another luxurious checkerboard where taro gardens alternate with banana patches and the landscape is adorned with clapboard houses. The town is known for **St. Gabriel's Church,** a simple structure made completely of sand and coral, dating from 1870.

Back on the main road, there's yet another picnic area and waterfall at **Puaakaa State Wayside** (22-mile marker). The cascade tumbles into a natural pool in a setting framed by eucalyptus and banana trees. Puaakaa means, by the way, "plenty of pigs."

HIDDEN ▶

Past here, another side road bumps three miles through picturesque **Nahiku** (25-mile marker) to a bluff overlooking the sea. The view spreads across three bays all the way back to Wailua. Directly below, the ocean pounds against rock outcroppings, spraying salt mist across a stunning vista. Set in one of the wettest spots along the entire coast, Nahiku village is inundated by rainforest and graced by yet another 19th-century church.

Several miles before Hana, be sure to stop at **Waianapanapa State Park**. Here you will find a black-sand beach and two lava tubes, **Waianapanapa** and **Waiomao caves**. Hawaiian mythology tells of a Hawaiian princess who hid from her cruel husband here, only to be discovered by him and slain. Now every spring the waters hereabouts are said to run red with her blood. Offshore you will also see several sea arches and nearby a blowhole that spouts periodically.

> Hana's three police officers report that the region's number one crime is driving without a seatbelt.

Just before the town of Hana, on the right, is **Helani Farm and Gardens**, a sprawling oasis of tropical plant life. Only a section of the gardens is currently open to the public, but it's worth a stop as there's a wealth of flowering plants, trees and vines. You'll also find fruit trees, baobab trees, papyrus, ginger plants and even a carp pond. Visits by appointment only. Admission. ~ Hana Highway; phone/fax 808-248-8274, 800-385-5241; e-mail bj4flowers@aol.com.

As you approach the town of Hana, take the Ulaino Road turnoff going left and follow it to the end. You'll cross a streambed that empties into a pristine freshwater pool, the **Blue Pool**, named for the cobalt color of its icy water. There's parking just beyond the streambed in the grassy meadow (perfect for a quiet picnic); the pool is on the left.

On your way to or from the pool along the same road, watch for the **Ka'eleku Caverns** sign and make a point to visit the island's largest underground lava tube system created from a flow 30,000 years ago. Maui Cave Adventures offers two tours: a one-hour scenic tour or a physically challenging two-and-a-half-hour tour. The latter does not allow anyone under 15 years of age; you have to crawl through a couple of tight spots and climb a ladder on this tour. Tour times vary: please inquire. The visitors center amidst tropical gardens is inviting for a picnic lunch, too. Admission. ~ P.O. Box 40, Hana, HI 96713; 808-248-7308; www.mauicave.com, e-mail info@mauicave.com.

To reach the secluded hamlet of **Hana**, you can take the old Hawaiian shoreline trail (see the "Hiking" section at the end of this chapter) or continue on along the highway. This Eden-like town, carpeted with pandanus, taro and banana trees, sits above an inviting bay. Known as "heavenly Hana," it's a ranch town inhabited primarily by part-Hawaiians. Because of its remote lo-

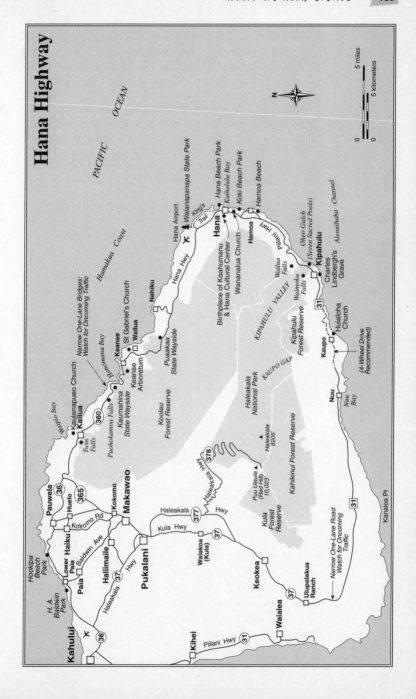

Hana Highway

PACIFIC OCEAN

5 miles

5 kilometers

N

Hamakua Coast

Hana Hwy

Hana Airport

King's Trail

Waianapanapa State Park

Hana Beach Park

Hana

Kaihulu Bay

Koki Beach Park

Hamoa Beach

Hamoa

Birthplace of Kaahumanu & Hana Cultural Center

Wananalua Church

Oheo Gulch (Seven Sacred Pools)

Kipahulu

Charles Lindbergh's Grave

Alenuihaha Channel

Nahiku

Wailua Falls

Waimoku Falls

Piilani Hwy

KIPAHULU VALLEY

Kipahulu Forest Reserve

Hualoha Church

St Gabriel's Church

Keanae
Wailua

Narrow One-Lane Bridges: Watch for Oncoming Traffic

Honomanu Bay

Kaulanapueo Church

Kailua

Puohokamoa Falls

Kaumahina State Wayside

Keanae Arboretum

Puaakaa State Wayside

Koolau Forest Reserve

Haleakala National Park

Kaupo

KAUPO GAP

Nuu
Nuu Bay

(4-Wheel Drive Recommended)

Waipio Bay

Twin Falls

360

31

31

Haleakala 8205'

Haleakala Hwy

378

Pauwela

36

365

Huelo

Kokomo

Makawao

Haleakala Hwy

377

Haleakala 6205'

Puu Ulaula (Red Hill) 10,023'

Kahikinui Forest Reserve

Kanaloa Pt

Lower Haiku

Kokomo Rd

Kula Hwy

Haliimaile

Baldwin Ave

Paia

Hookipa Beach Park

H. A. Baldwin Park

Pukalani

Waiakoa (Kula)

37

Kula Forest Reserve

Keokea

Utupalakua Ranch

Narrow One-Lane Road Watch for Oncoming Traffic

37

Haleakala Hwy

37

Kahului

36

Waialea

Kihei

Piilani Hwy

31

cation it has changed little over the years. The rain that continually buffets Hana makes it a prime agricultural area and adds
to the luxuriant, unsettling beauty of the place.

Because of its strategic location directly across from the Big
Island, Hana was an early battleground in the wars between the
chiefs of Maui and the Big Island, who conquered, lost and re-
gained the region in a succession of bloody struggles. During the
19th century it became a sugar plantation, employing different
ethnic groups who were brought in to work the fields. Then, in
1946, Paul Fagan, a San Francisco industrialist, bought 14,000
acres and created the Hana Ranch, turning the area into grazing
land for Hereford cattle and opening the exclusive Hotel Hana-
Maui.

Head down to **Hana Bay**. Here you can stroll the beach, explore the wharf and take a short path along the water to a plaque
that marks the **Birthplace of Kaahumanu**, King Kamehameha I's
favorite wife and a key player in the 1819 overthrow of the an-
cestral Hawaiian religious system. To reach this sacred spot, pick
up the trail leading from the boat landing on the right side of the
HIDDEN ▶ bay. It leads along the base of **Kauiki Hill**, a cinder cone covered
with ironwood trees that was the scene of fierce battles between
Kahekili, the renowned Maui chief, and the Big Island chief
Kalaniopuu.

Near the Hotel Hana-Maui (where you can request a key to
open the gate), you can drive or hike up a short road to **Mount
Lyons** (that camel-humped hill with the cross on top). From this
aerie, a memorial to Paul Fagan, there's a fine view of Hana Bay
and the surrounding coastline.

The **Hana Cultural Center**, an enticing little museum, displays
such artifacts from Hana's past as primitive stone tools, rare shells
and Hawaiian games. There are antique photographs and elab-
orately stitched quilts. ~ 4974 Uakea Street; 808-248-8622.

Also on the grounds, the old **Court House**, built in 1871, is a
modest but appealing structure containing five small benches and
the original desk for the judge.

Wananalua Church, a lovely chapel built from coral blocks
during the mid-19th century, has been beautifully refurbished.
Today, services are conducted in English and Hawaiian. Located
atop an ancient *heiau*, stately and imposing in appearance, it is
a perfect expression of the days when Christianity was crushing
the old Hawaiian beliefs. ~ Hauoli Street and Hana Highway.

FROM HANA TO ULUPALAKUA The backroad from Hana
around the southeast side of Maui is one of the island's great adventures. It leads along the side of Haleakala past dense rainforest and tumbling waterfalls to an arid expanse covered by lava
flows, and then opens onto Maui's vaunted Upcountry region.

Since a five-mile stretch is unpaved and other sections are punctuated with potholes, car rental companies generally do not permit driving on parts of this route; so check with them in advance or be prepared to take your chances. Also check on road conditions: The road is sometimes closed during periods of heavy rain.

Past Hana, the road, now designated the Piilani Highway and renumbered as Route 31 (with mileage markers that descend in sequence), worsens as it winds toward an overgrown ravine where **Wailua Falls** (45-mile marker) and another waterfall pour down sharp cliff faces.

At **Oheo Gulch** (known to some as Seven Sacred Pools) in the Kipahulu District of the Haleakala National Park (42-mile marker), a series of waterfalls tumbles into two dozen pools before reaching the sea. The pools are rock-bound, some are bordered by cliffs, and several provide excellent swimming holes. This is an eerie and beautiful place from which you can see up and down the rugged coastline. Used centuries ago by early Hawaiians, they still offer a cool, refreshing experience.

Every tourist to Maui dreams of visiting the "Seven Sacred Pools." In fact, says Mark Tanaka-Sanders, a ranger who helps manage a coastal section of Haleakala National Park, "there are 24 pools in the area." Who's responsible for the miscount? "Blame it on the tourist industry," he says. "It's also important to know that the Hawaiian people do not consider these pools sacred." They refer to them as the pools at Oheo.

Another special spot, **Charles Lindbergh's grave** (41-mile marker), rests on a promontory overlooking the ocean. The great aviator spent his last days here and lies buried beside Palapala Hoomau Church. The whitewashed chapel and surrounding   ◄ HIDDEN

sights

AUTHOR FAVORITE

For a cultural treat, turn off Route 360 at Ulaino Road following the signs to the **Kahanu Garden**, part of the National Tropical Botanical Gardens. The focus here is on native Hawaiian plants and culture. A highlight of the 90-minute tour is a look at the massive **Piilanihale heiau**, which overlooks a moody stretch of coast. The football field–sized platform, built of moss- and algae-covered lava rocks, is the largest of the ancient *heiau* sites remaining in Hawaii. The power of the past can be felt here, especially with the soulful expertise that tour guides impart on a visit. The sense of authenticity makes this a true encounter with Polynesian Hawaii. You can only visit the garden on a guided tour, which runs twice daily. Closed Saturday and Sunday. Admission. ~ 808-248-8912.

shade trees create a place of serenity and remarkable beauty. (To find the grave, continue 1.2 miles past Oheo Gulch. Watch for the church through the trees on the left. Turn left onto an unpaved road and drive several hundred yards, paralleling a stone fence. Turn left into the churchyard.)

Not far from here, in **Kipahulu**, the paved road gives way to dirt. It's five miles to the nearest pavement, so your car should have good shock absorbers; sometimes the weather makes it impassable. The road rises along seaside cliffs, some of which are so steep they jut out to overhang the road. This is wild, uninhabited country, ripe for exploration.

HIDDEN ►   **Huialoha Church**, built in 1859, rests below the road on a wind-wracked peninsula. The last time I visited this aging worship hall, horses were grazing in the churchyard. Nearby you'll encounter the tinroof town of **Kaupo**, with its funky general store. Located directly above the town is **Kaupo Gap**, through which billowing clouds pour into Haleakala Crater.

The road bumps inland, then returns seaward to **Nuu Bay's** rocky beach. From here the rustic route climbs into a desolate area scarred by lava and inhabited with scrub vegetation. The sea views are magnificent as the road bisects the **1790 lava flow**. This was the last volcanic eruption on Maui; it left its mark in a torn and terrible landscape that slopes for miles to the sea.

It's several miles farther until you reach **Ulupalakua Ranch**, a lush counterpoint to the lava wasteland behind. With its grassy acres and curving rangeland, the ranch provides a perfect introduction to Maui's Upcountry region.

LODGING   Along the Hana Highway out in Paia, about seven miles from Kahului, sits **Nalu Kai Lodge**. Tucked behind the Wine Corner Liquor Store near the town hub, this seven-unit resting place is a real sleeper. The rooms are often occupied by long-term renters. But if you snag one of the vacant rooms, you'll check into a small, plain cubicle with no carpeting and little decoration. And only one of the rooms has a double bed. Sound unappealing? Well, even bare walls sometimes look good at the right price. ~ Nalu Lane, off Hana Highway; 808-579-8009. BUDGET.

HIDDEN ►   Owners of North Shore Maui's Mama's Fish House have installed picturesque beachfront cottages next to their restaurant, naming the small complex **The Inn at Mama's Fish House**. Located just east of Paia at Kuau Cove, The Inn consists of four two-bedroom units, all facing the ocean, plus two one-bedroom garden-view units. True to form, the owners have named each cottage after a Hawaiian fish. Their beachfront property is known for its lush, tropical gardens and swaying coconut palm grove. Each unit is furnished in bold, Hawaiian print decor, including fresh tropical flowers as well as a complete kitchen and private lanai. ~ 799

Poho Place, Paia; 808-579-9764, 800-860-4852, fax 808-579-
8594; www.mamasfishhouse.com. DELUXE TO ULTRA-DELUXE.

A very convenient accommodation located on the Hana Highway in Keanae is the Maui YMCA's **Camp Keanae**. For just $15
a night, both men and women are welcome to roll out their sleeping bags on bunks in the dormitory or one of five cabins. The camp
overlooks the sea, and comes with hot showers, laundry facilities,
full-size gym, kitchen and outdoor cooking area. Sorry, the maximum stay here is three nights. Guests must make reservations and
provide their own bedding. ~ Hana Highway, Keanae; 808-242-
9007, 808-248-8355, fax 808-244-6713; e-mail ymcacampkeanae
@aol.com. BUDGET.

Aloha Cottages, perched on a hillside above Hana Bay, has   ◄ HIDDEN
two-bedroom cottages and one three-bedroom cottage that are
situated among banana trees and feature hardwood floors and
redwood walls. The decor is simple, the kitchens are all-electric
and many of the furnishings are rattan. Representing one of Hana's
best bargains, the cottages have been recommended many times
over the years by readers and friends. There are only five units
at this small complex, so advance reservations are a good idea.
~ 73 Keawa Place; 808-248-8420. MODERATE.

You can also consider heading down toward the water to the
Hana Kai Maui Resort. Located smack on a rocky beach, this pair
of two-story buildings sits amid lush surroundings. The ornamental
pool is a freshwater affair fed by toe-dipping
spring water. The location and exotic grounds rate   The honor system is
a big plus. Both studio apartments and one-bedroom   alive and well at the
condominiums are available. ~ 1533 Ukea Road; 808-   untended self-serve
248-8426, 800-346-2772, fax 808-248-7482; www.   coconut stand near
hanakaimaui.com. DELUXE TO ULTRA-DELUXE.   Hana Highway's 48-
                                                          mile marker.
Hana Accommodations and Plantation Houses has
cottages and studios. Scattered throughout the Hana area
are homes with either mountain or ocean views; each unit
is fully equipped with (or has access to) a kitchen. Many of the
accommodations are decorated with tapa-cloth designs and
Hawaiian paintings. Most are cooled with ceiling fans and all
have outdoor grills perfect for a private feast. Some facilities are
within walking distance of the beach and ancient Hawaiian fishponds. Gay-friendly. ~ Locations throughout Hana; 808-248-
7868, 800-228-4262, fax 808-248-8240; www.hana-maui.com.
MODERATE TO DELUXE.

Hana Alii Holidays offers a similar selection of accommodations
—including studios and homes—in several price ranges. Here you
can settle into a place on Hana Bay or on an idyllic hillside. Some
guest units sit atop lava-rock bluffs overlooking the ocean, others are found in secluded five-acre settings. Most accommodations come with lanais, outdoor barbecues and full kitchens. ~

103 Keawa Place; 808-248-7742, 800-548-0478, fax 808-248-8595; www.hanaalii.com, e-mail info@hanaalii.com. MODERATE TO ULTRA-DELUXE.

One of Hawaii's finest resting places is the **Hotel Hana-Maui**, a luxurious retreat on a hillside above the bay. From ocean views to tropical landscape to rolling lawn, this friendly inn is a unique, world-class resort. Spread across the 66-acre grounds are 76 cottages, all elegantly designed and devoid of clocks, radios and TVs. The hotel's health and fitness complex sponsors a variety of hiking excursions and nature walks. The adjacent 25-meter pool, landscaped with lava walls and monkeypod trees, enjoys a spectacular setting. The staff has been here for generations, lending a sense of home to an enchanting locale. Rates for this getaway of getaways are stratospheric, but I highly recommend the Hotel Hana-Maui. ~ P.O. Box 9, Hana, HI 96713; 808-248-8211, 800-321-4262, fax 808-248-7202; www.hotelhanamaui.com. ULTRA-DELUXE.

Don't forget the cabins at **Waianapanapa State Park** (for information, refer to the "Beaches & Parks" section later in this chapter).

GAY LODGING   The road to Hana is also home to several bed and breakfasts that cater to a gay, lesbian and straight clientele. **Golden Bamboo Ranch** has three suites and a cottage amid seven acres of gardens. There are views of the ocean through a horse pasture. ~ 422 Kaupakalua Road, Haiku; 808-572-7824, phone/fax 800-344-1238; www.goldenbamboo.com. MODERATE.

Halfway to Hana House is a private and secluded studio with a mini-kitchen overlooking the ocean. Guests enjoy a great sunrise view. Stay seven nights or longer and you'll get a 10 percent discount. ~ P.O. Box 675, Haiku, HI 96708; 808-572-1176, fax 808-572-3609; www.halfwaytohana.com, e-mail gailp@maui.net. MODERATE.

Kailua Maui Gardens, a gay-owned, mixed-clientele guest house, has everything from a one-room cottage to a three-bedroom house with a pool. It's set in a tropical garden with shaded paths

AUTHOR FAVORITE

Speaking of scenery, **Heavenly Hana Inn** is blessed indeed. Located in Hana Town, this hostelry offers three suites and is entered through a Japanese gate. On either side, stone lions guard a luxuriant garden. The interior mirrors this elegance. Each suite is decorated in a Japanese style with futon beds, shoji screens and tiled bathrooms with soaking tubs. Continental breakfast, picnic lunches, tea and early dinner are provided for a fee. ~ Hana Highway; phone/fax 808-248-8442; e-mail hanainn@maui.net. ULTRA-DELUXE.

and bridges plus a spa. Two-night minimum; rates drop with length of stay. ~ S.R. 1 Box 9, Haiku, HI 96708; 808-572-9726, 800-258-8588; www.maui.net/~kmg. MODERATE.

The **Huelo Point Lookout** is set on two acres and bounded by the ocean on three sides. There's lodging in three cottages—the Rainbow, Start and Haleakala, each with a full kitchen. Also available is a lookout house, a two-story home complete with a full kitchen, dining room, and space for up to eight people. You can also enjoy the hot tub and pool. ~ P.O. Box 117, Paia, HI 96779; 808-573-0914, 800-808-871-8645, fax 808-573-0227; www.maui vacationcottages.com, e-mail dreamers@maui.net. DELUXE TO ULTRA-DELUXE.

Napulani O'Hana offers spacious accommodations within a few miles of Hana. It's a ranch-style house set on four acres. Enjoy the pineapples and papaya served in season. ~ P.O. Box 118, Hana, HI 96713; 808-248-8935, 800-628-7092, fax 808-248-7494. BUDGET TO MODERATE.

Paia, an artsy little town located just a few miles out on the Hana Highway, has several restaurants to choose from. If you don't select any of them, however, be forewarned—there are no pit stops between here and Hana.

DINING

If you're craving a tasty fish sandwich, the **Paia Fish Market** is the place to go. When you're not in the mood for seafood, this eatery also offers hamburgers, pasta and Mexican dishes such as fajitas. It's is a casual place with plenty of greenery, and prints of water sports on the walls. ~ Corner of Baldwin Avenue and Hana Highway; 808-579-8030. BUDGET TO MODERATE.

For box lunches, drop in at **Picnics**. Open for breakfast, lunch and dinner, this light and airy café serves a variety of items including spinach-nut burger and mahimahi sandwiches. The menu also offers patrons basic breakfast selections, deli sandwiches, vegetarian options and plain old burgers. ~ 30 Baldwin Avenue, Paia; 808-579-8021; e-mail picnics@aloha.net. BUDGET.

The **Vegan Restaurant** is the prime address hereabouts for vegetarian food. Place your order at the counter—there are salads, sandwiches and hot entrées that include Thai specialties. ~ 115 Baldwin Avenue, Paia; 808-579-9144. BUDGET.

Bangkok Cuisine promises "authentic Thai food." They certainly sport an authentically attractive dining room decorated with tiles and pastel walls. There's also a patio where you can dine alfresco beneath an umbrella of palm trees. Oh, and the menu—Cornish game hen in a sauce of garlic and black pepper, eggplant beef and evil prince shrimp. Dinner only Saturday and Sunday. ~ 120 Hana Highway, Paia; 808-579-8979. BUDGET TO MODERATE.

Since 1971, **Charley's** has been a favorite spot to drop in for breakfast (and lunch and dinner). Macadamia-nut pancakes, french toast, Tex-Mex omelettes—you name it, they've got it. At lunch you can try the Woofer burger (Charley is named after a Great Dane); if you prefer the meatless menu, there are veggie burgers, salads or sandwiches. Dinner entrées include "catch of the day," New York steaks, pasta, pizza and calzones. It's a comfortable atmosphere to dine in and practically open all the time. ~ 142 Hana Highway, Paia; 808-579-9453. MODERATE.

You can also try **Mama's Fish House** outside Paia. This oceanfront nook is simply decorated: shell leis, an old Hawaiian photo here, a painting there, plus potted plants. During lunch, the varied menu includes Hawaiian seafood sandwiches and salads as well as fresh fish specialties. Other than a few steak and poultry dishes, the dinner menu is entirely seafood. Evening entrées include bouillabaisse, seafood provençal and fresh Hawaiian lobster. There are always at least four varieties of fresh fish, prepared ten different ways. ~ Hana Highway; 808-579-8488, 800-860-4852, fax 808-579-8594. DELUXE TO ULTRA-DELUXE.

If you plan to stay in Hana for any length of time, pack some groceries in with the raingear. You'll find only four restaurants along the entire eastern stretch of the island. Luckily, they cover the gamut from budget to ultra-deluxe.

HIDDEN ►   **Tutu's At Hana Bay**, within whistling distance of the water, whips up French toast and *loco moco* (rice, hamburger and an egg smothered with gravy) for breakfast and plate lunches, sandwiches and burgers for lunch. ~ Hana Bay; 808-248-8224. BUDGET.

Hana Ranch Restaurant is a small, spiffy establishment decorated with blond wood and providing great ocean views. There's a flagstone lanai for outdoor dining. Open daily for lunch, they serve steak and seafood for dinner every Friday and Saturday. On Wednesday night they serve pizza. Lunch is buffet style or à la carte; in the evening they offer fresh fish, steak and baby-back ribs. ~ Hana Highway; 808-248-8255. DELUXE TO ULTRA-DELUXE.

AUTHOR FAVORITE

At **Jacques Bistro**, the look is decidedly young and attractive. The Pacific Rim menu of chef Jacques Pauvert hints of French and Italian origins. The fresh fish means a variety of things, depending on the catches of the day. Rich-sauced pastas like chicken farfalle are hard to resist. Reasonable prices make Jacques a find for value as well as taste. If you're headed back to the coast after a Haleakala sunset, stop here for dinner. You won't regret it. ~ 89 Hana Highway, Paia; 808-579-6255. MODERATE TO DELUXE.

There's also a **takeout stand** serving breakfast and lunch, with picnic tables overlooking the ocean. ~ Hana Bay. BUDGET.

Hana's premier restaurant is the dining room of the **Hotel Hana-Maui**. This extraordinary resort, perched on a hillside over-looking the ocean, provides three gourmet meals a day to its guests and the public alike. The evening menu features pan-seared veal chops, bamboo-steamed seafood and baked Hunan-style lamb. The menu changes seasonally. ~ Hana Highway; 808-248-8211, fax 808-248-7202. DELUXE TO ULTRA-DELUXE.

There are few restaurants and even fewer stores in this remote **GROCERIES** region, so stock up where you can. On the Hana Highway in Paia, **Nagata Store** has a small supply of groceries. It's open Monday through Friday 6 a.m. to 7 p.m., Saturday from 6 a.m. to 6 p.m., and Sunday from 6 a.m. to 1 p.m. ~ Hana Highway, Paia; 808-579-9252. If you can't find what you need here, check the **H&P Market & Seafood**, which keeps the same hours as the Nagata Store. ~ In the Nagata Store, Hana Highway; 808-579-8362. You can also try the **Paia General Store**. It's open from 6 a.m. to 9 p.m. during the week, and from 7 a.m. to 9 p.m. on weekends. ~ Hana Highway, Paia; 808-579-9514.

Mana Foods has a complete range of health foods and organic produce. Open from 8 a.m. to 8 p.m. every day. ~ 49 Baldwin Avenue, Paia; 808-579-8078.

With a limited stock of grocery items are **Hana Ranch Store**, open daily from 7 a.m. to 7 p.m. ~ Mill Street, Hana; 808-248-8261; and **Hasegawa General Store**, open Monday through Saturday from 7 a.m. to 7 p.m., and Sunday from 8 a.m. to 6 p.m. ~ 5165 Hana Highway, Hana; 808-248-8231.

Clear across the island, along the back road from Hana, there's a sleeper called **Kaupo General Store** that's open from 9:30 a.m.   ◄ *HIDDEN* to 5:30 p.m. "most of the time." You'll find it tucked away in the southeast corner of the island. Selling a limited range of food, drinks and wares, this store, founded in 1925, fills the gaps on the shelves with curios from its illustrious history. Closed Sunday. ~ Base of Kaupo Gap; 808-248-8054; e-mail kaupostore@yahoo.com.

Paia, just seven miles outside Kahului, is my favorite place to   **SHOPPING** shop on Maui. Many fine artisans live in the Upcountry area and come down to sell their wares at the small shops lining the Hana Highway. The town itself is a work of art, with old wooden build-ings that provide a welcome respite from the crowded shores of Kaanapali and Kihei. I'll mention just the shops I like most. Browse through town to see for yourself. If you discover places I missed, please let me know.

On display at the **Maui Crafts Guild** is a range of handmade items all by local artists. Here you'll find anything from pressed hibiscus flowers to sculptures. There are also fabrics, ceramics, jewelry, baskets, woodwork and other Maui-made items. ~ 43 Hana Highway, Paia; 808-579-9697.

Paia Trading Company has a few interesting antiques and a lot of junk. Among the more noteworthy items: turquoise and silver jewelry, wooden washboards, apothecary jars and antique glassware. Closed Sunday. ~ 106 Hana Highway, Paia; 808-579-9472.

Hawaiians called Maui's isthmus *Kula o ka Mao Mao*, "the land of mirages."

Around the corner on Baldwin Avenue lies another shop worth browsing. **Maui Girl and Co.** features a fine selection of women's beachwear. ~ 12 Baldwin Avenue, Paia; 808-579-9266.

One of my favorite shops in Hana is the **Hana Coast Gallery**, located in the Hotel Hana-Maui. It features native Hawaiian art and artifacts and fine paintings by Hawaiian artists, as well as pieces by the novelist Henry Miller. Also here are beautiful serigraphs, model racing canoes in *koa*, ceremonial objects, feathered art, fiber collages and painted tapa cloth. ~ Hana Highway, Hana; 808-248-8636.

Also on the grounds of Hotel Hana-Maui is **Susan Marie**, specializing in linen clothing, hand-painted items and handmade jewelry. Closed Sunday. ~ Hana Highway, Hana; 808-248-7231.

For everything you could possibly want or need, drop by the **Hasegawa General Store**. This store stocks everything from groceries, clothing, sandals and hardware to placemats, movie rentals, film, cards and gas. The original Hasegawa's burned down years ago, but the name is still famous. ~ 5165 Hana Highway, Hana; 808-248-8231.

NIGHTLIFE If you're looking for something to do in the evening, **Charley's** often offers live music at night. Check to see if they have something scheduled. You might even run into Willie Nelson, who favors dining at this local restaurant when he's in town. ~ 142 Hana Highway, Paia; 808-579-9453.

In the early evening, you can enjoy a duo singing Hawaiian music at the Hotel Hana-Maui's **Paniolo Bar**. As relaxed as Hana itself, this low-key establishment is always inviting. ~ Hana Highway, Hana; 808-248-8211.

BEACHES & PARKS **H. A. BALDWIN PARK** This spacious county park is bordered by a playing field on one side and a crescent-shaped beach on the other. Palm and ironwood trees dot the half-mile-long beach. There's good shell collecting and a great view of West Maui. The swimming is good, as is the bodysurfing, but beware of currents; the snorkeling cannot be recommended. For surfing there are winter breaks, with a right slide. Fishing for threadfin, mountain bass, goatfish and *ulua* is good. Facilities include a picnic area with large pavilion, showers and restrooms. ~ Located about seven miles east of Kahului on the Hana Highway.

HOOKIPA BEACH PARK For serious surfers, kitesurfers and windsurfers this is one of the best spots on Maui. The beach itself is little more than a narrow rectangle of sand paralleled by a rocky shelf. Offshore, top-ranked windsurfers or kitesurfers may be performing airborne stunts. On any day you're likely to see a hundred sails with boards attached skimming the whitecaps. The swimming is good only when the surf is low. There are picnic areas, restrooms and showers. ~ Located just off the Hana Highway about three miles east of Paia near Mama's Fish House.

HONOMANU BAY A tranquil black-sand-and-rock beach surrounded by pandanus-covered hills and bisected by a stream, Honomanu Bay is a beautiful and secluded spot. There are no facilities, and the water is often too rough for swimming, but it's a favorite with surfers. ~ Located off the Hana Highway, about 30 miles east of Kahului. Turn off onto the dirt road located east of Kaumahina State Wayside; follow it to the beach.

◄ HIDDEN

WAIANAPANAPA STATE PARK Set in a heavenly seaside locale, this park is one of Hawaii's prettiest public facilities and is a very popular spot. The entire area is lush with tropical foliage and especially palmy pandanus trees. There's a black-sand beach, sea arches, a blowhole and two legendary caves. But pack your parkas; wind and rain are frequent. Swimming and snorkeling are good—when the water is calm—and the fishing is good. Facilities here include a picnic area, restrooms and showers. ~ Located just off the Hana Highway about four miles north of the town of Hana.

▲ There are sites for up to 60 people on a grass-covered bluff overlooking the sea. There are also plain but attractive accommodations renting for $45 for up to four people. Two additional people are allowed at $5 each. Each cabin contains a small bed-

SPRING TRAINING, HANA STYLE

In 1946, Hana hosted the only mainland American baseball team ever to conduct spring training in Hawaii. That was the year that financier Paul Fagan brought the Pacific Coast League's San Francisco Seals to the islands. Arriving with the players was a squadron of sportswriters who sent back glowing dispatches on "Heavenly Hana," helping to promote the destination and the Hotel Hana-Maui, owned of course by Paul Fagan.

room with two bunk beds, plus a living room that can double as an extra bedroom. All cabins are equipped with bedding and complete kitchen facilities, and some have ocean views. A state permit is required. The cabins are rented through the Division of State Parks. ~ 54 South High Street, Suite 101, Wailuku, Maui, HI 96793; 808-984-8109.

HANA BEACH PARK Tucked in a well-protected corner of Hana Bay, this park has a large pavilion and a curving stretch of sandy beach. It's a great place to meet local people. Swimming is fine; snorkeling is good near the lighthouse; and beginning surfers will find both summer and winter breaks on the north side of the bay (left slide). Some days are very calm, however. Bonefish, *ulua* and *papio* are routinely taken here and *moilii* run in the months of June and July. As well as the picnic area, there are restrooms and showers and there is a snack bar across the street. ~ Located off the Hana Highway at Hana Bay.

HIDDEN ▶   **RED SAND BEACH** Known to the Hawaiians as Kaihalulu ("roaring sea") Beach, this is one of the most exotic and truly secluded beaches in all Hawaii. It is protected by lofty cliffs and can be reached only over a precarious trail. A volcanic cinder beach, the sand is reddish in hue and coarse underfoot. Most dramatic of all is the lava barrier that crosses the mouth of this natural amphitheater, protecting the beach and creating an inshore pool. This beach is popular with nudists. Swimming, snorkeling and fishing are all good. Technically, visiting this beach is illegal. There are no facilities. ~ This is one place where getting to the beach becomes a grand adventure. It is located on the far side of Kauiki Hill in Hana. Follow Uakea Road to its southern terminus. There is a grassy plot on the left between Hana School and the parking lot for the Hotel Hana-Maui's sea ranch cottages. Here you will find a trail leading into the undergrowth. It traverses an overgrown Japanese cemetery and curves around Kauiki Hill, then descends precipitously to the beach. Be careful!

America's first domestic rubber plantation opened in Nahiku in 1905. You can still see a few remaining rubber plants in the area.

HAMOA BEACH Located at the head of Mokae Cove, this stretch of salt-and-pepper sand with rock outcroppings at each end is a pretty place. Unfortunately, the Hotel Hana-Maui uses the beach as a semiprivate preserve. There are restrooms for guests and separate facilities for everybody else and a dining pavilion that is available only to guests, so a sense of segregation pervades the beach. ~ Follow the Hana Highway south from Hana for a little over a mile. Turn left on Haneoo Road and follow it for a mile to Hamoa.

KOKI BEACH PARK ⚓ 🏊 A sandy plot paralleled by a grassy park, this beach is more welcoming than Hamoa. Backdropped by lofty red cinder cliffs, Koki can be very windy and is plagued by currents. With a small island and sea arch offshore, it is also very pretty. Swimmers should exercise caution. ~ Located half a mile back up the Haenoo Road toward the highway.

▲ Primitive beach camping is allowed.

OHEO GULCH 🏃 ⚓ The stream that tumbles down Haleakala through the Oheo Gulch forms several large pools and numerous small ones. The main pools descend from above the Hana Highway to the sea. This is a truly enchanting area swept by frequent wind and rain, and shadowed by Haleakala. It overlooks Maui's rugged eastern shore. You can swim in the chilly waters and camp nearby. There are picnic facilities and outhouses; bring your own drinking water. ~ Located in the National Park's Kipahulu section (about ten miles south of Hana).

▲ Primitive, meadow-style camping is available on a bluff above the sea. No permit is required and there are no restrictions on the number of occupants but there is a three-day limit.

NINE

Upcountry and Haleakala

Maui's Upcountry is a verdant mountainous belt that encircles Haleakala along its middle slopes. Situated between coastline and crater rim, it's a region of ample rainfall and a sparse but growing population that is ideal for camping, hiking or just wandering. Here the flat fields of sugar cane and pineapples that blanket central Maui give way to open ranchland where curving hills are filled with grazing horses.

Farmers plant tomatoes, cabbages, carrots and the region's famous Maui onions. Proteas, those delicate flowers native to Australia and South Africa, grow in colorful profusion. Hibiscus, jacarandas, silver oak and other wildflowers sweep along the hillsides like a rainstorm. And on the region's two ranches—35,000-acre Haleakala Ranch and 35,000-acre Ulupalakua Ranch—Angus, Hereford and Brangus cattle complete a picture far removed from Hawaii's tropical beaches. Brangus cattle, by the way, are a Brahma–Angus hybrid.

Home to *paniolos*, Hawaii's version of the Western cowboy, the Upcountry region lies along the highways that lead to the crest of Haleakala. Route 37, Haleakala Highway, becomes the Kula Highway as it ascends to the Kula uplands.

It's impossible to tell from the road the beauty within at the **Enchanting Floral Garden**. This eight-acre floral fantasy, however, is in spectacular bloom much of the year, thanks to dedicated owners Kazuo and Kazuko Taketa, who have spent nearly a decade planting and nurturing an amazing array of flowers. They drip from vines and trees in great swaths of vibrant color with the Maui lowlands for a backdrop. Admission. ~ Route 37, 10-mile marker, Kula; 808-878-2531, fax 808-878-1805; www.qpg.com/e/enchanting.

The **Church of the Holy Ghost** (12-mile marker), a unique octagonal chapel, was built here in 1897 for Portuguese immigrants working on Maui's ranches and farms.

This roadway angles southwest through Ulupalakua Ranch to the ruins of the **Makee Sugar Mill**, a once flourishing enterprise built in 1878. A currently flourishing business, **Tedeschi Vineyards**, which produces a pineapple wine called Maui

Blanc, sits just across the road. The tasting room is located in a building that served as a retreat for King Kalakaua, also known as "The Merry Monarch" because of his passion for composing hula music. Here at Hawaii's oldest winery you can stop for a taster's tour. ~ 808-878-6058; www.maui.net/~winery.

In Maui's Upcountry, you may spot axis deer, Hawaiian owls and pheasants.

Just past Keokea Park on Kula Highway (Route 37), you'll see **Grandma's Coffee House**, a local gathering place. Four generations of the Franco family, owners of the coffee shop, have been growing coffee on the slopes of Haleakala and picking the beans by hand. These beans are roasted at the shop in a century-old roaster. Boasting panoramic views, Grandma's Coffee House can also brag about its homemade breakfasts, fresh-baked goodies, and hot lunch specials; the coffee, of course, is very good, too. ~ 153 Kula Highway; 808-878-2140.

Pull out of Grandma's back onto Route 37, and after a short drive, on the right you'll see a sign for **Sun Yat Sen Park**. What will really draw your attention, though, are the statues that seem to pop up out of the dry grass. They have a distinctly Asian flair because they are monuments to the Chinese immigrants who first settled Upcountry Maui. China's leader from the early 20th century, Sun Yat Sen actually visited Maui and stayed at the Pioneer Hotel in Lahaina, which may be one more reason why the park was named after him.

You can also turn up Route 377 to **Kula Botanical Gardens**. An excellent place for picnicking, the landscaped slopes contain an aviary, a pond and a "Taboo Garden" with poisonous plants and over 60 varieties of protea, the flowering shrub that grows so beautifully in this region. Admission. ~ Kula; 808-878-1715.

Several farms, including **Sunrise Protea Farm**, devoted primarily to proteas, are located nearby. ~ Haleakala Crater Road; 808-876-0200; www.sunriseprotea.com.

If you make a right from Route 377 onto the road marked for Polipoli before you get to Kula Botanical Gardens, you'll eventually reach **Polipoli Spring State Recreation Area**. This recreation area is the starting point for uncrowded, easy hikes on Haleakala's upper slopes. Head to Polipoli in the morning and you'll likely catch sight of hang gliders taking off on flights to the lowlands below. Note: The final half of the road to Polipoli is extremely rough; a four-wheel-drive vehicle is recommended. For more information on trails, see "Hiking" detailed at the end of the chapter.

Another intriguing place is the tiny town of **Makawao**, where battered buildings and falsefront stores create an Old West atmosphere. This is the capital of Maui's cowboy country, similar to Waimea on the Big Island, with a rodeo every Fourth of July.

From Makawao the possibilities for exploring the Upcountry
HIDDEN ▶   area are many. There are two **loop tours** I particularly recommend.
The first climbs from town along Olinda Road (Route 390) past
Pookela Church, a coral sanctuary built in 1843.

It continues through a frequently rain-drenched region to the
Tree Growth Research Area, jointly sponsored by state and federal forestry services. You can circle back down toward Makawao on Piiholo Road past the **University of Hawaii Agricultural
Station**, where you will see more of the area's richly planted
acreage.

The second loop leads down Route 365 to the Hana Highway. Turn left on the highway for several miles to Haiku Road, then
head left along this country lane, which leads into overgrown
areas, across one-lane bridges, past banana patches and through
the tinroof town of **Haiku**.

LODGING   A mountain lodge on the road to the summit of Haleakala offers
a cold-air retreat that is well-situated for anyone who wants to
catch the summit sunrise. For years, **Kula Lodge** has rented five
chalets, some with fireplaces, sleeping lofts and sweeping ocean
and mountain views. The individual chalets are carpeted wall-to-
wall and trimmed with stained-wood paneling. The central lodge
features a cheery restaurant, bar and stone fireplace. An appealing mountain hideaway. ~ Haleakala Highway, Kula; 808-878-
1535, 800-233-1535, fax 808-878-2518; www.kulalodge.com.
DELUXE.

What more could an urban cowpoke ask for than a bed and
breakfast with trail rides that begin in the front yard? That's the
HIDDEN ▶   scene up at **Silver Cloud Ranch**, a nine-acre spread located at 3000-
feet elevation on the slopes of Haleakala. In addition to a broad
swath of cattle country, the ranch looks out over several neighboring islands. Accommodations include six bedrooms in a big ranch
house, a bunkhouse with five studio units and a private cottage.
Full breakfast, pardner. There's a $15 surcharge for one-night
stays. ~ R.R. 2, Box 201, Kula, HI 96790; 808-878-6101, 800-
532-1111, fax 808-878-2132; www.silvercloudranch.com. MOD-
ERATE TO DELUXE.

DINING   There are several good dining spots in Pukalani Terrace Center.
Among them is **Nick's Place**, a breakfast-and-lunch-only cafeteria
serving Japanese-Chinese-American fare. Choose from such à la
carte items as *chow fun*, tempura, Portuguese sausage, stew or
corned-beef hash; together they make a hearty meal. At breakfast,
try the eggs with Portuguese sausage. ~ Pukalani Terrace Center,
Haleakala Highway, Pukalani; 808-572-8258. BUDGET.

HIDDEN ▶   A good local restaurant for breakfast or lunch is the **Up Country Café**. The theme here is bovine all the way, with the restaurant

Upcountry

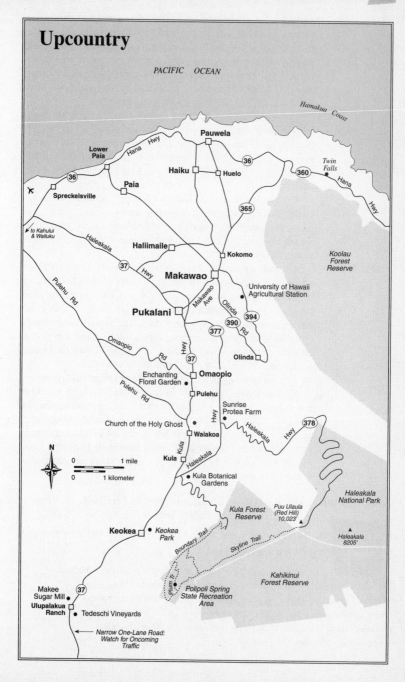

PACIFIC   OCEAN

Hamakua Coast

Pauwela

Lower
Paia

Hana   Hwy

36

360

Twin
Falls

Haiku

Huelo

Hana

Hwy

Paia

36

Spreckelsville

365

to Kahului
& Wailuku

Haleakala

Haliimaile

Kokomo

Koolau
Forest
Reserve

37

Hwy

Makawao

Makawao Ave

University of Hawaii
Agricultural Station

Pukalani

Olinda

Rd

390

394

377

Pulehu   Rd

Omaopio

Rd

Hwy

37

Olinda

Enchanting
Floral Garden

Omaopio

Pulehu   Rd

Pulehu

Sunrise
Protea Farm

378

Haleakala

Hwy

Church of the Holy Ghost

Waiakoa

Hwy

N

Kula

Kula

Haleakala

0   1 mile

0   1 kilometer

Kula Botanical
Gardens

Haleakala
National Park

Kula Forest
Reserve

Puu Ulaula
(Red Hill)
10,023'

Keokea

Keokea
Park

Boundary   Trail

Skyline   Trail

Haleakala
8205'

Kahikinui
Forest Reserve

Plum Tr.

Makee
Sugar Mill

37

Ulupalakua
Ranch

Tedeschi Vineyards

Polipoli Spring
State Recreation
Area

Narrow One-Lane Road:
Watch for Oncoming
Traffic

decked out in everything from cow bells to cow salt-and-pepper shakers. Breakfast is pretty predictable; lunch includes a half-dozen entrées such as teriyaki beef and New York steak, as well as such nonbovine fare as chicken curry with fresh country vegetables, sautéed mahimahi and vegetarian lasagna. Also open for dinner Monday through Saturday. ~ Haleakala Highway and Aewa Place, Pukalani; 808-572-2395. BUDGET TO MODERATE.

For something a step more upscale, consider the **Makawao Steak House**. Knotty pine walls and a comfortable lounge lend the place an air of refined rusticity. The popular menu serves a mix of surf-and-turf dishes; unfortunately there are no vegetarian dishes. Dinner only. ~ 3612 Baldwin Avenue, Makawao; 808-572-8711. DELUXE.

Go Mediterranean at **Casanova Italian Restaurant & Deli**, a stylish bistro that serves Italian-style seafood, pasta dishes, and pizza. For something faster, cheaper and more casual, you can try the adjacent deli. ~ 1188 Makawao Avenue; 808-572-0220. MODERATE TO DELUXE.

HIDDEN ▶   Or head across the street to **Polli's Restaurant**. This sombreros-on-the-wall-and-oilcloth-on-the-tables eatery offers a full selection of Mexican dishes for three meals a day. A local gathering place popular with residents throughout Maui's Upcountry region, Polli's has become an institution over the years. It will inevitably be crowded with natives dining on tacos, burritos and tamales, as well as burgers, sandwiches and ribs. ~ 1202 Makawao Avenue, Makawao; 808-572-7808. BUDGET TO MODERATE.

On the lower slope of Haleakala, **Kula Lodge Restaurant** enjoys a panoramic view of the island. Through picture windows you can gaze out on a landscape that rolls for miles to the sea. The exposed-beam ceiling and stone fireplace lend a homey feel, as do the homemade pastries. Specialties include rack of lamb, pasta dishes and vegetarian entrées. ~ Haleakala Highway, Kula; 808-878-1535, 800-233-1535; e-mail info@kulalodge.com. MODERATE TO DELUXE.

GROCERIES   Along the Haleakala Highway there's a **Foodland**, open from 5 a.m. to midnight. ~ Pukalani Terrace Center; 808-572-0674.

AUTHOR FAVORITE

Upcountry's contribution to Hawaii Regional cuisine is **Haliimaile General Store**. A former plantation store that has been converted into a chic gathering place, it puts a creative spin on contemporary cuisine and serves roast duckling, fresh island fish and beef from the Big Island. No lunch on Saturday and Sunday. ~ 900 Haliimaile Road, Haliimaile; 808-572-2666. DELUXE.

You can also count on **Down to Earth Natural Foods** for health foods and New Age supplies. Open from 8 a.m. to 8 p.m. ~ 1169 Makawao Avenue, Makawao; 808-572-1488.

Baldwin Avenue in the western-style town of Makawao has developed over the years into a prime arts-and-crafts center. Housed in the falsefront stores that line the street you'll find galleries galore and a few boutiques besides. **SHOPPING**

The Courtyard, an attractive woodframe mall, contains **Hot Island Glass** (808-572-4527), with a museum-quality collection of handblown glass pieces made in the store. Also here is **Viewpoints Gallery** (808-572-5979), which puts many of the higher-priced Lahaina galleries to shame. ~ 3260 Baldwin Avenue, Makawao.

Gecko Trading Company is a small boutique that features contemporary fashions at reasonable prices, as well as other gift items. ~ 3621 Baldwin Avenue, Makawao; 808-572-0249.

The kids will love **Maui Child Toys & Books** for its puppets, art supplies, wooden toys and music tapes. ~ 3643 Baldwin Avenue, Makawao; 808-572-2765.

Check out **Goodie's** for gift items: crystal mobiles, locally made jewelry, picture frames. There are also women's fashions, men's shirts and handmade Hawaiian baskets. ~ 3633 Baldwin Avenue, Makawao; 808-572-0288.

Miracles Bookery specializes in self-discovery and New Age books and gifts for local Upcountry soul seekers and travelers searching for the meaning of life. ~ 3082 Baldwin Avenue, Makawao; 808-572-2317.

On the outskirts of Makawao, the 1917 Mediterranean-style Baldwin mansion is home to the **Hui Noeau Visual Arts Center**. Here you can view rotating educational exhibits, purchase works by Maui artists or take the plunge yourself at one of the regular workshops on painting, printmaking, pottery, sculpture and much, much more. Closed Monday. ~ 2841 Baldwin Avenue, Makawao; 808-572-6560; e-mail hui@maui.net.

In the Kula Lodge complex, the **Curtis Wilson Cost Gallery** sells prints, limited editions and originals by Curtis Wilson Cost. The emphasis is on local landscapes and ocean scenery. ~ Haleakala Highway, Kula; 808-878-6544.

Proteas of Hawaii specializes in gift boxes, Proteas and tropical floral arrangements. They also sell orchids. ~ 210 Mauna Place, Kula; 808-878-2533.

There are live bands on Friday and Saturday nights and deejay music Wednesday and Thursday at **Casanova Italian Restaurant.** One of Upcountry's only nightspots, it features a range of live acts—from local Mauian to internationally known. Cover. ~ 1188 Makawao Avenue, Makawao; 808-572-0220. **NIGHTLIFE**

BEACHES & PARKS

POLIPOLI SPRING STATE RECREATION AREA 🏃 Located at 6200-foot elevation on the slopes of Haleakala, this densely forested area is an ideal mountain retreat. Monterey and sugi pine, eucalyptus and Monterey cypress grow in stately profusion; not far from the campground there's a grove of redwoods. From Polipoli's ethereal heights you can look out over Central and West Maui, as well as the islands of Lanai, Molokai and Kahoolawe. Miles of trails, some leading up to the volcano summit, crisscross the park. Polipoli has a picnic area, restrooms and running water. ~ From Kahului, take Haleakala Highway (Route 37) through Pukalani and past Waiakoa to Route 377. Turn left on 377 and follow it a short distance to the road marked for Polipoli. About half of this ten-mile road to the park is paved. The second half of the track is extremely rough and often muddy. It is advisable to take a four-wheel-drive vehicle.

▲ There is meadow-style camping (a state permit is required) for up to 20 people; the cabin houses up to ten people and rents on a sliding scale from $10 single and $14 double up to $50 for ten people. The spacious cabin (three bedrooms) is sparsely furnished and lacks electricity. It does have a wood heating stove, gas cooking stove, gas lanterns, kitchen utensils and bedding. It can be rented from the Division of State Parks. It's recommended to bring in drinking water.

KEOKEA PARK This is a pleasant picnic spot on Route 37 in Keokea. There's a rolling lawn with picnic tables and restrooms.

▼▼▼▼▼▼▼▼▼▼▼▼▼▼▼▼

Haleakala National Park

It seems only fitting that the approach to the summit of Haleakala is along one of the world's fastest-climbing roads. From Kahului to the summit rim—a distance of 40 miles along Routes 37, 377 and 378—the macadam road rises from sea level to over 10,000 feet, and the silence is broken only by the sound of ears popping from the ascent.

At the volcano summit, 10,023-feet in elevation, you look out over an awesome expanse—seven miles long, over two miles wide, 21 miles around. This dormant volcano, which last erupted around 1790, is the central feature of a 28,808-665-acre national park that extends all the way through the Kipahulu Valley to the sea. The crater floor, 3000 feet below the rim, is a multihued wasteland filled with cinder cones, lava flows and mini-craters. It's a legendary place, with a mythic tradition that's as vital as its geologic history. It was from Haleakala ("House of the Sun") that the demigod Maui lassoed the sun and slowed its track across the sky to give his mother more daylight to dry her tapa cloth.

Technically, by the way, this area is an "erosional depression," not a crater. The converging headwaters of eroding valleys met at the top of the mountain and scooped out the seven-mile by two-mile bowl. Later eruptions studded the floor with cinder cones and lava flows. "Erosional depression" is cumbersome compared to "crater," so if you are like me and still say crater, you can at least claim to know the difference.

In the afternoon the volcano's colors are most vivid, but during the morning the crater is more likely to be free of clouds. Before going up Haleakala, call 808-871-5054 for a weather report. Then you can decide what time of day will be best for your explorations. Remember that it takes an hour and a half to two hours to reach the summit from Kahului, longer from the Kaanapali–Kapalua area. Be sure to bring warm clothes since the temperature drop from sea level to 10,000 feet can be 30° or more, which means the temperature may be below freezing. You might even encounter snow.

On the way up to the summit you'll pass **Hosmer's Grove** (6800-feet), a picnic area and campground surrounded by eucalyptus, spruce, juniper and cedar trees.

SIGHTS

National Park Headquarters, located at the 7030-foot elevation, contains an information desk and maps, and makes a good starting point. You may be lucky enough to see the Hawaiian state bird, the nene, which frequents the area around headquarters. Be sure to keep your distance during nesting season. ~ 808-572-4400.

The first crater view comes at **Leleiwi Overlook**, an 8800-foot perch from where you'll be able to see all the way from Hana across the island to Kihei. Here at sunrise and sunset, under correct meteorological conditions, you can see your shadow projected on the clouds and haloed by a rainbow. To experience this "Specter of the Brocken," stand atop the volcano rim looking toward the cloud-filled crater with the setting sun at your back.

◆◆

GIDDY UP

If you'd rather not do the walking, why not mount a steed and ride the trail into the depths of Haleakala? **Pony Express** offers rides down the trail into the crater. On the seven-and-a-half-mile roundtrip (which takes three and a half to four hours) you'll learn about the unique plant and animal life found in the crater, as well as Hawaiian myths and stories. Remember: the altitude is 10,000 feet so dress in layers (you need long pants and closed-toe shoes) because it gets hotter as you go down the trail. (No pregnant women allowed and you must be at least 13 to ride.) ~ Crater Road, Kula; 808-667-2200.

Up the hill, a side road leads to **Kalahaku Overlook**, a 9324-foot aerie that offers a unique view of several cinder cones within the volcano. Just below the parking lot are numerous **silverswords**. Related to sunflowers, these spike-leaved plants grow only on Maui and the Big Island. They remain low bristling plants for 20 years or more before blooming into a flowering stalk. Each plant blossoms once, sometime between May and November, and then dies.

The best view of the wilderness area is farther up the road at the **Haleakala Visitors Center**, 9745-feet elevation, where you'll find an information desk, as well as a series of exhibits about the volcano. From this vantage point you can gaze out toward Koolau Gap to the north and Kaupo Gap to the south. Several peaks located along the volcano loom out of the clouds; cinder cones, including 600-foot Puu o Maui, rise up from the crater floor.

From the visitors center a short trail heads up to **White Hill**. Composed of andesite lava and named for its characteristic light color, this mound is dotted with stone windbreaks once used as sleeping places by Hawaiians who periodically visited the summit of Haleakala.

It's a short drive to the summit at **Puu Ulaula Overlook**. From the plate-glass lookout you can view the Big Island, Molokai, Lanai, West Maui and wilderness area itself. On an extremely clear day this 360° panorama may even include a view of Oahu, 130 miles away.

Perched high above atmospheric haze and the lights of civilization, Haleakala is also an excellent spot for stargazing. If you can continue to the end of Skyline Drive, past the **Haleakala Observatory**, you'll see that it is also an important center for satellite tracking and television communications.

While the views along the volcano rim are awesome, the best way to see Haleakala is from the inside looking out. With 36 miles of hiking trails, two campsites and three cabins, the wilderness provides a tremendous opportunity for explorers. Within the belly of this monstrous volcano, you'll see such geologic fea-

LATE SLEEPERS, TAKE NOTE

One of Maui's favorite rituals is a predawn trip to the top of Haleakala to watch the sun rise. Unfortunately, the weather can be foggy and cold. Besides that, getting up early is probably the last thing you want to do on vacation. If so, consider the alternative: Sleep late, take your time getting to the top and arrive in time for sunset. But, then again, you'll miss a dazzling, almost religious experience. In any case, call **808-871-5054** to check on the weather before making the trip up!

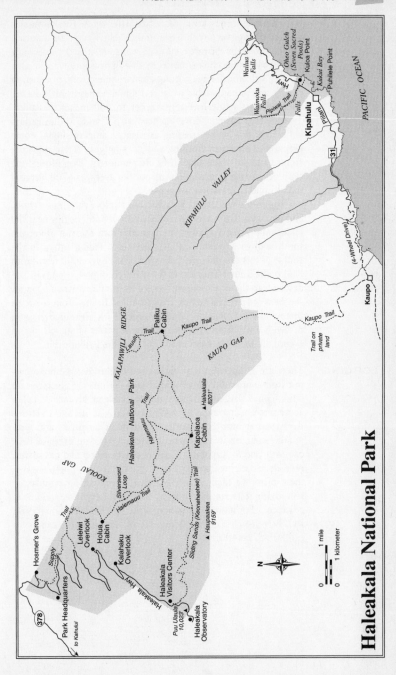

PACIFIC OCEAN

Wailua Falls

Oheo Gulch
(Seven Sacred Pools)
Kuloa Point
Kukui Bay
Puhilele Point

Waimoku Falls

AMH

Pipiwai Trail

Falls

Kipahulu

Piilani

31

(4-Wheel Drive)

KIPAHULU VALLEY

Kaupo

KALAPAWILI RIDGE

Lauulu Trail

Paliku Cabin

Kaupo Trail

Kaupo Trail

KAUPO GAP

Trail on
private
land

▲Haleakala
8201'

Halemauu Trail

Kapalaoa
Cabin

Haleakela National Park

Silversword
Loop

Halemauu Trail

Sliding Sands (Keoneheehee) Trail

▲ Haupaakea
9159'

KOOLAU GAP

Hosmer's Grove

Supply
Trail

Leleiwi
Overlook

Holua
Cabin

Kalahaku
Overlook

Haleakala
Visitors Center

Puu Ulaula
10,023'

Haleakala
Observatory

Haleakala Hwy

378

Park Headquarters

to Kahului

N

0   1 mile

0   1 kilometer

Haleakala National Park

tures as cinder cones, lava tubes and spatter vents. The Hawaiians marked their passing with stone altars, shelters and adze quarries. You may also spy the rare nene (a Hawaiian relative of the Canada goose), as well as chukar partridges and pheasants.

HIDDEN ►   The **volcano floor** is a unique environment, one of constant change and unpredictable weather. Rainfall varies from 12 inches annually in the southwestern corner to 200 inches at Paliku. Temperatures, usually hovering between 55° and 75° during daylight, may fall below freezing at night. Campers should come prepared with warm clothing and sleeping gear, a tent, poncho, lantern and stove (no open fires are permitted). Don't forget the sunblock, as the elevation on the bottom averages 6700 feet and the ultraviolet radiation is intense.

Within the wilderness area you can explore three main trails. **Sliding Sands Trail**, a steep cinder and ash path, begins near the Haleakala Visitors Center. It descends from the rim along the south wall to Kapalaoa cabin, then on to Paliku cabin. In the course of this ten-mile trek, the trail drops over 3000 feet. From Paliku, the **Kaupo Trail** leaves the crater through Kaupo Gap and descends to the tiny town of Kaupo, eight miles away on Maui's southeast coast. **Halemauu Trail** (8 miles) begins from the road three-and-a-half miles beyond National Park Headquarters and descends 1400 feet to the crater floor. It passes Holua cabin and eventually joins Sliding Sands Trail near the Paliku cabin.

LODGING   There are campgrounds at **Holua** and **Paliku** that require a permit from National Park Headquarters. Permits are given out on a first-come, first-served basis (not available in advance), so plan accordingly. Camping is limited to two days at one site and three days total at both. The campgrounds have pit toilets and non-potable running water. There is also a 12-person cabin at each campsite and at **Kapalaoa**. Equipped with wood and gas stoves, pit toilets, cooking utensils, bunks and limited nonpotable water, these primitive facilities are extremely popular. So popular, in fact, that guests are chosen by a monthly lottery three months in advance. ~ For more information, write Haleakala National Park, P.O. Box 369, Makawao, Maui, HI 96768, attention: cabins; or call 808-572-4400.

TEN

Lanai

Eight miles from Maui, across the historic whaling anchorage at Lahaina Roads, lies the pear-shaped island of Lanai. In profile the island, formed by an extinct volcano, resembles the humpback whales that frequent its waters. It rises in a curved ridge from the south, then gradually tapers to the north. The east side is cut by deep gulches, while the west is bounded by spectacular sea cliffs rising 1500 to 2000 feet. Lanaihale, the island's tallest peak, stands 3370 feet above sea level.

First discovered by Captain Cook's men in 1779, Lanai was long avoided by mariners, who feared its reef-shrouded shores and saw little future in the dry, barren landscape. You can still see testaments to their fear in the rotting hulks that lie off Shipwreck Beach.

Ancient Hawaiians believed Lanai was inhabited only by evil spirits until Kaululaau, son of the great Maui chief Kakaalaneo, killed the spirits. Kaululaau, a Hawaiian-style juvenile delinquent who chopped down fruit trees with the gay abandon of young George Washington, had been exiled to Lanai by his father for his destructive behavior. After the wild youth redeemed himself by making the island safe from malevolent spirits, Lanai was settled by Hawaiians and controlled by powerful Maui chiefs.

Most archaeologists doubt that the native population, which lived from taro cultivation and fishing along the eastern shore, ever exceeded 2500. Even periods of peak population were punctuated by long intervals when the island was all but deserted. Lying in Maui's wind shadow, Lanai's rainfall ranges from 40 inches along its northeast face to a meager 12 inches annually in the barren southwest corner.

Like Molokai, its neighbor to the north, Lanai for centuries was a satellite of Maui. (Even today it is part of Maui County.) Then in 1778 it was overwhelmed by the forces of Kalaniopuu, the king of the Big Island. Later in the century, an even more powerful monarch, Kamehameha the Great, set up a summer residence along the south coast in Kaunolu.

During the 19th century, Lanai was a ranchers' island with large sections of flat range land given over to grazing. Missionaries became active saving souls and securing property in 1835 and by the 1860s one of their number had gained control of Lanai's better acreage. This was Walter Murray Gibson, a Mormon maverick whose life story reads like a sleazy novel. Despite being excommunicated by the Mormon church, Gibson went on to become a formidable figure in Hawaiian politics.

Gibson was not the only man with a dream for Lanai. George Munro, a New Zealand naturalist, came to the island in 1911 as manager of a plantation complex that originally tried to grow sugar on the island and then turned to cattle raising. While his herds grazed the island's tablelands, Munro worked in the rugged highlands. He extended the native forest, planting countless trees to capture moisture and protect eroded hillsides. He restored areas ravaged by feral goats and imported the stately Norfolk pines that still lend a mountain ambience to Lanai City. And, most important, Munro introduced an ecological awareness that hopefully will continue to pervade this enchanting island.

The land that Gibson and Munro oversaw changed hands several times until James Dole in 1922. Dole, descended from missionaries, was possessed of a more earthly vision than his forebears. Pineapples. He converted the island to pineapple cultivation, built Lanai City, and changed the face of Lanai forever.

Filipinos, now about 50 percent of the island's population, were imported to work the fields. They bent to their labors all over Lanai, wearing goggles and gloves to protect against the sharp spines that bristled from the low-lying plants. Pineapples are cultivated through plastic sheets to conserve precious water and harvesting is done by hand. Up until the early 1990s, you could see hundreds of acres covered in plastic. Downtown Lanai would roll up the streets at 9 p.m., but the lights would burn bright in the pineapple fields as crews worked through the night loading the hefty fruits onto conveyor belts.

That was yesterday, back when Lanai retained something of an ambiguous reputation. Most tourists, hearing that Lanai was nothing but pineapples and possessed only 20 miles of paved roads and a single ten-room hotel, left the place to the antelopes and wild goats.

Now, however, the sleeping midget has awakened. You still rent your car in an old gas station with scuffed floors and deer trophies on the wall. And there are still only three paved roads on the island. But nothing else here is the same.

Stores have been renovated, old plantation homes have received fresh coats of paint, and two small clusters of homes have been constructed on the outskirts of town. Castle & Cooke, the conglomerate that now owns the island, has poured $350 million into the place, building two resorts and transforming little Lanai into luxurious Lanai. The Manele Bay Hotel, a 250-room oceanfront extravaganza, opened in 1991 just one year after the christening of The Lodge at Koele, a rustic but refined 102-room resort situated along Lanai's forested mountain slopes.

Meanwhile the days of pineapple cultivation are over. The output has dropped from a peak of about 16,000 acres to a mere 200 acres, sufficient to supply island needs and give visitors a glimpse at what life was like "back when." Fields are being converted to alfalfa and oats; cattle raising is being reintroduced; and the island's Filipino and Japanese population is quitting the plantation and going to work

serving the visitors who make their way to Lanai to enjoy the two posh resort hotels and a plethora of outdoor activities like golf, tennis, biking and horseback riding.

In the midst of all the change, this lovely little isle retains its charm. Even now
only a fraction of Lanai's 140 square miles is developed. The rest of the island is
covered with a network of jeep and hiking trails guaranteed to keep the heartiest
adventurer happy.

Here is an entire island that fits the description "hidden Hawaii." Almost all
of Lanai's 3200 citizens live in rustic Lanai City at the island's center and most
tourists are concentrated at the lodge at Koele one mile away or along Hulope Beach
at the Manele Bay Resort. Just beyond these clusters lie mountains, rainforests,
ranchlands and remote beaches—untouched realms ripe for exploration.

Situated at 1645 feet, **Lanai City** is a trim community of
corrugated-roof houses and small garden plots. Tourist
brochures present the place as a quaint New England village, but until the Lodge at Koele was built the town was rather
drab. Most of the houses were constructed around the 1920s in
traditional company-town fashion. They are square boxes topped

Lanai City

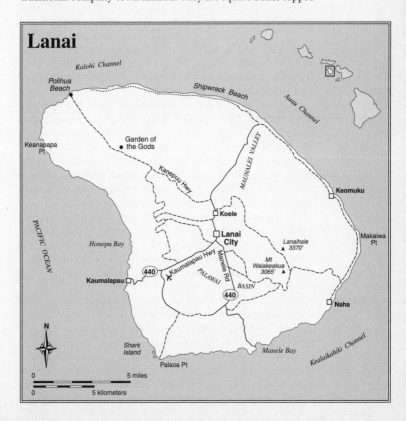

with tin roofs and tend to look alike. Norfolk pines break the monotony, and now that Lanai is much more self-conscious, many homes are freshly painted in a rainbow assortment of hues.

It is still a company town, but today the company is harvesting tourists instead of planting pineapples. Several housing developments and condominium complexes have been built on the outskirts to house hotel employees. With everything centered around the town square, Lanai City embraces almost the entire population of the island. Situated at the center of the island at an elevation midway between the beach and the mountain peaks, it is cool and breezy with a temperate climate.

Nevertheless, the really interesting places on Lanai lie outside town, and most require driving or hiking over jeep trails. It's advisable to get specific directions wherever you go, since the maze of pineapple roads can confuse even the most intrepid pathfinder. Where possible, I've included directions; otherwise, check with the jeep rental shop in Lanai City or at the hotels.

To be extra safe, ask about road conditions, too. The slightest rain can turn a dusty jeep road into a slick surface, and a downpour can transmogrify it into an impassable quagmire. I once dumped a jeep into a three-foot ditch when the trail to Polihua Beach collapsed. It had been raining steadily for three days and the soft shoulder couldn't support the weight of a vehicle. I was 11 miles from Lanai City with the wheels hopelessly embedded and an hour left until dark.

The way back led past pretty menacing country, heavily eroded and difficult to track through. Rain clouds brought the night on in a rush. I gathered up my poncho and canteen, convinced myself that the worst to come would be a cold and wet night outdoors, and began trekking back to civilization. Fortunately, after five miserable hours I made it. But the entire incident could have been avoided if I had first checked road conditions and had allowed at least several hours of daylight for my return.

This shouldn't discourage you, though. With the proper precautions, exploring Lanai can be a unique experience, challenging but safe. To make things easy, I'll start with a journey to the island's northeastern shore, part of which is over a paved road. Then I'll continue clockwise around the island.

LODGING

HIDDEN ►

Once the only inn on the entire island, the **Hotel Lanai** is a modest mountain retreat. Set 1600 feet above sea level and surrounded by Norfolk pines, it offers clean, medium-sized rooms equipped with private baths. The lodge was built in the '20s, as was most of Lanai City, but was refurbished several years ago. It features a restaurant and lounge, and is a local gathering place at dinnertime. A lot of folks hang out in the lobby here, making for a warm, friendly atmosphere, and the staff is congenial. Choose between small- and medium-sized standard accommodations and rooms with lanais. There's a cottage in the back and a U-shaped structure with only ten rooms, so reservations can be troublesome. It's advisable to arrange transportation with the hotel at the time of making reservations. ~ 828 Lanai Avenue; 808-565-7211, 800-795-7211, fax 808-565-6450; www.onlanai.com. MODERATE TO DELUXE.

The Lodge at Koele, a fashionable 102-room hideaway, is a study in style and decorum. The most noteworthy feature is the lobby, a vaulted-ceiling affair faced on either end with a stone fireplace that rises to the roofline. Etched-glass skylights extend the length of the room, illuminating the "great hall." The plantation-style guest rooms are done with four-poster beds, hand-stenciled

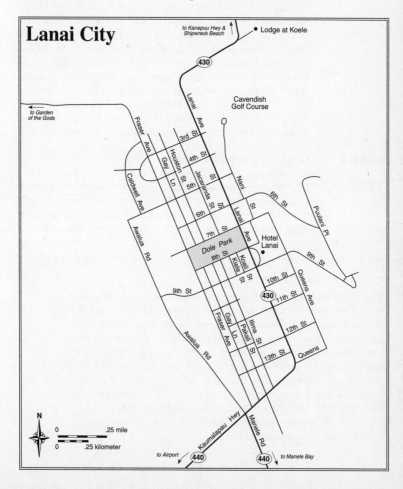

Lanai City

walls, statuettes and decorative plates. To make sure you remember that even here amid the Cook pines you are still in Hawaii, an overhead fan beats the air in languid motions.

Backdropped by mountains and surrounded by miles of grasslands, the emphasis at The Lodge is on staying put. There are porches lined with wicker chairs, a croquet court, a swimming pool and two jacuzzis that look out on field and forest, and a congenial staff to take care of every request. Five-night minimum at Christmastime. ~ P.O. Box 630310, Lanai City, HI 96763; 808-565-7300, 800-321-4666, fax 808-565-3868; www. lanairesorts.com. ULTRA-DELUXE.

You can discover for yourself whether **Dreams Come True on Lanai**. That's what Michael and Susan Hunter, two local jewelry makers, claim can happen when you stay in the six-bedroom house they transformed into one of the island's only bed and breakfasts. Set in Lanai City and surrounded by fruit trees and flowering gardens, the house is decorated with hand-carved screens and furniture that the owners transported from Sri Lanka and Bali. There's a large living room for guests as well as a selection of single and double rooms, some with canopied four-poster beds. Swedish and Shiatsu massage available. ~ 547 12th Street, Lanai City; 808-565-6961, 800-566-6961, fax 808-565-7056; www.circumvista.com/dreamscometrue.html, e-mail hunters@aloha.net. MODERATE.

DINING

HIDDEN ►

Henry Clay's Rotisserie at the Hotel Lanai offers wholesome dinners featuring an assortment of steak, seafood, pasta, ribs and other selections. Its knotty pine walls decorated with island photographs, this is a cozy place to share a meal. You can strike up a conversation with a local resident, sit back and enjoy the mountain air or bask in the glow of the restaurant's two fireplaces. Dinner

CULTURE RESORT-STYLE

The Lanai Visiting Artist Program has embarked upon an odyssey that brings celebrity authors, performers, musicians and chefs to the secluded isle for *complimentary* performances. It's a great way for guests and the Lanai community to interact with distinguished artists in an accessible, comfortable atmosphere. The program occurs monthly throughout the calendar year. Performances usually take place over the weekend, between 8:30 and 9:30 p.m., while chefs offer cooking classes on Sundays at 3:30 p.m. Featured artists in the past have included author Tom Robbins, soprano Marie Plette, film critic Roger Ebert, syndicated columnist Ellen Goodman, and chef Ron Siegel. For information, call Lanai Resorts at 800-321-4666; www.lanairesorts.com.

only. ~ 828 Lanai Avenue; 808-565-7211, fax 808-565-6450. MODERATE TO ULTRA-DELUXE.

If the hotel restaurant is closed, Lanai City has a few other alternatives. First there is **S. & T. Property Inc**, a luncheonette where locals drop in for breakfast and lunch. They swear S. & T. has the best hamburgers in town. ~ 419 7th Street; 808-565-6537. BUDGET.

A New York style–deli by day, an Italian restaurant at night, **Pele's Other Garden** is another establishment locals frequent. ◄ HIDDEN During the day you can get overstuffed, made-to-order sandwiches, pasta, salads, pizzas, soup and much more. Come nightfall, table-cloths transform the deli into an Italian bistro; you'll find a variety of appetizers, salads and pizzas as well as pasta dishes. The desserts and coffee are tempting. Pele's also offers "Off Road" picnic basket lunches for the adventurers in the crowd. ~ 8th and Houston streets; 808-565-9628; e-mail pogdeli@wave.hicv.net. BUDGET TO MODERATE.

The **Blue Ginger Café** rests in an old plantation house and ◄ HIDDEN serves three solid meals a day. Traditional paintings and simple drawings of tropical fish adorn the place and the red paint on the cement floor has worn away almost completely. But the white walls shine and the dinners are served piping hot. Breakfasts and plate lunches are pretty standard, but the evening meal is sophisticated enough to include New York steak, *kalbi* short ribs and mixed plates. ~ 409 7th Street; 808-565-6363, fax 808-565-6306; e-mail gabilay@aloha.com. BUDGET TO MODERATE.

On Lanai, isolation is the engine of ingenuity. Confronted with all that land and so few people, The Lodge at Koele transformed sections of the island into an organic garden, hog farm and cattle ranch. After adding a master chef, they had the ingredients for two gourmet restaurants that would be the pride not only of tiny Lanai but any island. Meals in The Terrace and The Formal Dining Room (jackets are required) are as enticing as the hotel's sumptuous surroundings.

The **Terrace** serves breakfast, lunch and dinner in a fairly casual atmosphere. Here the day begins with sweet rice waffles, breakfast bread pudding, or bacon and eggs fresh from the farm. By evening the chef progresses to oysters on the half shell and oven-braised lamb shank with herbed polenta, as well as vegetarian specialties. ~ The Lodge at Koele; 808-565-7300, fax 808-565-4561; www.lanairesorts.com. DELUXE TO ULTRA-DELUXE.

The **Formal Dining Room** serves dinner only; feast on roasted rack of lamb or Lanai venison loin with mashed sweet potatoes. Both restaurants overlook the back of the lodge grounds, with views of the fishpond, fountain and orchid house. ~ The Lodge at Koele; 808-565-7300, fax 808-565-4561; www.lanairesorts.com. ULTRA-DELUXE.

GROCERIES For standard food needs, try **Richard's Shopping Center**. This "shopping center" is really only a small grocery store with a dry goods department. Richard's is open Monday through Wednesday from 8:30 a.m. to noon and from 1:30 to 6:30 p.m., and Thursday through Saturday from 8:30 a.m. to 6:30 p.m. Closed Sunday. ~ 8th Street; 808-565-6047.

If, by some strange circumstance, you can't find what you're seeking here, head down the street to **Pine Isle Market**. Open Monday through Thursday from 8 a.m. to noon and 1:30 to 7 p.m., and Friday and Saturday from 8 a.m. to 7 p.m. Closed Sunday. ~ 356 8th Street; 808-565-6488.

Lanai City International Food & Clothing Center sells fresh meat, produce and canned goods as well as liquor, beer and wine. They are open 8 a.m. to 6 p.m. Monday through Friday, and Sunday 8 a.m. to 1:30 p.m. Closed Saturday. ~ 833 Ilima Avenue; 808-565-6433.

You can also pick up deli meat, cheese and other delectables at **Pele's Other Garden**. ~ Corner of 8th and Houston streets; 808-565-9628.

There's also a "Saturday Market" in Dole Park each week.

SHOPPING Granted, it doesn't have much competition, but **Heart of Lanai Art Gallery** would be remarkable regardless of where it was located. Many of the paintings and sculptures were done by local artists and depict the plantation culture that was once Lanai's lifeblood but is now fast becoming its legacy. Call ahead. Closed Sunday. ~ 758 Queens Street (behind Hotel Lanai); 808-565-6678.

Don't miss **Gifts with Aloha** on the corner of 8th and Houston streets. This boutique, run by the genial Duprees, features Lanai and Hawaiian artists. Watercolor originals, pottery and wood pieces along with tempting jams, jellies and sauces, hats and casual resort wear round out the offerings at this Lanai-style (i.e., laidback) store. ~ 811B Houston Street; 808-565-6589.

Art and nature are celebrated in the paintings by local artist **Michael Carroll**. Stop by and see his work at Gifts from Aloha or at his studio (by appointment only). ~ 808-565-8126; e-mail mike@studiomike.com.

In the heart of Dole Park is **The Local Gentry**, a small clothing boutique. If you forgot your swimsuit or sandals, or if you're short on shorts, they have them. They feature clothing from San Francisco City Lights, Putumayo, Tiki, Big Blue, Picante and others. ~ 363 7th Street; 808-565-9130; e-mail thelocalgentry@aloha.net.

Coffee Works Lanai offers gourmet coffee beans and teas to take home. If you're tired of all of this shopping, stop in for an espresso or ice cream. ~ Corner of Ilima and 6th streets; 808-565-6962.

Otherwise, you will have to seek out the gift shop at **The Lodge at Koele** (808-565-7300) or the **Hotel Lanai** (808-565-7211).

Munro Trail

Named for New Zealand naturalist George Munro, this seven-mile jeep trail climbs through rainforest and stands of conifers en route to **Lanaihale**, the highest point on Lanai. From this 3370-foot perch you can see every major Hawaiian island except Kauai.

On the way to Lanaihale, about two miles up the trail, you'll pass **Hookio Gulch**. The ridge beyond is carved with a defense work of protective notches made by warriors who tried futilely to defend Lanai against invaders from Hawaii in 1778.

A footpath leads to an overlook above 2000-foot deep **Hauola Gulch**, Lanai's deepest canyon. Here you may see axis deer clinging to the sharp rockfaces, seeming to defy gravity as they pick their way along the heights.

This knife-edge ridge, little more than 100 feet wide in places, is studded with ironwood and eucalyptus trees, as well as the stately Norfolk pines that New Zealand naturalist George Munro personally planted along the heights. From this aerie the slopes fall away to reveal the twin humps of Maui. The Big Island rests far below you, anchored in open ocean. The sea itself is a flat, shimmering expanse.

From Lanaihale you can either turn around or continue and descend through open fields to Hoike Road, which connects with Route 440. The Munro Trail begins in Koele off Route 430 (Keomuku Road) about a mile north of Lanai City. Be sure to check road conditions and try to go early in the morning before clouds gather along the ridgetop. While it's rough going at times, the trail affords such magnificent views from its windswept heights that it simply must not be ignored by the adventurous sightseer.

NIGHTLIFE Visitors find this a great spot to get the sleep they missed in Lahaina or Honolulu. If rest isn't a problem, Lanai may be a good
place to catch up on your reading or letter writing. One thing is
certain—once the sun goes down, there'll be little to distract you.
You can have a drink while listening to local gossip at the **Hotel
Lanai** (808-565-7211) or while mixing with the gentry at **The
Lodge at Koele** (808-565-7300), where the lounge possesses a
kind of gentlemen's library atmosphere with an etched-glass-and-
hardwood interior. But on an average evening, even these night
owl's nests will be closed by midnight (*pupus* are served until 11
p.m.). In addition to its plush lounge, The Lodge at Koele features hula dancers on weekends at lunchtime or other live entertainment in the lobby (the "great hall") at night.

▼▼▼▼▼▼▼▼▼▼▼▼▼▼▼

Northeast—Shipwreck Beach and Naha

From Lanai City, Route 430 (Keomuku
Road) winds north through hot, arid country. The scrub growth and red soil in this
barren area resemble a bleak southwestern
landscape, but the sweeping views of Maui and Molokai could
be found only in Hawaii.

By the way, those stones piled atop one another along the road
are neither an expression of ancient Hawaiian culture nor proof of
the latest UFO landing. They were placed there by imaginative hikers. Each one is an *ahu*, representative of a local tradition in which
columns of three or so stones are built to help ensure good luck.

SIGHTS Near the end of the macadam road you can turn left onto a dirt
road. This track leads past colonies of intermittently inhabited
squatters' shacks, many built from the hulks of vessels grounded on nearby **Shipwreck Beach**. The
coral reef paralleling the beach has been a nemesis
to sailors since whaling days. The rusting remains of
a barge and a 1950s-era oil tanker still bear witness to
the navigational hazards along this coast. Needless to say,
this is one of the best areas in Hawaii for beachcombing.
Look in particular for the Japanese glass fishing floats that
are carried here on currents all the way from Asia.

When James Dole bought
Lanai in 1922, he paid
$1.1 million for the
entire island.

At the end of the dirt road, a path marked with white paint
HIDDEN ▶ leads to clusters of ancient **petroglyphs** depicting simple island
scenes. Those interested in extensively exploring the coast can
hike all the way from Shipwreck eight miles west to Polihua Beach
along jeep trails and shoreline.

Back on the main road (continuing straight ahead as if you had
never made that left turn that led to Shipwreck Beach) you will
discover that the macadam gives way to a dirt road that leads
along the northeast shore for 12 teeth-clicking miles. It was along
this now-deserted coast that the ancient Hawaiian population

lived. Numbering perhaps 2000 in pre-Western times, they fished the coast and cultivated taro.

The ghost town of **Keomuku**, marked by a ramshackle church that's been partly refurbished, lies six miles down the road. It's another mile and a half to **Kahea Heiau**, a holy place that many claim is the reason Keomuku was deserted. It seems that stones from this temple were used to build the nearby Maunalei Sugar Company plantation despite warnings against disturbing the sacred rocks. So when the plantation failed in 1901 after its sweet water mysteriously turned brackish, the Hawaiians had a heavenly explanation. It was shortly after this incident that most of the rest of Lanai's populace moved up to Lanai City, leaving only spirits along the coast.

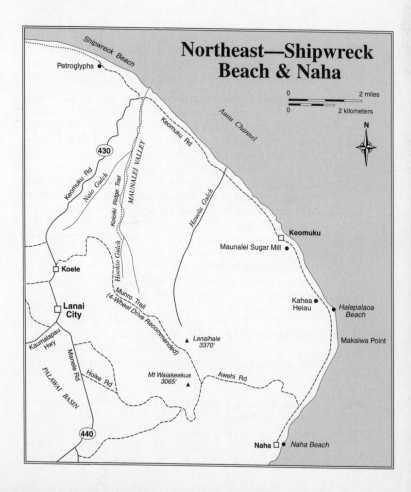

Northeast—Shipwreck Beach & Naha

Several miles farther, past numerous salt-and-pepper-colored beaches, the road ends at the old Hawaiian village of **Naha**. Today nothing remains of this once prosperous colony.

BEACHES & PARKS

SHIPWRECK BEACH This strand is actually a string of small sandy patches that stretches for eight miles along the north coast, all the way to Polihua Beach. The glass fishing balls, driftwood and occasional nautilus shells on the beach make this a beachcomber's paradise. The remains of misguided ships that gave the beach its name also add to the allure. It's often windy. You can swim here but the water is shallow and you must beware of sharp coral—a protecting reef is 200 yards offshore. Snorkeling is not advised because of sharks. There's good diving for lobsters, but again, be cautious! You'll find good fishing for *ulua*, *papio* and octopus in the area between the squatters' houses and the petroglyphs. There are no established facilities at the beach. ~ Ten miles north of Lanai City. Head north on Route 430 (Keomuku Road) and turn left at the end of the paved road. (See the "Northeast—Shipwreck Beach and Naha" section above for more details.)

HALEPALAOA BEACH AND NAHA BEACH A string of salt-and-pepper-colored sand beaches lies along the 12-mile dirt road to Naha. While most are unattractive and crowded with shoals, they do offer great views of Molokai, Maui and Kahoolawe. The Naha road winds in and out along the seafront, with numerous access roads leading to the shore. The prettiest strand is Halepalaoa Beach, a mile-long white-sand corridor partially bordered by sand dunes. These are swimming beaches; most are well-protected by shoals, but the waters are shallow. Snorkeling is a possibility here but beware of currents. You can also fish here. Several beaches, including Naha, have small picnic areas. ~ Take Route 430 north from Lanai City and continue on after it turns southward and becomes a dirt road. The dirt road extends for about 12 miles, ending at Naha; Halepalaoa Beach is about seven miles out along the dirt road.

Southeast—Manele Bay

Heading south from Lanai City on Route 440 (Manele Road), you'll be traveling through the Palawai Basin, the caldera of the extinct volcano that formed the island. This was also the heart of Lanai's once extensive pineapple plantation.

SIGHTS

HIDDEN ►

The explorer can detour off the main highway to the **Luahiwa petroglyphs**. Finding them requires obtaining explicit directions, then driving through a field, and finally climbing a short distance up a steep bluff. But the Luahiwa petroglyphs—portraying human figures, deer, paddles and turtles—are among the finest rock carvings in Hawaii and are definitely worth the search. As you approach each cluster of boulders, you'll see pictographic stories begin to unfold. One in particular depicts a large outrigger canoe, sails unfurled, being loaded Noah-style with livestock. Preparing, perhaps, for the ancient migration north to the Hawaiian Islands? To locate the petroglyphs, head south from Lanai City on Route 440. Turn left at the first dirt road. Follow the lower road as it curves along the bottom of the hillside. After passing below a watertank and pipeline, the road forks and you follow the left fork. The road goes into a horseshoe curve; when you come out of the curve there will be black boulders on the hillside above you to the left. Spread across a few acres, they contain the petroglyphs.

The main road leads through agricultural fields and winds down to the twin bays at **Manele Small Boat Harbor** and **Hulo-**

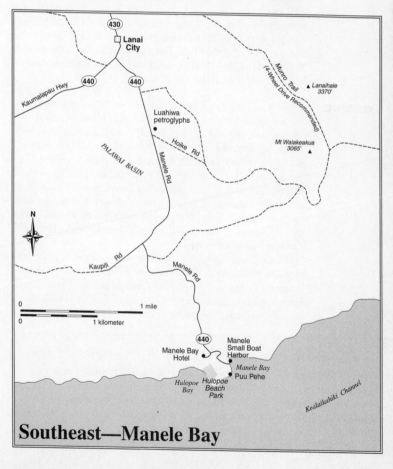

Southeast—Manele Bay

poe Bay, which together comprise a marine life conservation area. Just offshore from the cinder cone that separates these two harbors is a sea stack, **Puu Pehe**, known not only for its beauty but its legends as well. Puu Pehe was a lovely Maui girl kidnapped by a Lanai warrior who kept her hidden in a sea cave. One day when he went off in search of water, a huge sea wave swept the girl to her death. Stricken with grief and remorse, the young warrior buried her on top of the rock island and then jumped to his death from its heights.

The small-boat harbor at Manele, rimmed by lava cliffs along the far shore, contains ruins of ancient Hawaiian houses. You'll also see an old wooden chute protruding from the rocks, a loading platform used years ago to lead cattle onto ships. Today this rock-rimmed anchorage is a mooring place for fishing boats and yachts. Hulopoe offers the island's finest beach, a crescent of white sand with gentle waves, crystalline waters and a fine park facility. You'll find the stone ruins of an ancient Hawaiian home and canoe house at the north end of the beach. Just above the beach, on the grounds in front of the plush Manele Bay Hotel, stands the remains of an *ahu* or traditional Hawaiian shrine.

LODGING While The Lodge at Koele is situated at 1600-feet elevation in Lanai City, eight miles from the ocean, Lanai's other fashionable resting spot, the **Manele Bay Hotel**, is a traditional beachfront resort. Set on a bluff overlooking the best beach on the island, it is a 250-room extravaganza designed along both Asian and Mediterranean lines and surrounded by artistically planted gardens. Elegance here is in no way subdued: It speaks from the stone floors and white columns, the dark-paneled library and the recessed ceilings. The two-tiered lobby combines art deco windows with stylized Asian murals; the lower level is a terrace with glass doors that open onto ocean views.

Guest accommodations look out either on the beach or the grounds, which are sculpted into five different theme gardens— Japanese, Bromeliad, Hawaiian, Chinese and Kamaaina. Each room is spacious, done in pastel hues and decorated with Asian armoires and color sketches of Hawaiian flora. The four-poster

HOME, HOME ON THE RANGE

While touring Lanai you're bound to meet more of the island's wildlife than its human citizenry. Asian Axis deer roam everywhere while the mouflon, which look like big horn sheep, tend to be found in the lower elevations of the island. Also keep an eye out for wild turkeys and ring-neck pheasants.

beds are accented with quilts and upholstered throw pillows. Add a four-leaf-clover-shaped pool, six tennis courts, spa and workout room and you will realize that once-sleepy little Lanai has joined the 21st century. ~ 1 Manele Bay Drive; 808-565-7700, 800-321-4666, fax 808-565-3868; www.lanairesorts.com. ULTRA-DELUXE.

DINING

Outside Lanai City the dining choices—a grand total of three—are concentrated at the Manele Bay Hotel. Here, ladies and gentlemen, lunch is served at the **Pool Grille** on a bougainvillea-covered terrace. Set poolside just above the beach, this patio dining facility features island salads, including a seasonal fruit offering. There is also a standard assortment of sandwiches, as well as grilled mahimahi on *nori* bread and other specialties. Lunch only. ~ 808-565-7700, fax 808-565-2483. MODERATE.

This spacious resort offers more formal dining in the **Hulopoe Court Restaurant,** a high-ceiling dining room equipped with glass doors that open onto a veranda overlooking the ocean. Island murals adorn the walls and pineapple-motif chandeliers dominate the room. The decor blends Asian and Polynesian styles while the menu features Hawaiian regional cuisine. Breakfast and dinner only. ~ 808-565-7700, fax 808-565-2483. ULTRA-DELUXE.

Sweeping views of Hulopoe Bay star at the **Ihilani Dining Room**. The menu features Mediterranean cuisine and specializes in lamb, bouillabaisse, and fresh fish dishes. The service is formal, and the wine list and cheese cart extensive. Jacket required. Dinner only. Closed Sunday and Monday. ~ 808-565-7700, 808-565-2996, fax 808-565-2483. ULTRA-DELUXE.

NIGHTLIFE

Down along Hulopoe Beach at the Manele Bay Hotel, the **Hale Ahe Ahe Lounge** combines several different settings, each equally inviting. The lounge itself has dark textured walls, a hardwood bar and a clubby ambience. It features piano or contemporary Hawaiian music Tuesday through Saturday. Out on the terrace you can settle into a comfortable armchair or lean against the rail and enjoy the ocean view. The adjacent **Holokai Room** is a game room complete with backgammon board and an air of relaxed elegance. ~ 808-565-2000, fax 808-565-2483.

BEACHES & PARKS

HULOPOE BEACH PARK 🐾 🛶 🛁 💧 Lanai's finest beach also possesses the island's only fully developed park. Set in a half-moon inlet and fringed with *kiawe* trees, this white-sand beach is an excellent spot for all sorts of recreation. It is also the site of the 250-room Manele Bay Hotel, which rests on a bluff about 50 yards above the waterfront. Part of a marine life conservation area, Hulopoe has a lava terrace with outstanding tidepools along its eastern point. There is also a wading area for children at this end of the park. If you continue a short distance along this eastern shoreline you'll encounter **Puu Pehe Cove**, a small beach with abundant marine life that is excellent for swimming and snorkeling. Little wonder that Hulopoe is the island's favorite picnic spot. It's also recommended for surfing and fishing. Prime catches are threadfin, *ulua* and bonefish. This is the most accessible surf-casting beach on the island. There are restrooms and showers. ~ Take Route 440 (Manele Road) south from Lanai City for seven miles.

▲ This is it—the only campground on the island! There are campsites at the far end of the beach. Expect to pay a $5 registration fee plus a charge of $5 per camper per day. Permits are issued by the Lanai Company. ~ P.O. Box 310, Lanai City, Lanai, HI 96763; 808-565-3978, fax 808-565-3984.

MANELE BAY 🏊 🦅 🛶 Primarily a small-boat harbor, this cliff-fringed inlet is populated by sailboats from across the Pacific. Carouse with the crews, walk along the jetty or scramble up the rocks for a knockout view of Haleakala on Maui. It's a very good place for swimming since the harbor is well protected, but you need to be wary of boat traffic. Because Manele Bay is part of a marine preserve the snorkeling is notable and the fishing is limited. Only pole fishing is allowed—no nets. There's a park for picnicking, and just around the corner at Hulopoe Beach are facilities for camping, swimming and other sports. ~ Located Route 440 south of Lanai City.

▼▼▼▼▼▼▼▼▼▼▼▼▼▼▼▼
Southwest—Kaumalapau Harbor & Kaunolu

A southwesterly course along Route 440 (Kaumalapau Highway) will carry you steadily downhill for about six miles to **Kaumalapau Harbor**. This busy little harbor was built by pineapple interests and used primarily to ship the fruit on barges to Honolulu. During the heyday of Lanai's pineapple industry, more than a million pineapples a day were loaded onto waiting ships. On either side of Kaumalapau, you can see the *pali*, which rises straight up as high as 1000 feet, protecting Lanai's southwestern flank. These lofty sea cliffs are an ideal vantage point for watching the sunset.

The most interesting point along this route involves a detour near the airport and a journey down a *very* rugged jeep trail to

HIDDEN ▶ **Kaunolu Village**. A summer retreat of Kamehameha the Great and now a national historic landmark, this ancient fishing community still contains the ruins of more than 80 houses as well as stone shelters, petroglyphs and graves. Pick your way through it carefully, lest you step on a ghost. Kamehameha's house, once perched on the eastern ridge, looked across to **Halulu Heiau** on the west side of Kaunolu Bay. Commanding a dominant view of the entire region, these rocky remains are bounded on three sides by cliffs that vault 1000 feet from the ocean.

From nearby **Kahekili's Leap,** warriors proved their courage by plunging more than 60 feet into the water below. If they cleared a 15-foot outcropping and survived the free fall into 12 feet of water, they were deemed noble soldiers worthy of their great king.

Just offshore from this daredevil launching pad lies **Shark Island,** a rock formation that bears an uncanny resemblance to a shark fin. Could it be that warriors skilled enough to survive Kahekili's Leap had then to confront the malevolent spirit of a shark?

From Lanai City, a graded pineapple road passes through an eerie stand of iron-wood trees, then disintegrates into an ungraded dirt track that leads about seven miles to the **Garden of the Gods.** This heavily eroded area resembles the Dakota Badlands and features multihued boulders that change color dramatically during sunrise and sunset. A fantasy land

▼▼▼▼▼▼▼▼▼▼▼

Northwest— Polihua Beach

◄ HIDDEN

Southwest— Kaumalapau Harbor & Kaunolu

of stone, the Garden of the Gods is planted with ancient lava flows tortured by the elements into as many suggestive shapes as the imagination can conjure. The colors here vibrate with psychedelic intensity and the rocks loom up around you as though they were the gods themselves—hard, cold, dark beings possessed of untold power and otherworldly beauty. This is a spot not to be missed.

Past this surreal and sacred spot, Polihua Trail, a rugged jeep road, descends several miles to the ocean. **Polihua Beach,** stretching more than a mile and a half, is the longest and widest white-sand beach on the island. Once a prime nesting beach for green sea turtles, it is an excellent spot to watch whales as they pass close by the shoreline

BEACHES & PARKS

HIDDEN ►

POLIHUA BEACH A wide white-sand beach situated along Lanai's northwest shore, this isolated strand, with a stunning view of Molokai, rivals Kauai's trackless beaches. Swimming is allowed here but exercise caution—strong winds and currents prevail throughout this region. The water here is sometimes muddy but when it's clear, and when the Fish and Game Division declares it "in season," you can dive for lobsters. According to local anglers, this is the best spot on the island for fishing. Common catches include *papio*, *ulua*, bonefish, threadfin and red snapper. There are no facilities here. ~ It's about 11 miles from Lanai City through pineapple fields and the Garden of the Gods. The last half of the drive is over a rugged jeep trail. For specific directions and road conditions, check with the jeep rental garages.

▼▼▼▼▼▼▼▼▼▼▼▼▼▼
Outdoor Adventures

CAMPING

With so much virgin territory, Lanai should be ideal for camping. But here, as on the other islands, landowners restrict outdoors lovers. The villain is the outfit that manages the island. It permits island residents to camp where they like, but herds visitors into one area on the south coast. This campsite is located at Hulopoe Beach; reservations are recommended; $5 for camping permit plus $5 per person per day. ~ Lanai Company, P.O. Box 310, Lanai City, HI 96763; 808-565-3978, fax 808-565-3984.

If you have a hankering to catch marlin, mahi or ono, contact **Spinning Dolphin Charters of Lanai,** a private sportfishing charter out of Lanai. Ahi and aku (tuna) are found year-round in the waters around Lanai. You can go out for half-day, three-quarter-day or full-day runs. They also offer whale-watching and snorkel tours. ~ 808-565-6613.

FISHING

If you have a hankering to catch marlin, mahi or ono contact **Spinning Dolphin Charters of Lanai,** a private sportfishing charter out of Lanai. Ahi and aku (tuna) are found year-round in the waters around Lanai. You can go out for half-day, three-quarter-day or full-day runs. They also offer whale-watching and snorkel tours. ~ 808-565-6613.

Lanai EcoAdventure Centre features sea kayaking/snorkel combo trips. Explore the reef and the shipwreck on the island's east side or the volcanic history to the west. ~ 328 8th Street, Lanai City; 808-565-7737; www.adventurelanai.com.

KAYAKING

Lanai EcoAdventure Centre offers scuba tours. ~ 328 8th Street, Lanai City; 808-565-7737; www.adventurelanai.com. Also, a number of outfitters that operate out of Maui provide everything you'll need (including refreshments) to test the waters off Lanai. One area—Cathedrals—is considered the best dive site in Hawaii. Expect to float among Hawaiian green turtles, butterfly fish, black sturgeons and eels. Trip departure times can vary by season.

DIVING

    Trilogy Excursions conducts a snorkel/sail trip from Lahaina Harbor to Hulopoe Beach Park on Lanai. Guests enjoy a barbecue chicken lunch and an hour-long guided van tour around the island. When conditions are good, introductory scuba dives are an option for non-certified divers. Diving equipment is available but costs extra. ~ Lahaina Harbor, Maui; 808-661-4743, fax 808-667-7766.

    Scotch Mist Sailing Charters offers half-day snorkeling trips from Maui to various locations, at the captain's discretion. ~ Lahaina Harbor, slip 2, Maui; 808-661-0386; www.scotchmist2.com.

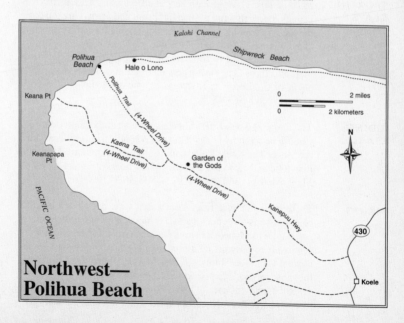

Northwest—Polihua Beach

Catering to all levels of experience, **Dive Maui** explores over 30 locations, including the Cathedrals. ~ 900 Front Street, Lahaina, Maui; 808-667-2080; www.divemauiscuba.com.

GOLF

Golfers won't be disappointed when they tee off in Lanai. The premier course on the island is one designed by Greg Norman and Ted Robinson, **The Experience at Koele.** Set against the backdrop of forested hills and steep gorges, it lies in the verdant central highlands. Green 17 is completely surrounded by a lake. Reserve tee times up to 30 days in advance. ~ Lanai City; 808-565-7300.

The nine-hole **Cavendish Golf Course**—where the locals play— is open to the public as well. ~ Lanai City.

Or try **Challenge at Manele,** an 18-hole golf course at the Manele Bay Hotel. Designed by Jack Nichlaus, it lies on natural lava outcroppings and follows towering cliffs. The signature hole, number 12, demands a 200-yard tee shot across the ocean. Reserve tee times up to 30 days in advance. ~ 808-565-7700.

TENNIS

Call the County Department of Parks and Recreation for information on the public courts in Lanai City. ~ 808-565-6979.

Courts are available to guests at **The Lodge at Koele** ~ Lanai City, 808-565-7300; and the **Manele Bay Hotel** ~ near Hulopoe Beach, 808-565-7700.

ARCHERY & SPORTING CLAYS

Ready to test your skills at a medieval sport? **Lanai Pine Archery** has a 12-target range for archers of all skills and ages. Instructors provide safety tips and pointers. If bows and arrows are too tame for you, try your luck at shooting clay targets **Lanai Pine Sporting Clays.** Games include skeet, wobble traps and compact sporting. Clays are launched to simulate running patterns of various animals and birds. The staff offers instruction. ~ Located one mile north of the Lodge at Koele on Keamoku Highway; 808-559-4600, fax 808-565-4808.

RIDING STABLES

The Lodge at Koele offers horseback riding and equestrian tours. Choose between five rides that take you on various trails around the lodge. The Koele Ride is an hour-long leisurely walking ride that follows a wooded trail and gives riders stunning views of Maui, Molokai and Lanai City. ~ 808-565-7300.

BIKING

There are a few nice rides from Lanai City, but all are steep in places and pass over pockmarked sections of road. One goes south eight miles to Manele Bay and the beach at Hulopoe, another diverts west to busy little Kaumalapau Harbor, and the last heads north 14 miles to Shipwreck Beach. The **Munro Trail** is perfect for those in good shape and into mountain biking.

Road and mountain bike tours and rentals are available through **Lanai EcoAdventure Centre.** ~ 328 8th Street, Lanai City;

808-565-7737; www.adventurelanai.com. You can also rent them from **The Lodge at Koele.** ~ Lanai City; 808-565-7300.

Lanai City Service Inc. is a good place to obtain information concerning Lanai roads. ~ 808-565-7227.

HIKING

Hikers on Lanai are granted much greater freedom than campers. Jeep trails and access roads are open to the public; the only restriction is that hikers cannot camp along trails. Since most of the trails lead either to beaches or points of interest, you'll find them described in the regional sightseeing and "Beaches & Parks" sections above. All distances for hiking trails are one way unless otherwise noted.

Covered in scrub vegetation along much of its surface, Lanai still supports several rare endemic bird species.

In addition to these listings, there are two other trails to consider. The **Ancient Graveyard Trail** (.5 mile) winds to a picturesque graveyard that has been used since ancient times.

The **Koloiki Ridge Trail** (5 miles) leads through forest lands and the Cathedral of Pines (a group of pines resembling a gothic church) to a ridge that runs between Naio Gulch and Maunalei Valley. This moderately difficult hike provides views of Molokai and Maui.

Guided hikes, including overnight camping trips, are offered by **Lanai EcoAdventure Centre.** ~ 328 8th Street, Lanai City; 808-565-7737; www.adventurelanai.com.

Transportation

AIR

Planes to Lanai land at **Lanai Airport** amid an endless maze of grassland and tilled fields four miles from downtown Lanai City. This tiny landing strip has a small gift shop and a courtesy telephone for car rentals (you'll be picked up in a shuttle). There are no lockers or public transportation. A few rooms house airline offices. Hawaiian Airlines, Aloha Airlines and Pacific Wings offer service to the islands; IslandAir flies propeller-driven planes and features competitive rates. ~ 808-565-6757.

If you're staying at any of the island hotels, they will provide transportation into town, as will any of the island's car rental agencies if you're renting a vehicle from them.

BOAT

A ferry service called **Expeditions** operates out of Maui and links Lahaina with Manele Bay on Lanai. There are five boats per day in each direction. The 45-minute crossing provides a unique way to arrive on the island and if you're lucky, a chance to spy spinner dolphins and flying fish. ~ P.O. Box 10, Lahaina, HI 96767; 808-661-3756.

CAR & JEEP RENTALS

Lanai City Service Inc., which is affiliated with Dollar Rent A Car, rents automatic compact cars with free mileage. But renting a car on Lanai is like carrying water wings to the desert: there's simply nowhere to go. Rental cars are restricted to pavement, while most of Lanai's roads are jeep trails: four-wheel drive is the only way to fly. ~ 1036 Lanai Avenue; 808-565-7227.

Once known as the "Pineapple Isle," Lanai is now dubbed "The Secluded Island" since the pineapple fields have all but disappeared.

The first time I visited the island of Lanai, I rented a vintage 1942 jeep. The vehicle had bad brakes, no emergency brake, malfunctioning windshield wipers and no seat belts. It was, however, equipped with an efficient shock absorber—me. Today, **Lanai City Service Inc.**, described above, rents new and reliable jeeps. You can also try **Lanai EcoAdventure Centre** for jeep rentals. ~ 328 8th Street, Lanai City; 808-565-7737. (Be aware that the rental car collision insurance provided by most credit cards does not cover jeeps.)

BOAT TOURS

There are boat tours of Lanai offered by the Maui-based outfit **Trilogy Excursions**. They'll take you on a full-day excursion, leaving from Lahaina Harbor. Breakfast and lunch is provided, as well as snorkeling equipment and instruction. You'll also go on a one-hour van tour of the island. ~ 808-661-4743.

HITCHING

Officially, it's illegal, but actually it's common. The folks in these parts are pretty friendly, so rides are easy to get. The trick lies in finding someone who's going as far as you are—like all the way to Shipwreck Beach or out to the Garden of the Gods.

GUIDED TOURS

If you'd rather not do the driving, **Rabaca's Limousine Service** offers tours around the island in limousines ($73.50 an hour) or, if you prefer, 4 x 4s ($50 an hour). There's a two-hour minimum. They also offer 24-hour service. ~ 808-565-6670.

Hawaiian Hummer Xcursions, based out of the Hotel Lanai, has tours ranging from a two-hour visit to the Garden of the Gods, Shipwreck Beach and Lanai City to a more extensive six-hour excursion that goes to the Garden of the Gods, Shipwreck Beach, Keomuku Village, Awehi Trail and the Munro Trail. The rates are $150 an hour, with a two-hour minimum. ~ Hotel Lanai; 808-565-7211.

ELEVEN

Molokai

Between the bustling islands of Oahu and Maui lies an isle which in shape resembles Manhattan, but which in spirit and rhythm is far more than an ocean away from the smog-shrouded shores of the Big Apple. Molokai, Hawaii's fifth-largest island, is 38 miles long and 10 miles wide. The slender isle was created by three volcanoes that mark its present geographic regions: one at West End where the arid Mauna Loa tableland rises to 1381 feet, another at East End where a rugged mountain range along the north coast is topped by 4970-foot Mount Kamakou, and the third, a geologic afterthought, which created the low, flat Kalaupapa Peninsula.

Considering that the island measures a modest 260 square miles, its geographic diversity is amazing. Arriving at Hoolehua Airport near the island's center, travelers feel as though they have touched down somewhere in the American Midwest. Red dust, dry heat and curving prairie surround the small landing strip and extend to the west end of Molokai. This natural pastureland gives way in the south-central region to low-lying, relatively swampy ground and brown-sand beaches with murky water.

The prettiest strands lie along the western shore, where Papohaku Beach forms one of the largest white-sand beaches in the state, and at the east end around Halawa Valley, a region of heavy rainfall and lush tropic vegetation. To the north is the vaunted pali, which rises in a vertical wall 3000 feet from the surf, creating the tallest sea cliffs in the world. Here, too, is an awesome succession of sharp, narrow valleys cloaked in velvet green.

Kaunakakai, a sleepy port town on the south shore, is the island's hub. From here a road runs to the eastern and western coasts. Kalaupapa and the northern *pali* are accessible overland only by mule and hiking trails.

Even in a region of islands, Molokai has always been something of a backwater. To the early Hawaiians it appeared desiccated and inhospitable. The rich Halawa Valley was settled in the 7th century and the island developed a haunting reputation for sorcery and mystical occurrences. In ancient times it was also called *pule-oo*, or "powerful prayer," and was revered for the potency of its priests.

When Captain James Cook "discovered" the island in November 1778, he found it bleak and inhospitable. Not until 1786 did a Western navigator, Captain George Dixon, bother to land. When Kamehameha the Great took it in 1795, he was actually en route to the much grander prize of Oahu. His war canoes are said to have loomed along four miles of shoreline when he attacked the island at Pakuhiwa Battleground and slaughtered the island's outnumbered defenders.

The next wave of invaders arrived in 1832 when Protestant missionaries introduced the Polynesians to the marvels of Christianity. Around 1850 a German immigrant named Rudolph Meyer arrived in Molokai, married a Hawaiian chieftess, and began a reign as manager of the Molokai Ranch that lasted for almost a half-century.

Leprosy struck the Hawaiian Islands during the 19th century, and wind-plagued Kalaupapa Peninsula became the living hell to which the disease's victims were exiled. Beginning in 1866, lepers were torn from their families and literally cast to their fates along this stark shore. Here Father Damien de Veuster, a Belgian priest, the Martyr of Molokai, came to live, work and eventually die among the afflicted.

For years Molokai was labeled "The Lonely Isle" or "The Forgotten Isle." By 1910 a population that once totaled 10,000 had decreased to one-tenth the size. Then in 1921, Polynesians began settling homesteads under the Hawaiian Homes Act, which granted a 40-acre homestead to anyone with over 50 percent Hawaiian ancestry. Molokai eventually became "The Friendly Isle," with the largest proportion of native Hawaiians anywhere in the world (except for the island of Niihau, which is closed to outsiders). With them they brought a legacy from old Hawaii, the spirit of aloha, which still lives on this marvelous island. Young Hawaiians, sometimes hostile on the more crowded islands, are often outgoing and generous here.

During the 1920s, while Hawaiians were being granted the hardscrabble land that had not already been bought up on the island, Libby (which later sold out to Dole) and Del Monte began producing pineapples across the richer stretches of the island. The company towns of Maunaloa and Kualapuu sprang up and Molokai's rolling prairies became covered with fields of spike-topped fruits. Over the years competition from Asia became increasingly intense, forcing Dole to shut its operation in 1975 and Del Monte to pull out in 1982.

As elsewhere in Hawaii, the economic powers realized that if they couldn't grow crops they had better cultivate tourists. During the 1970s thousands of acres along the island's western end were allocated for resort and residential development and the sprawling Kaluakoi Resort was built. In 1996, vandals opposed to this sort of development destroyed five miles of water pipes on Molokai Ranch, which had earlier closed access to several beaches and evicted a number of former plantation workers from their homes.

Today the island's population numbers under 7000. There isn't a single traffic light here, and the weak economy has saved Molokai from the ravages of development that plagued the rest of Hawaii during the 1980s. Change is coming, but like everything on Molokai, it is arriving slowly. Time still remains to see Hawaii as it once was and to experience the trackless beaches, vaulting seacliffs, sweeping ranchlands and forested mountains that led ancient Hawaiians to believe in the mystical powers of Molokai.

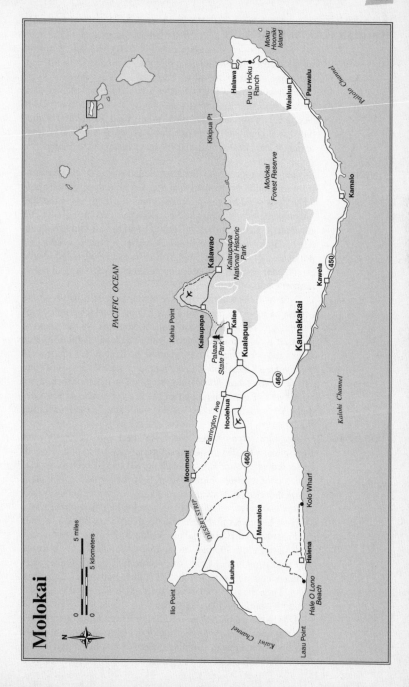

▼▼▼▼▼▼▼▼▼▼▼▼▼▼▼▼

Kaunakakai to East End

You don't need a scorecard, or even a map for that matter, to keep track of the sightseeing possibilities on Molokai. Across its brief expanse, the Friendly Isle offers several rewards to the curious, none of which are difficult to find.

First of course is the falsefront town of Kaunakakai, a commercial hub that more resembles a way station on the road to Dodge City. From here a simple two-lane road, Route 450 (Kamehameha V Highway), threads its way along the southern shore in search of the Halawa Valley at the far east end of the island.

SIGHTS

It is only too appropriate that **Kaunakakai** gained its greatest fame from someone who never existed. Known for a song written about "The Cock-eyed Mayor of Kaunakakai," the town has in fact had only one mayor—whether he was cock-eyed, no one will say. This somnolent village, with its falsefront buildings and tiny civic center, is administered from Maui. Poor but proud, it possesses a population of fewer than 3000, and has a main drag (Ala Malama Street) that extends a grand total of three blocks but still represents the hub of Molokai.

Nearby is the **wharf**, extending seaward almost a half-mile and offering a mooring place for a few fishing boats, charter outfits, and private sailboats. A good place to gaze out on the island of Lanai, it is also an ideal vantage from which to take in the green slopes that rise toward the ridgeline of Molokai. Kids love to swim off the Kaunakaki Wharf, where a roped off area keeps them safe from the boats. It's also a great place to meet local children.

Close to the pier landing rest the rocky remains of **Kamehameha V's Summer Home**, where Hawaii's king luxuriated during the late-19th century.

HIDDEN ►

For birdwatching, you'll want to check out the **Wastewater Reclamation Facility**, where the nutrient-rich (read bug-infested) water is a year-round hit with endangered species such as the Hawaiian coot and stilt. In the winter, keep an eye out for the occasional shoveler, green-winged teal, wandering tattler and other migratory waterfowl. ~ Located off Maunaloa Highway on the ocean side just before Kaunakakai; 808-553-5341, fax 808-553-4251.

From Kaunakakai to Halawa Valley, a narrow macadam road leads past almost 30 miles of seascapes and historic sites. Route 450 runs straight along the south shore for about 20 miles, presenting views across the Kalohi and Pailolo channels to Lanai and Maui. Then the road snakes upward and curves inland before descending again into Halawa Valley.

Due to the calm, shallow waters along the southeastern shoreline, this area once supported one of the greatest concentrations of fishponds in Hawaii. Numbering as many as five dozen during the pre-Western period, these ancient aquaculture structures were

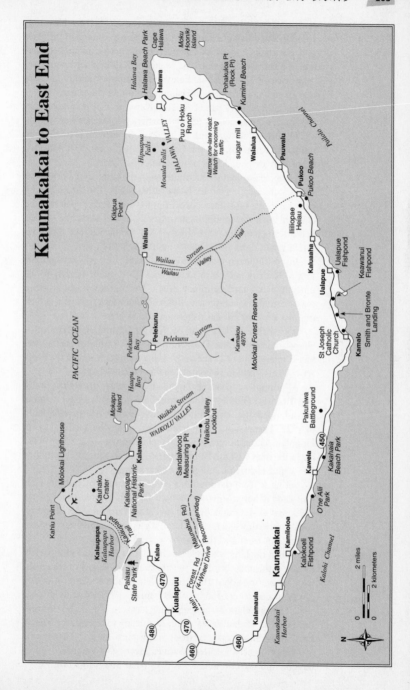

Kaunakakai to East End

PACIFIC OCEAN

Kahiu Point

Molokai Lighthouse

Kaupapapa Point

Mokapu Island

Haupu Bay

Pelekunu Bay

Kikipua Point

Wailau

Halawa Bay

Halawa Beach Park

Cape Halawa

Moku Hooniki Island

Pohakuloa Pt (Rock Pt)

Kumimi Beach

Halawa

Puu o Hoku Ranch

Hipuapua Falls

Moaula Falls

HALAWA VALLEY

Narrow one-lane road: Watch for oncoming traffic

sugar mill

Wailua

Pauwalu

Pailolo Channel

Pukoo

Pukoo Beach

Iliiliopae Heiau

Trail

Wailau Stream

Wailau Valley

Wailau

Pelekunu

Pelekunu Stream

Kamakou 4970

Molokai Forest Reserve

Kalaupapa

Kauhako Crater

Kalaupapa National Historic Park

Kalaupapa Harbor

Kalawao

Waikolu Stream

WAIKOLU VALLEY

Waikolu Valley Lookout

Sandalwood Measuring Pit

Kalae

Palaau State Park

Kualapuu

480

470

460

Main (Mauhui Rd) Forest Rd (4-Wheel Drive Recommended)

Kalamaula

Kaunakakai

Kamiloloa

Kalokoeli Fishpond

Kaunakakai Harbor

Kalohi Channel

One Alii Park

Kakahaia Beach Park

450

Kawela

Pakuhiwa Battleground

St Joseph Catholic Church

Kamalo

Smith and Bronte Landing

Ualapue

Ualapue Fishpond

Keawanui Fishpond

Kaluaaha

2 miles

2 kilometers

0

0

N

built of lava and coral by commoners to raise fish for Hawaiian royalty. Small fish were trapped within these stone pens, fattened and eventually harvested. You will see the rebuilt remains of several as you drive along the coast, including **Kalokoeli Fishpond**, two miles east of Kaunakakai, **Keawanui Fishpond**, about 12 miles east of town, and **Ualapue Fishpond**, a mile farther east.

About five miles from town lies **Kawela**, once an ancient city of refuge, now known as the place where two battles were fought at **Pakuhiwa Battleground**. In his drive to become Hawaii's first monarch, Kamehameha the Great launched a canoe flotilla that reportedly extended four miles along this shore.

For a face-to-feather encounter with the endangered nene, Hawaii's state bird, swing by **Nene O Molokai**. This nonprofit facility raises the birds on a beachfront location and is open for educational visits (by appointment only). ~ Located past Mile Marker 4 off Kamehameha V Highway; 808-553-5992, fax 808-553-9029; www.aloha.net/~nene, e-mail nene@aloha.net.

Just past the ten-mile marker (indicating that you are ten miles east of Kaunakakai), a dirt road leads to **Kamalo Wharf**, an old pineapple and cattle shipping point. This natural harbor, once a major commercial center (by Molokai standards!), is now a gathering place for occasional fishermen and boats.

It's a half-mile farther to **St. Joseph Catholic Church**, a tiny chapel built by Father Damien in 1876. A statue of the bespectacled priest, clad in a cape and leaning on a cane, graces the property. A small cemetery completes this placid tableau.

A monument (past the 11-mile marker) designates the **Smith and Bronte Landing**, an inhospitable spot where two aviators crash-landed after completing the first civilian transpacific flight in 1927. The 25-hour flight from California, scheduled to land in Honolulu, ended abruptly when the plane ran out of gas. (An opening in the trees past the 12-mile marker reveals the aforementioned Keawanui Fishpond, one of Molokai's largest.)

Set back from the road in a clearing framed by mountains is **Our Lady of Seven Sorrows Catholic Church**, located 14 miles east of Kaunakakai. Originally built by Father Damien in 1874 and reconstructed almost a century later, it's a pretty chapel surrounded by coconut trees and flanked by a small cemetery.

HIDDEN ▶ One of the largest temples in the islands, **Iliiliopae Heiau**, rests hidden in the underbrush on private land just inland from the highway. Measuring about 100 yards in length and 40 yards in width, it was once a center of sorcery and human sacrifice that today consists of a stone platform and adjoining terraces. This is also the trailhead for the Wailau Valley Trail. According to legend, the *heiau*'s stones were all transported from this distant valley and assembled in a single night. ~ Located 15 miles east of Kaunakakai; for permission and directions, call Pearl Petro at 808-558-8113.

The best way to visit this ancient site is on the **Molokai Wagon Ride,** a horse-drawn-wagon or horseback tour conducted by several delightful local fellows. ~ Mapulehu Mango Grove, about 15 miles east of Kaunakakai; 808-558-8132; e-mail wgnride@ aloha.net.

The Molokai Wagon Ride also visits the nearby **Mapulehu Mango Grove,** a stand of over 2000 fruit trees that were planted in 1926 and now represent one of the largest such groves in the world. The wagon ride winds up at a picturesque beach where guests enjoy a Molokai-style lunch on the beach complete with coconut husking and Hawaiian net throwing.

The ruins of the island's first **sugar mill** stand near Route 450's 20-mile marker. All that remains of this early factory, which burned down about a century ago, is a solitary stack.

Just beyond the 20-mile marker is Kumimi Beach, which presents your first view of **Moku Hooniki Island** as well as otherworldly vistas of Maui.

The road now begins a sinuous course along a string of pearl-white beaches, then climbs above a rocky coastline. As you curve upward into Molokai's tropical heights, the roadside flora becomes increasingly colorful and dense. First you encounter the open pastures and rolling ranchland of 14,000-acre **Puu o Hoku Ranch,** then dive into the tropical foliage of Molokai's windblown northeast coast.

As the road winds high above **Halawa Valley** it offers several vista points from which to view this V-shaped canyon bounded by green walls. Directly below, tropical greenery gives way to white

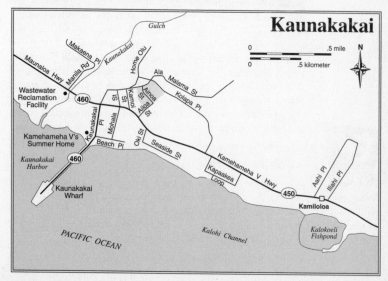

surf and then aquamarine ocean. A river bisects this luxuriant region. At the far end, surrounded by sheer walls, two waterfalls—**Hipuapua** and **Moaula**—spill down the mountainside. Obviously East End has withheld its most spectacular scenery until the last.

Archaeologists believe that Molokai's first settlement was established here, possibly as early as the 7th century. The ancient Hawaiians terraced the surrounding slopes, planting taro and living off the largesse of the sea.

In 1946 (and again in 1957) a tidal wave swept through the valley, leveling buildings and leaving salt deposits that destroyed the agricultural industry. Today you can drive down into the valley, where you'll find a park, a lovely curve of sandy beach, freshwater Halawa Stream, an old church and several other structures. A hiking trail leads to 250-foot Moaula Falls and 500-foot Hipuapua Falls, which lie to the interior of this awesomely beautiful vale. Please note, however, that this trail has been closed by the landowner and is not open to the public. You may, however, embark on a guided tour of the area by contacting **Pilipo's Halawa Falls and Cultural Hike**. Closed Sunday. ~ 808-553-4355.

LODGING   Two miles east of Kaunakakai is the 45-room **Hotel Molokai**, a lowrise hotel with faux-Polynesian architectural details. The accommodations are small but comfortable, and have rattan furnishings, tropical prints, refrigerators and ceiling fans; some units also have kitchenettes. There is an oceanside pool and a pleasant lounge area with an adjacent restaurant and cocktail lounge. The hotel fronts a narrow beach, and shallows offshore are not suitable for ocean swimming, but they're great for fishing. The grounds are nicely landscaped with plenty of tall palms that provide a tropical feel. ~ Kamehameha Highway; 808-553-5347, 800-367-5004, fax 808-553-5047; www.hotelmolokai.com. MODERATE TO DELUXE.

If privacy is what you're after, you'll love **Kamalo Plantation Bed & Breakfast**. Set on five acres of orchards and tropical gardens, the secluded cottage lies in the middle of lush grounds. Screen windows let in the tropical smell of the flowering trees, and a private lanai is perfect for the breakfast of homemade bread and fresh fruit from the orchard. ~ HCO1 Box 300, Kaunakakai,

sights

AUTHOR FAVORITE

I love to wander the windswept beach at the edge of **Halawa Valley**, or hike deep into the valley, which has been inhabited by Hawaiians for 1300 years. Ancient *heiaus*, two spectacular waterfalls and the remains of a once-rich agricultural industry are some of the highlights of this lush rainforest. See pages 205–206 for more information.

HI 96748; phone/fax 808-558-8236; e-mail kamaloplantation@ aloha.net. MODERATE TO DELUXE.

Ten miles farther east on a sandy beach ideal for whale-watching is the **Moanui Beach House**. Decorated Polynesian style, with vaulted ceilings, the house has two bedrooms with king-size beds, a bathroom, a living and dining area and a large kitchen. All the home amenities, including TV and VCR, as well as beach gear and grill, are included. There's a three-night minimum. ~ HCO1, Box 300, Kauanakakai, HI 96748; phone/fax 808-558-8236; e-mail kamaloplantation@aloha.net. DELUXE.

In a tropical garden east of Kaunakakai is **A'ahi Place Bed and Breakfast.** Here you'll find a cedar cottage with kitchen and bath, two full-sized beds, and lanais surrounded by fragrant tropical flowers and swaying palms. Best of all—there are no TVs or phones to interrupt your thoughts. Continental breakfast is included. ~ P.O. Box 528, Kaunakakai, HI 96748; 406-549-8345; e-mail mitty@aloha.net. MODERATE.

On the south shore near the five-mile marker, **Ka Hale Mala** (The Garden House) is a quick walk to the beach. Gourmet breakfasts are included in the moderate host rate, or you can stay there on your own for a budget price. The spacious four-room apartment (that sleeps up to four) is surrounded by a tempting tropical garden—tangelos, pommelos, figs, kau oranges, papayas, limes, breadfruit and more—that you're allowed to pick from. Yum. ~ P.O. Box 1582, Kaunakakai, HI 96748; 808-553-9009; www.molokai-bnb.com, e-mail cpgroup@aloha.net. BUDGET TO MODERATE.

CONDOS

If you're traveling with several folks or want kitchen facilities, there are also condominiums: **Marc Molokai Shores Suites** offers oceanfront accommodations with full kitchen, lanai and color television. A series of low-slung buildings that forms a U-shaped configuration around a landscaped lawn extending to the beach sits among palm trees, a swimming pool, shuffleboard and barbecue areas. Rates start at $144. ~ Phone/fax 808-553-5954, 800-535-0085; www.marcresorts.com.

DINING

A gourmet will starve on Molokai, but someone looking for a square meal at fair prices should depart well-fed. The budget restaurants are clustered along Ala Malama Street in Kaunakakai.

◄ HIDDEN

Kanemitsu's Bakery serves tasty meals at appetizing prices. A local institution, it's a simple café with molded seats, formica tables and an interesting folk-art mural presenting a map of Molokai. The lunch special varies but the price is low whether you are dining on pork chops, beef teriyaki, breaded mahi or fried chicken. Kanemitsu's is a favorite with the breakfast crowd, which is drawn in by the bakery as well as by the menu of omelettes, hot cakes and egg dishes served with Portuguese sausage or that island favorite, Spam. No dinner. Closed Tuesday. ~ Kaunakakai; 808-553-5855. BUDGET.

Outpost Natural Foods has a takeout counter at the back of its tiny health food store. Here you can fuel up with delicious sandwiches, salads and smoothies that are both nutritious and inexpensive. There are also burritos and daily specials. Open 10 a.m. to 3 p.m. No dinner. Closed Saturday. ~ 70 Makaena Place, Kaunakakai; 808-553-3377, fax 808-553-5857. BUDGET.

HIDDEN ▶

Molokai Pizza Cafe is an excellent neighborhood pizzeria located just outside of town. Clean and modern, this local hangout is a great place for a tasty lunch or a quick-and-easy dinner. On Wednesday, Mexican standards are featured, while on Sunday, prime rib is added to the menu. Try one of their homemade pies for dessert. ~ Kaunakakai Place, Kaunakakai; 808-553-3288, fax 808-553-5400. BUDGET TO MODERATE.

You're hungry? You want take-out? Why not try **Molokai Drive Inn**. At breakfast you'll find the usual (eggs and hotcakes) or the unusual (shrimp omelettes, fried rice, banana pancakes or eggs and Spam). For lunch or dinner try the ox tail, Chinese plate or barbecue pork chops—or stick to burgers if you must. ~ 857 Kamoi Street, Kaunakakai; 808-553-5655. BUDGET.

Kamuela's Bar & Grill is a family-owned and -operated restaurant serving breakfast, lunch and dinner daily. Here you'll find local and mainland dishes to fit a budget-sized pocketbook. You'll understand why they call this the Friendly Isle when you step inside. ~ Kaunakakai; 808-553-4286; e-mail purdy@aloha.net.

GROCERIES   The nearest Molokai approaches to a supermarket is **Misaki's**, a medium-sized grocery store on Kaunakakai's main drag, Ala Malama Street. The prices are higher and the selection smaller here than at the chain markets, so it's wise to bring a few provisions from the larger islands. Open 8:30 a.m. to 8:30 p.m., Sunday 9 a.m. to noon. ~ 78 Ala Malama Street, Kaunakakai; 808-553-5505, fax 808-531-6447.

AUTHOR FAVORITE

If you're into Filipino fare, try **Oviedo's Lunch Counter**. This mom-and-pop restaurant serves up spicy steaming dishes at low prices. You'll find plank board walls surrounding a few plastic chairs and yellow formica tables. The steam-tray cuisine includes chicken papaya, pig's feet, turkey tail adobo and mango beans. Open for lunch and early dinner. ~ Ala Malama Street, Kaunakakai; 808-553-5014. BUDGET.

Outpost Natural Foods, down the street and around the corner from Misaki's, offers a friendly atmosphere as well as juices, herbs, dried fruit, fresh local produce and other health food items. Closed Saturday. ~ 70 Makaena Place, Kaunakakai; 808-553-3377, fax 808-553-5857.

Try **Kanemitsu's Bakery** for delicious raspberry jelly, bread and pastries. ~ Ala Malama Street, Kaunakakai; 808-553-5855.

On the East End, **Neighborhood Store 'n Counter** has groceries and a stock of liquor. Open 8 a.m. to 6 p.m. daily. ~ Kamehameha Highway (near the 17-mile marker); 808-558-8498.

You needn't worry about falling into the shop-till-you-drop syndrome on Molokai. Long before you have even begun to think about being tired you will have visited every store on the island. Shopping is still an adventure here, since the few stores operating are all owned by local people and provide a window into life on Molokai.

SHOPPING

Ala Malama Street, Kaunakakai's main street, offers a modest row of shops. **Molokai Island Creations** specializes in clothing, jewelry, glassware and gift items made by Molokai artists. ~ 63 Ala Malama Street, Kaunakakai; 808-553-5926.

In the same complex, **Molokai Fish & Dive**, "home of the original Molokai T-shirt designs," features its signature clothing and souvenirs as well as beach items and sporting equipment. ~ 63 Ala Malama Street, Kaunakakai; 808-553-5926; www.molokai-aloha.com/fishdive.

Imports Gift Shop features casual wear, cultured and mabe pearls, and Hawaiian heirloom jewelry. ~ 828 Ala Malama Street, Kaunakakai; 808-553-5734.

For surfwear you can try **Molokai Surf**. Closed Sunday. ~ 130 Kamehameha Highway, Suite 103, Kaunakakai; 808-553-5093.

Be sure to stop by the **Kamakana Fine Arts Gallery**, located above the American Savings Bank in Kaunakakai. Finely turned bowls, blown glass, hula implements, *pahu* drums, *lauhala* hats, baskets, painted spirit paintings and marine sculptures are just some of the objects you'll find. Over 90 of Molokai's artists are featured here. ~ 40 Ala Malama Street, Kaunankakai; 808-553-8520; e-mail kgallery@aloha.net.

O'NE ALII PARK 🏊 🌊 🎣 ⚓ This spacious park features a large grass-covered field and coconut trees plus a narrow beach with an excellent view of Lanai. A reef far offshore makes this area very shallow and affords ample protection. It's excellent for children. Snorkeling, though, is only mediocre. As for surfing, all the action is far out on the reef and it's rarely any good. Surf-casting isn't bad here but it's even better farther to the east. The most common catches are *manini*, red and white goatfish, parrotfish,

BEACHES & PARKS

papio, *ulua*, milkfish and mullet. The facilities here include a picnic area, restrooms, showers and electricity at the pavilion. ~ Located four miles east of Kaunakakai on Route 450; 808-553-3204, fax 808-553-3206.

▲ Mainly tent camping; no hookups, $3 per person per night. Very popular and therefore sometimes crowded and noisy. County permit required.

KAKAHAIA BEACH PARK This is a long, narrow park wedged tightly between the road and the ocean; it's the site of the Kakahaia National Wildlife Refuge. Since the water is both shallow and murky, swimming and snorkeling are not recommended. Picnicking, surfing and fishing are much the same as at O'ne Alii Park. Day use only. ~ Located six miles east of Kaunakakai on Route 450.

PUKOO BEACH This crescent-shaped strand is mirrored by another curving beach just to the west. Maui lies directly across the channel and there are also marvelous views of Lanai. With a shallow, rocky bottom, this beach provides only mediocre swimming. However, it's very popular with anglers. There are no facilities. ~ The old Neighborhood Store 'n' Snack Bar, located on Route 450 near Mile Marker 16, is your landmark. Just past here, traveling east, turn into the second driveway on the right. This access road leads a short distance to the beach.

KUMIMI BEACH, POHAKULOA POINT AND OTHER EAST END BEACHES Beginning near the 18-mile marker on Route 450, and extending for about four miles, lies this string of small sandy beaches. These are among the island's loveliest, featuring white sands and spectacular views of the islands of Maui and Lanai. The swimming is very good, but beware of heavy currents and high surf. Plentiful coral makes for great snorkeling and good lobster diving. There are numerous surfing breaks throughout this area. Pohakuloa Point (or Rock Point), located eight-tenths of a mile past the 20-mile marker, is one of Molokai's top surfing spots. Barracuda are sometimes caught in the deeper regions. Also bonefish, mountain bass, threadfin, *manini*, red and white goatfish, *ulua*, *papio*, parrotfish, milkfish and mullet. There is a small market near Mile Marker 15. ~ These pocket beaches are located along Route 450 between the 18- and 22-mile markers.

HALAWA BEACH PARK Set in lush Halawa Valley, one of Molokai's most splendid areas, the park is tucked neatly between mountains and sea on a grassy plot dotted with coconut palms and ironwood trees. Cliffs, waterfalls, two pocket beaches—altogether a heavenly spot, though sometimes rainy and almost always windy. This is an okay place to swim because it is partially protected by the bay, but exercise caution anyway. Snorkeling is good, though the water is sometimes murky. It's one of the very best spots on the island for surfing. Fishing is also notable; the reefs studding this area make it a prime locale for many of the species caught along East End Beaches. The park is a bit weatherbeaten and overgrown and although there are a picnic area and restrooms, the running water must be boiled or treated chemically. ~ Located 30 miles east of Kaunakakai on Route 450.

▲ Not permitted in the park, but people camp on the other side of Halawa Stream on property owned by Puu o Hoku Ranch (808-558-8109). You will have to park and carry your gear to where you want to camp.

Kaunakakai to West End

Generally, if you are not pointed east on Molokai, you are headed westerly. The thoroughfare that carries you across the prairie-like plains of west Molokai is Route 460, also called the Maunaloa Highway, another two-lane track. Along the way you can venture off in search of the plantation town of Kualapuu and the vista point overlooking Kalaupapa, but eventually you will arrive at road's end out in the woodframe town of Maunaloa. From this red-dust municipality it's a short jaunt to Papohaku Beach, Molokai's western shore.

SIGHTS

Just a mile west of the cock-eyed town of Kaunakakai on Route 460 is the **Kapuaiwa Coconut Grove**, planted in the 1860s by Kamehameha V. This magnificent stand of coconut palms, once 1000 in number, consists of particularly tall trees. The grove creates the sensation of being in a tropical dream sequence, with hundreds of palm trees flashing green and yellow fronds and extending to the lip of the ocean. Some appear to stand in columns, but others have bent so far to the wind they have fallen out of formation. Pay a visit toward sunset, when the palms are memorably silhouetted by tropic skies for a wonderful end-of-day setting. Watch out for falling coconuts: these trees are not the trimmed-back kind made safe for the unwary. Adjacent to the coconut grove is the **Kalanianaole Community Hall**, a unique early-20th-century cultural landmark that still serves the community. ~ Route 460.

> According to legend, Molokai was the child of the god Wakea and his mistress Hina, whose cave still lies along the southeastern edge of the island.

Strung like rosary beads opposite the grove are seven tiny churches. This **Church Row** includes Protestant, Mormon, Jehovah's Witness and several other denominations. Like sentinels protecting the island from the devil, they too are gathered in rows. The most intriguing are the oldest, tiny woodframe structures with modest steeples. These one-room chapels lack worldly frills like stained glass and are furnished with creaky wooden pews that seat a few dozen parishioners. Stop by and inquire about services; visitors are always welcome.

Molokai Plumerias is a family-run company that will take you on a tour of their one-acre plumeria farm. Plumeria, with the scent of heaven, are the primary flowers used in lei making. Your guide will teach you about the flower, allow you to pick your own and provide you with the necessary tools to create a lei. There are no regularly scheduled tours, so make reservations in advance. ~ Kalamaula, about two miles west of Kaunakakai; 808-553-3391.

A side trip along Route 470 leads past the tinroof town of **Kualapuu**. Filled with modest plantation houses, it harkens back to an earlier era when Molokai cultivated pineapples rather than tourists. Today its claim to fame is a 1.4-million-gallon reservoir that is reportedly the largest rubber-lined water tank in the world.

If you tire of Hawaii's relaxed pace and long for a jolt of java, arrange a tour at **Coffees of Hawaii**. Walking and mule-drawn wagon tours are offered here; you'll be led around the 500-acre coffee plantation to witness the roasting process "from seed to cup." The tour wraps up in the tasting room, where an espresso bar churns out samples. Reservations required. ~ P.O. Box 160, Kualapuu, HI 96757; 800-346-5051, fax 808-567-9270; www.coffee hawaii.com, e-mail coffees@aloha.net.

Molokai's West End was once a rich adze quarry. The rock, vital to a Stone Age society, was fashioned into tools that were in turn used to create weapons, canoes, bowls and other necessities.

Farther up Route 470, Kalae is home to the R. W. Meyer Sugar Mill, which is the highlight of the **Molokai Museum and Cultural Center**. There is an 1878 steam-generated operation that has been restored in sparkling fashion. The mule-driven cane crusher, copper clarifiers and dependable old steam engine are ready and waiting for Molokai to return to its old ways. There are also well-presented displays and heirlooms of the German immigrant family that owned the mill, as well as native Molokai artifacts. Closed Sunday. Admission. ~ Route 470, Kalae; 808-567-6436.

Route 470 ends at the **Kalaupapa Lookout**. Here cliffs as green as Ireland fall away in dizzying fashion to reveal a softly sloping tableland 1600 feet below, the Kalaupapa Peninsula. Fringed by white-sand beaches, this geologic afterthought extends more than two miles out from the foot of the *pali*. A lighthouse and landing strip occupy the point of the peninsula. Nearer the cliffs, a cluster of houses comprises the famous leper colony; while neighboring Kauhako Crater, a nicely rounded circle far below you, represents a vestige of the volcano that created this appendage. Ringed by rock and water, protected by the tallest sea cliffs in the world, Kalaupapa Peninsula is a magnificent sight indeed.

A short hike from the lookout, **Phallic Rock** protrudes obscenely from the ground amid an ironwood stand as thick as pubic hair. This geologic formation, so realistic it almost seems sculpted,

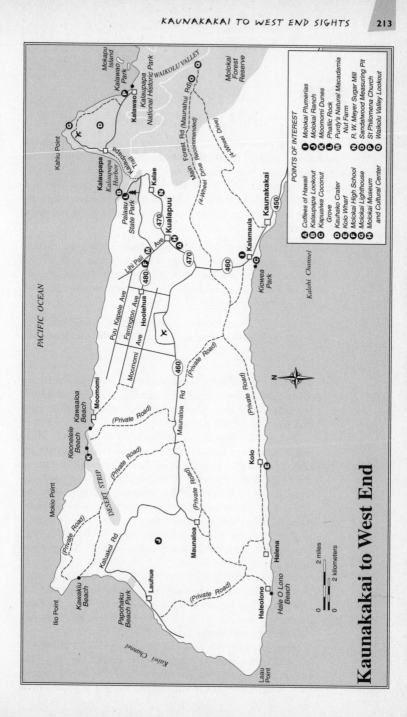

Kaunakakai to West End

POINTS OF INTEREST

- Ⓐ Coffees of Hawaii
- Ⓑ Kalaupapa Lookout
- Ⓒ Kapuaiwa Coconut Grove
- Ⓓ Kauhako Crater
- Ⓔ Kolo Wharf
- Ⓕ Molokai High School
- Ⓖ Molokai Lighthouse
- Ⓗ Molokai Museum and Cultural Center
- Ⓘ Molokai Plumerias
- Ⓙ Molokai Ranch
- Ⓚ Moomomi Dunes
- Ⓛ Purdy's Natural Macadamia Nut Farm
- Ⓜ Phallic Rock
- Ⓝ R. W. Meyer Sugar Mill
- Ⓞ Sandalwood Measuring Pit
- Ⓟ St Philomena Church
- Ⓠ Waikolu Valley Lookout

DRIVING TOUR
Molokai's Outback

For a splendid tour of Molokai's mountainous interior, take a drive or hike on the Main Forest Road (Maunahui Road), located four miles west of Kaunakakai. This bumpy dirt road requires four-wheel-drive vehicles along its ten-mile length. To reach the Main Forest Road, take Route 460 west from Kaunakakai. There is a white bridge a little more than three and a half miles from town, just before the four-mile marker. Take a right on the dirt road right before the bridge and you're on the Main Forest Road.

MOLOKAI FOREST RESERVE   Deer, quail, pheasant, doves and chukkar partridge populate the route. Numerous secondary roads and trails lead to the very edge of the mammoth Molokai Forest Reserve, through which the main road passes. These side roads offer excellent possibilities for adventurous hikers.

LUA MOKU ILIAHI   After nine miles, the main road passes Lua Moku Iliahi, known to the English-speaking world as the **Sandalwood Measuring**

was said to represent the Hawaiian fertility god, who was turned to stone when his wife caught him admiring a beautiful young girl. Legend says that a woman offering gifts and spending the night here will return home pregnant.

Route 480 will take you into the town of Hoolehua, where you'll find **Purdy's Natural Macadamia Nut Farm**. Located right behind the island's only high school, this small grove of 70-year-old macadamia nut trees is open to the public for free tours and tastings. The owner will explain the growing cycles of the trees and demonstrate harvesting and cooking techniques. Visitors can taste the raw product and also sample the nut after it's been naturally roasted, a process that cuts down greatly on the fat and calories found in nuts sold in stores. Closed Sunday. ~ Lihipali Avenue, Hoolehua; phone/fax 808-567-6601.

Route 460 continues over dry rolling plains toward Molokai's West End. This arid plateau, windswept and covered by deep red, iron-rich soil, was once planted in pineapple. Today Molokai Ranch, which still owns much of the region, has turned to hay cultivation to feed cattle.

If nothing else, the West End is rich in myth and history. As Hawaiian storytellers recount, the region around Maunaloa, the volcano that formed this side of the island, was once a cultural focus of the Polynesians. It was here that the hula originated; from

Pit. This depression, dug into the earth to match the hull size of an old sailing vessel, was used by 19th-century Hawaiians to gauge the amount of sandalwood needed to fill a ship.

WAIKOLU VALLEY LOOKOUT   It's another mile to **Waikolu Picnic Grove**, a heavily wooded retreat ideal for lunching or camping. Here you'll find picnic facilities and an outhouse. (State permit required to camp.) Across the road, Waikolu Valley Lookout perches above Waikolu Valley, which descends precipitously 3000 feet to the sea.

KAMAKOU PRESERVE   Here you can also explore Kamakou Preserve, a 2774-acre sanctuary managed by The Nature Conservancy. Home to more than 200 plants that live only in Hawaii, the preserve is a lush rainforest and an important watershed for Molokai. There are several forest birds, including the *apapane* and *amakihi*. For information on visiting the reserve or to check the condition of the Main Forest Road (which may be closed in wet weather), call 808-553-5236, fax 808-553-9870; www.tnc-hawaii.com.

the slopes of Maunaloa the goddess Laka spread knowledge of the sensuous dance to all the other islands.

Like the pineapple industry itself, Route 460 ends in **Maunaloa**. With the departure of Dole's operations in 1975, this company town assumed the dusty, falsefront visage of the Wild West after the mines petered out and the saloons shut down. That's all begun to change in the past few years as the Molokai Ranch, which owns just about all of Maunaloa, has started a revitalization program that has seen the more ramshackle plantation houses replaced by contemporary homes, some of the town's more historic buildings upgraded, and several new buildings added, including a lovely 22-room lodge and Molokai's first movie theater. The old post office and general store provide links to Maunaloa's days as a pineapple town, and the overall feeling remains rustically charming, albeit with an increasingly gentrified air.

Any tour of West End should of course finish at the west end. **Papohaku Beach**, a sparkling three-mile long swath of white sand, would be a fitting finale to any tour. Reached by taking Kaluakoi Road from Route 460 and driving through the rolling hills of sprawling Kaluakoi Resort, Papohaku is one of the largest beaches in the state. During World War II troops practiced shore landings along this coast. But today you will have the beach and surrounding sand dunes almost entirely to yourself.

LODGING   Far from the madding crowd on the west end of Molokai, you will find a 6700-acre master-planned complex, the **Kaluakoi Resort**. Divided into the 116-room Kaluakoi Hotel & Golf Club, the cottage-like condos of Kaluakoi Villas, and two other condominium complexes, it is set near a luxurious three-mile-long beach. This is Molokai's premier resting spot, offering both seclusion and comfort. Here you'll find the essence of plush living: wasp-waisted pool, golf course, a view of Oahu across the channel, and an oceanfront lounge and restaurant. The hotel rooms are located in a two-story building and have all the necessities: lanai, color TV, tile bathroom, overhead fan, rattan furniture. For an ultra-deluxe price tag, you can buy a piece of that ocean view in a studio unit with a kitchenette. The villas are more spacious, also include a kitchenette and are priced deluxe. ~ Kaluakoi Hotel & Golf Club: 808-552-2555, 888-552-2550, fax 808-552-2821, www.kaluakai.com; Kaluakoi Villas: 808-552-2721, 800-367-5004, fax 808-552-2201, www.castle-group.com.

Ke Nani Kai Resort, a 120-unit condominium, has one- and two-bedroom units starting at $149 per night. Over Christmas there's a two-night minimum. The complex includes a pool, tennis courts, a putting green and an outdoor party area with barbecues. ~ Kepuhi Place; 808-552-2761, 800-888-2791, fax 808-552-0045; www.kenanikai.com.

Nearby **Paniolo Hale** has 25 condos starting at $95 per night. Located just off the shore of Kepuhi Beach, they offer oak floors and beamed ceilings and walls of glass doors that open onto screened lanais. Access to a pool, barbecue area and paddle tennis round out the traditional amenities (dishwasher, washer and dryer). ~ Kakaako Road; 808-552-2731, 800-367-2984; www.paniolohaleresort.com, e-mail stay@paniolohaleresort.com.

The two-story **Lodge at Molokai Ranch** in Maunaloa was designed and decorated with the town's plantation past in mind—the 22-room lodge exudes a sense of intimacy and charm, with rattan furnishings and '30s-style Hawaiian prints. Rooms are spacious and individually decorated with cheerful upcountry decor. All offer long, unobstructed views of West Molokai's rolling hills, with the ocean in the distance. The eight-acre property includes

AUTHOR FAVORITE

Camping isn't quite the same at **Molokai Ranch**. Their oceanview tent company and outdoor adventures make me think I'm a kid again, riding the range in cowboy movies—but this time with a Hawaiian *paniolo* theme. See page 217 for more information.

KAUNAKAKAI TO WEST END DINING

a day spa, swimming pool, game room and lounge. ~ P.O. Box 259, Maunaloa, HI 96770; 877-726-4656, fax 808-552-2773; www. molokai-ranch.com. ULTRA-DELUXE.

If there is such a thing as luxury camping, a stay at **The Camps at Molokai Ranch** would be it. Their idea of "roughing it" includes spacious wood-frame "tentalows," canvas-sided bungalows that come with queen-size beds, overhead fans, solar-heated bathrooms and private wooden decks for lounging about. Three hearty meals are served in the communal cookhouse at each of the three campsites. **Paniolo Camp** is located several miles from Maunaloa, while **Kaupoa** is adjacent to a private white sand beach. **Kolo Cliffs** also has an oceanside setting on a hillside overlooking the south coast. Equally appealing are the wide range of activities offered to guests: mountain biking, horseback riding, kayaking and cultural hikes. There are also unique options like The Ropes Challenge, an adventurous obstacle course; the Paniolo Roundup, where guests participate in a cattle roundup; and the Cattle Drive, where you'll join *paniolos* as they move cattle from one pasture to another. The staff couldn't be more friendly or helpful, and time flies as one beautiful day flows into the next. ~ P.O. Box 259, Maunaloa, HI 96770; 877-726-4656, fax 808-552-2773; www. molokai-ranch.com. ULTRA-DELUXE.

Now just a take-out joint, **Kamuela's Cookhouse** fills the bill when you're hungry. Homemade corned beef hash tops your eggs, if you want, or there's buttermilk pancakes, french toast, breakfast sandwiches and omelettes at breakfast. Lunch and dinner bring teriyaki plates, katsu, lemon chicken, mahimahi plates and sandwiches. Friendly folks. ~ Uwao Street, Kualapuu; 808-567-9655; e-mail purdy@aloha.net. BUDGET TO MODERATE.

The Maunaloa Village Grill offers dining amidst a plantation-town setting with wood floors, a screened-in dining veranda, a wonderful old brass bar, Hawaii's first stonegrill, plus *paniolo* memorabilia to provide a sense of place. The ranch-style cuisine ranges from well-prepared standards like prime rib and fresh catch to burgers. ~ Maunaloa; 808-552-0012, fax 808-552-2413. MODERATE TO ULTRA-DELUXE.

The Kaluakoi Hotel, on the island's far west end, has a penny-saver **snack bar** with sandwiches. ~ BUDGET.

That's just light artillery to back up the hotel's big gun, the **Ohia Lodge**, Molokai's finest restaurant. This multilevel, handsomely appointed establishment (high-beamed ceiling, rattan furnishings) looks out on the distant lights of Oahu. You can order from an extensive surf-and-turf menu that includes orange-glazed almond chicken, seafood linguine, tenderloin of beef with bearnaise sauce and rack of lamb with black-bean beurre blanc. Seeking a place to splurge? This is it. Breakfast and dinner. Dinner

DINING

reservations required. ~ 808-552-2555, fax 808-552-2821; www.
kaluakoi.com. MODERATE TO ULTRA-DELUXE.

GROCERIES   In Kualapuu, check out **Kualapuu Market**. Open Monday through
Saturday 8:30 a.m to 6 p.m. ~ Farrington Highway; 808-567-6243.

Out West End way, **Maunaloa General Store**, in Maunaloa a
few miles away from Kaluakoi Resort, has a limited stock of grocery items. Open 8 a.m. to 6 p.m. Closed Sunday. ~ 200 Maunaloa Highway; 808-552-2346.

SHOPPING   Over on Molokai's West End in the red-dust town of Maunaloa
you'll stumble upon two great shops that share the same building and the same telephone. **Big Wind Kite Factory** has an astonishing assortment of high flyers. There are diamond kites,
dancer kites, windsocks and rainbow tail kites. You can even pick
up flags and banners here. At **The Plantation Gallery** there are
aloha shirts, batik sarongs, tribal art, shell necklaces and other original pieces by over 30 Molokai craftspeople. They also have the
largest collection of books about Hawaii and Hawaiian culture
on the island. ~ Maunaloa Highway; 808-552-2364.

The **Kaluakoi Hotel** has a sundries store. Also on the grounds
is the **Laughing Gecko**, offering local artwork and handicrafts, as
well as T-shirts, *lauhala* jewelry and bracelets. ~ 808-552-2320.

NIGHTLIFE   To step out in style, head west to Kaluakoi Hotel's **Ohia Lounge**.
The rattan furnishings, carpets, overhead fans and marvelous view
of Honolulu, not to mention a local musician on the weekends,
make it *the* place. ~ 808-552-2555.

BEACHES   **KIOWEA PARK** ⛵🎣 Watch for falling coconuts in the beau-
& PARKS   tiful Kapuaiwa Grove, which is the centerpiece of this beach park.
Towering palm trees extend almost to the water, leaving little space
for a beach. The swimming here is only okay; the water is well-
protected by a distant reef, but the bottom is shallow and rocky,

MOLOKAI KA HULA PIKO

If you're in town in mid- to late-May, you'll want to experience **Molokai Ka
Hula Piko**, an event that honors the tradition that claims the hula was first
danced on Molokai. A mile-long hike to a sunrise ceremony on a hillside
leads to where the dances were said to have originated. Cameras are not
allowed and decorum is the rule at this spiritual rite. Later in the day
beachfront festivities at Papohaku Beach Park include hula and general
high spirits. It can be hard to find a room or car during the event, so
plan accordingly. Call the Molokai Visitors Association (800-800-6367)
for information and updates.

and the water is muddy. Beyond the reef, fishing yields mullet, *manini*, parrotfish, milkfish, and *papio*, plus red, white and striped goatfish; crabbing is good in the evening. (This park is generally restricted to homesteaders, but if you stop for a picnic you may be allowed by the locals to stay.) A nice place to visit, but I wouldn't want to fall asleep in the shade of a coconut tree. Facilities include a picnic area, restrooms and a pavilion. (Unfortunately, the park is closed for renovations until further notice.) ~ Located one mile west of Kaunakakai on Route 460; 808-560-6104, fax 808-560-6665.

▲ Camping is usually restricted to homesteaders. If the park is vacant however, the Hawaiian Homelands Department across the street will issue permits for a fee; hours are Monday through Friday from 7:45 a.m. to 4:30 p.m.

PALAAU STATE PARK Set in a densely forested area, this 233-acre park is ideal for a mountain sojourn. Several short trails lead to petroglyphs, a startling phallic rock, and the awesome Kalaupapa Lookout. The trail down to Kalaupapa Peninsula is also nearby. There are picnic area, restrooms and pavilion. ~ Take Route 460 six miles west from Kaunakakai, then follow Route 470 (Kalae Highway) about six more miles to the end of the road; 808-567-6923.

▲ State permit required. Tent camping only.

MOOMOMI BEACH A small, remote beach   ◄ *HIDDEN*
studded with rocks and frequented only by local people—what more could you ask? While Moomomi is a small pocket beach, many people use the name to refer to a three-mile length of coastline that extends west from the pocket beach and includes two other strands, Kawaaloa Beach and Keonelele Beach. Moomomi offers good swimming, but use caution because the bottom is rocky and the beach is only partially protected. The snorkeling is very good along reefs and rocks. As for surfing, there are fair breaks at the mouth of the inlet. There's good surf-casting from the rocky headland to the west; you must pay a $25 deposit (refundable) to the Nature Conservancy. Keonelele Beach forms the coastal border of the Moomomi Dunes, a unique series of massive sand dunes that extend as far as four miles inland, covering Molokai's northwestern corner. Also known as the Desert Strip, this unique ecosystem is overseen by the Nature Conservancy (808-553-5236, fax 808-553-9870; www.tnc-hawaii.com), which can provide information and tours. The preserve protects five endangered plant species and is a habitat for the endangered Hawaiian green sea turtle. You'll find no facilities. ~ Take Route 460 west from Kaunakakai to Hoolehua. Go right on Route 481 (Puupeelua Avenue), then left on Farrington Avenue. Farrington starts as a paved road, then turns to dirt. After 2.2 miles of dirt track, the road forks. Take the right fork and follow it a half-mile to the beach. A four-wheel drive vehicle may be required.

HIDDEN ▶ **HALENA AND OTHER SOUTH COAST BEACHES** 🚣 🚤 🎣
🏖️ 🏄 Don't tell anyone, but there's a dirt road running several miles along a string of trackless beaches on the south shore. (Note, however, that at last report this road was closed to the public.) The first one, **Halena**, is a very funky ghost camp complete with a dozen weatherbeaten shacks and a few primitive facilities. To the west lies **Hale O Lono Beach**, with its pleasant bay and lagoon. To the east is **Kolo Wharf** (an abandoned pier collapsing into the sea), plus numerous fishponds, coconut groves and small sand beaches. This is an excellent area to explore, camp, hike, fish (bass, threadfin, *enenue*, red goatfish) and commune with hidden Hawaii. The swimming is also good if you don't mind muddy water. It's wise to boil or chemically treat the water. *Note*: Only Hale O Lono Beach has a public-access road; the other two are located on Molokai Ranch and are open to guests only. ~ Take Route 460 to Maunaloa. As you first enter town (before the road curves into the main section), you'll see houses on the left and a dirt road extending perpendicularly to the right.

Now, to get to Halena, take a right at the fork, then a quick left (there are signs posted), then drive a few hundred yards to the end. The shore is nearby; simply walk west along the beach several hundred yards to the shacks.

To get to Hale O Lono Beach, walk about a mile west along the beach from Halena.

To get to Kolo Wharf and the other beaches, go straight where the road forks. Kolo is two miles east over an equally rugged road. Sand beaches, coconut groves and fishponds extend for another six miles past Kolo. Then the road turns inland, improving considerably, and continues for seven miles more until it meets the main road two miles west of Kaunakakai.

For current information about road access contact Molokai Ranch. ~ 808-552-2741.

HIDDEN ▶ **KAWAKIU BEACH** 🏃 🏊 🚤 🏄 This idyllic spot is my favorite Molokai campground. Here a small inlet, tucked away in Molokai's northwest corner, is edged by a beautiful beach with a sandy bottom. Nearby is a shady grove of *kiawe* trees, fringed by the rocky coastline. On a clear night you can see the lights of Oahu across Kaiwi Channel. This is a very good place to swim because the inlet offers some protection, but exercise caution. Snorkeling is good in summer near the rocks when the surf is low. People fish here for mountain bass, threadfin, *enenue* and red goatfish. There are no facilities here. ~ Take Route 460 west from Kaunakakai. At the Kaluakoi Hotel Golf Course, head to the road near the back 9. Drive north until you hit the beach. It's a tricky route, so you may want to check in with the hotel staff for further details; they warn against making the trip without a four-wheel drive. ~ 808-552-2555, 888-552-2550.

▲ That shady grove is a perfect site to pitch a tent.

PAPOHAKU BEACH PARK 🏖️ 🏊 🚻 This splendid beach extends for three miles along Molokai's west coast; it's an excellent place to explore, collect puka shells, or just lie back and enjoy the view of Oahu. Backed by *kiawe* trees and low sand dunes, Papohaku is the largest beach on the island, averaging 100 yards in width. Swimming is excellent, but use caution; sit out on the beach and observe the wave action before jumping in. There's not much rock or coral here so the snorkeling is only mediocre. You'll find good breaks for surfing when the wind isn't blowing from the shore. Use caution, especially in the winter months. The beach is also popular with bodysurfers. The fishing is good, usually for mountain bass, threadfin, *enenue* and red goatfish. There are picnic areas, restrooms and showers. ~ Take Route 460 for about 14 miles from Kaunakakai. Turn right onto the road to the Kaluakoi Resort. Continue past the hotel (don't turn onto the hotel road) and down the hill. Follow this macadam track, Kaluakoi Road, as it parallels the beach. Side roads from Kaluakoi Road and Pohakuloa Road (an adjoining thoroughfare) lead to Papohaku and other beaches.

▲ Tent only. County permit required.

The ultimate Molokai experience is the pilgrimage to the Kalaupapa leper colony located along the rugged north shore of the island. Isolated on a 12-square-mile lava tongue that protrudes from the north shore, this sacred and historic site can be reached only by foot, mule or plane.

Kalaupapa

Here about 68 victims of Hansen's Disease, a chronic infectious bacterial disease that causes sores and ulcers and destroys tissue, live in solitude. Doctors have controlled the affliction since 1946 with sulfone drugs, and all the patients are free to leave. But many are 60 to 90 years old, and have lived on this windswept peninsula most of their lives.

A PLACE TO CALL HOME—VACATION RENTALS

Molokai offers a variety of home and condo rentals, too many to mention in a guidebook. From one-bedroom facilities to spacious homes, you can probably find something to meet your budgetary needs. One place to look is www.visitmaui.com—check the Molokai listings. Property-management and realty companies are also available in Kaunakakai and Maunaloa. A few include Friendly Isle Realty (800-600-4158), Swenson Real Estate (800-558-3648) and Libra Resorts Properties (808-552-2244).

The story of the remaining residents goes back to 1866 when the Hawaiian government began exiling lepers to this lonely spot on Molokai's rain-plagued north coast. In those days Kalaupapa was a fishing village, and lepers were segregated in the old settlement at Kalawao on the windy eastern side of the peninsula. The place was treeless and barren—a wasteland haunted by slow death. Lepers were shipped along the coast and pushed overboard. Abandoned with insufficient provisions and no shelter, they struggled against both the elements and disease.

Pope John Paul II beatified Father Damien in recognition of his service to leprosy victims banished to Kalaupapa.

To this lawless realm came Joseph Damien de Veuster, Father Damien. The Belgian Catholic priest, arriving in 1873, brought a spirit and energy that gave the colony new life. He built a church, attended to the afflicted and died of leprosy 16 years later. In 1995, the Pope made Father Damien "The Blessed Father Damien." Perhaps it is the spirit of this "Martyr of Molokai" that even today marks the indescribable quality of Kalaupapa. There is something unique and inspiring about the place, something you will have to discover yourself.

SIGHTS

To visit Kalaupapa, you can fly, hike or ride muleback; there are no roads leading to this remote destination. Once there you must take a guided tour; no independent exploring is permitted. And no children under 16 are allowed. Bus tours are organized by **Molokai Mule Ride**. ~ 808-567-6088, 800-567-7550; www.mule ride.com. For flight information, check **Molokai Air Shuttle** from Honolulu. ~ 808-567-6847. **Paragon Air** (808-244-3356, 800-428-1231) and **Pacific Wings** (808-873-0877, 888-575-4546; www.pacificwings.com) fly from Maui.

As far as I'm concerned, the mule ride is the only way to go. The Molokai Mule Ride conducts tours daily, except Sunday when the park is closed, weather permitting. You saddle up near the Kalaupapa Lookout and descend a 1700-foot precipice, among the tallest sea cliffs in the world. Kalaupapa unfolds below you as you switchback through lush vegetation on a three-mile-long trail. The ride? Exhilarating, frightening, but safe. And the views are awesome.

On the tour you will learn that Kalaupapa has been designated a national historical park. Among the points of interest within this refuge are numerous windblasted structures, a volcanic crater and several monuments. You'll visit **St. Philomena Church**, built by Father Damien in the 1870s, and **Kalawao Park**, an exotically beautiful spot on the lush eastern side of the peninsula. **Father Damien's grave** is also located here.

Definitely visit Kalaupapa. Fly in and you'll undergo an unforgettable experience; hike and it will become a pilgrimage.

With so little development and such an expanse of untouched land, Molokai would seem a haven for campers. Unfortunately, large segments of the island are owned by Molokai Ranch and other private interests; with the exception of a few beaches on Molokai Ranch property, these tracts are closed off behind locked gates.

Outdoor Adventures

CAMPING

There are a few parks for camping. A county permit is required for Papohaku Beach and O'ne Alii Park. Permits are $3 per person a day (50 cents for children) and are obtained at the County Parks and Recreation office in Kaunakakai. Hours are 8 a.m. to 4 p.m., Monday through Friday, so get your permit in advance. ~ 808-553-3204, fax 808-553-3206.

Camping at Palaau State Park is free but requires a permit from the Department of Land and Natural Resources (808-984-8109) on Maui, or from the park ranger (808-567-6923).

For information on camping at Molokai Ranch, contact the **Outfitters Center, Molokai Ranch**, Monday through Friday 8 a.m. to 4:30 p.m. ~ P.O. Box 259, Maunaloa, HI 96770; 808-552-2741, fax 808-552-2773; www.molokairanch.com.

Molokai Fish & Dive sells camping gear. ~ 63 Ala Malama Street, Kaunakakai; 808-553-5926.

DIVING

If you're not traveling with gear, the following outfitters can rent you snorkeling equipment. Several provide snorkeling trips to prime spots around the island, and you might check with them regarding other activities such as scuba diving, kayaking and sailing. The best place for snorkeling on Molokai is at the 20-mile marker on the east side of the island. Here you're likely to see sturgeon, trumpetfish and a few green turtles.

Check out **Molokai Fish & Dive** for masks, fins and snorkels. ~ 61 Ala Malama Street, Kaunakakai; 808-553-5926. **Bill Kapuni's Snorkel and Dive Adventure** rents snorkel equipment. He leads dives to spots where it's not uncommon to see tiger sharks, hammerhead sharks and countless green turtles. He also teaches PADI classes. ~ 808-553-9867. **Molokai Action Adventures** offers three- to four-hour snorkeling expeditions. ~ Kaunakakai; 808-558-8184.

KAYAKING

For a scenic paddling adventure, **Lani's Kayak** has full-day North Shore trips that take in breathtaking sea cliffs and lush greenery. Its two-and-a-half-hour Southeast tour features turtles and waterfalls. ~ P.O. Box 826, Kaunakakai, HI 96748; 808-558-8563.

Molokai Action Adventures has half- and full-day kayaking trips. ~ Kaunakakai; 808-558-8184.

An exploration of the old Kolo wharf in an ocean kayak is offered by **Molokai Ranch**. Your guides will share their knowledge of the ancient Hawaiian fish ponds. ~ 888-729-0059.

One- and two-person kayak rentals are available at **Hotel Molokai's Outdoor Activities**. They also have car carriers for rent. ~ Kamehameha V Highway, Kaunakakai; 808-553-4477; www. hotelmolokai.com.

SAILING   Providing Molokai's only sailing adventure, **Molokai Charters** operates *Satan's Doll*, a 42-foot sloop that is docked on the wharf in Kaunakakai. Step aboard for sunset cruises, whale-watching tours and snorkeling excursions to Lanai. ~ 808-553-5852.

FISHING   Depending on the weather, deep-sea fishing charters will take you to various spots that are within ten to twenty miles of Molokai. Here you're likely to catch mahimahi, tuna, marlin and *ono*.

Molokai has the largest reef system in the United States and the highest bog in the world.

Alyce C Commercial and Sport Fishing offers half-, three-quarter, and full-day excursions—all equipment included. Bring your own food and drink. They also operate whale-watching tours from late November to late March. ~ Kaunakakai; 808-558-8377. **Molokai Action Adventures** provides all the equipment for half- or full-day charters. ~ Kaunakakai; 808-558-8184.

An expert in **netcasting** at **Molokai Horse and Wagon Ride** takes folks out by the reef for a half- or full-day excursion. You can lay nets, cast fish or learn how to throw a net. ~ 808-558-8380.

RIDING STABLES   **Molokai Wagon Ride** sponsors wagon and saddle tours to scenic and historic sites at Mapulehu on eastern Molokai; this outfit also rents horses with guides. ~ Mapulehu Mango Grove, about 15 miles east of Kaunakakai; 808-558-8380; e-mail wgnride@aloha. net. **Molokai Ranch** offers a variety of horseback rides including a paniolo round-up and a cattle trail drive. ~ 808-552-2741.

BIKING   Traffic is light and slow-moving, making Molokai an ideal place for two-wheeling adventurers. The roads are generally good, with some potholes out East End near Halawa Valley. The terrain is mostly flat or gently rolling, with a few steep ascents. Winds are strong and sometimes make for tough going.

For those in good shape and who like to climb, contact **Molokai Ranch** for their advanced mountain-bike tour on rugged terrain. Afternoon tours are for beginners and feature a single-track or ranch-road descent to Hale O Lono. All in all, the ranch features 100 miles of trails. ~ 888- 729-0059.

Bike Rentals   **Molokai Bicycle** sells, repairs and rents mountain and road bikes. Rentals include helmets, locks and maps. Closed Sunday, Monday and Friday. ~ 80 Mohala Street, Kaunakakai; 808-553-3931. **Hotel Molokai's Outdoor Activities** has bikes for younger children and buggies for tots. ~ Kamehameha V Highway, Kaunakakai; 808-553-4477; www.hotelmolokai.com.

Molokai features some splendid country and numerous areas that seem prime for hiking, but few trails have been built or maintained and most private land is off-limits to visitors. Some excellent hiking possibilities, but no official trails, are offered along the beaches described above. Palaau State Park also has several short jaunts to points of interest.

The only lengthy treks lead to the island's rugged north coast. Four valleys—Halawa, Wailau, Pelekunu and Waikolu—cut through the sheer cliffs guarding this windswept shore.

The **Pelekunu Trail** begins several hundred yards beyond the Waikolu Valley Lookout (see the Driving Tour on "Molokai's Outback"). It is unmaintained and extremely difficult. Traversing Nature Conservancy property, the trail leads to a lookout point and then drops into the valley. This is one to avoid.

The **Wailau Trail** is another very difficult trail; it takes about 12 hours and passes through some muddy rainforest regions. The trailhead is off Route 450 about 15 miles east of Kaunakakai. The trail extends across nearly the entire island from south to north. Dangers include deep mud and wild boar. To hike it, you must obtain permission from Pearl Petro. Send a self-addressed stamped envelope with a letter of nonresponsibility. ~ P.O. Box 125, Kaunakakai, HI 96748; 808-558-8113.

The **Kalaupapa Trail** is the easiest and best-maintained trail descending the north *pali*. A trail description is given in the "Kalaupapa" section in this chapter. To hike here you must obtain permission and pay $30 for a mandatory tour of the leper colony. Bring food and water along for this four-hour tour. Call Damien Tours for permission and information. ~ 808-567-6171, fax 808-567-9018.

The only valley accessible by car is Halawa. The **Halawa Valley Trail**, one of Molokai's prettiest hikes, extends for two miles from the mouth of the valley to the base of **Moaula Falls**. This 250-foot cascade tumbles down a sheer cliff to a cold mountain pool perfect for swimming. **Hipuapua Falls**, a sister cascade just a third of a mile north, shoots 500 feet down the *pali*. The trail can be accessed only through a guided tour. Call **Pilipo's Halawa Falls and Cultural Hike**. ~ 808-553-4355.

Historical Hikes West Molokai offers hikes to Molokai's west end. Guides integrate *mo'olelo* (or storytelling) into the tour to share their knowledge of the area's cultural heritage. You'll explore old fishing villages, ancient *heiaus*, petroglyphs and sacred monuments. Lunch is provided on the intermediate and advanced hikes. ~ 808-553-9803, 800-274-9303; www.molokai-aloha.com/bikes.

Transportation

AIR

When your plane touches down at **Molokai Airport**, you'll realize what a one-canoe island you're visiting. There's a snack bar and adjoining lounge, which seem to open and close all day, plus a few car rental and airline offices. It's seven miles to the main town of Kaunakakai. There's no public transportation available. However, shuttle service can be arranged through some of the hotels, and taxis are available.

The airport is served by Hawaiian Airlines in turbo prop planes. Aloha Island Air and Molokai Air Shuttle fly small prop planes.

Pacific Wings, Molokai Air Shuttle and Paragon have daily flights from Maui and Oahu. To fly direct from Honolulu to Kalaupapa, try IslandAir, which can always be relied upon for friendly service.

CAR RENTALS

The existing companies are **Dollar Rent A Car** (808-567-6156, 800-800-4000 from the mainland, 800-367-7006 in Hawaii) and **Budget Rent A Car** (808-567-6877, 800-283-4387 from the mainland, 800-451-3600 in Hawaii), and **Island Kine Auto Rentals** (808-553-5242).

JEEP RENTALS

Budget Rent A Car rents jeeps, but requires that you drive them only on paved roads! ~ 808-567-6877, 800-283-4387 from the mainland, 800-451-3600 in Hawaii. (Be aware that the rental car collision insurance provided by most credit cards does not cover jeeps.)

TOURS

Kukui Tours and Limousine Service (808-553-5133) offers half- and full-day tours (and limo service, if you want to go in style). **Molokai Off-Road Tours** (808-553-3369) will take you to see the Coffees of Hawaii plantation, a macadamia nut farm, St. Joseph's Church and the fishponds.

FERRY ACROSS THE CHANNEL

Sea Link of Hawaii has resurrected Molokai's lifeline to Maui, the ocean ferry. When state subsidies ran out in 1996, Sea Link's *Maui Princess* was forced to abandon its daily commuter shuttle between the two islands. Recognizing the tremendous need to boost Molokai's economy, Sea Link purchased a new 100-foot vessel, *Molokai Princess*, and began running the ferry service again. This Maui–Molokai ferry offers twice-a-day departures between Kaunakakai Harbor on Molokai and Lahaina Harbor on Maui, Monday through Saturday. ~ 808-661-8397, 800-275-6969; www.molokaiferry.com.

Addresses & Phone Numbers

MAUI ISLAND

Ambulance ~ 911

Fire Department ~ 911

Police Department ~ 911

County Department of Parks and Recreation ~ Wailuku; 808-270-7230, permits 808-270-7389

Division of State Parks ~ Wailuku; 808-984-8109

Maui Visitors Bureau ~ 1727 Wili Pa Loop, Wailuku; 808-244-3530, 800-525-6284

Weather Report ~ 808-877-5111 for entire island

LAHAINA–KAANAPALI–KAPALUA AREA

Books ~ Waldenbooks, Lahaina Cannery Mall, 1221 Honoapiilani Highway; 808-667-6172

Hospital ~ Maui Medical Group, 130 Prison Street, Lahaina; 808-661-0051

Laundromat ~ Kahana Koin-Op Laundromat, 4465 Honoapiilani Highway; 808-669-1587

Library ~ 680 Wharf Street; 808-662-3950

Pharmacy ~ Lahaina Pharmacy, Lahaina Shopping Center, 843 Wainee Street; 808-661-3119

Police Department ~ 1850 Honoapiilani Highway; 808-661-4441

Post Office ~ 1760 Honoapiilani Highway; 800-275-8777

KIHEI–WAILEA–MAKENA AREA

Hospital ~ Urgent Care Maui, 1325 South Kihei Road #103, Kihei; 808-879-7781

Laundromat ~ Lipoa Laundry Center, 41 East Lipoa Street #1, Kihei; 808-875-9266

Library ~ 35 Waimahaihai Street, Kihei; 808-875-6833

Pharmacy ~ Kihei Professional Pharmacy, 41 East Lipoa Street #23, Kihei; 808-879-8499

Police Department ~ 55 Mahalani Street, Wailuku; 808-244-6400

Post Office ~ 1254 South Kihei Road, Kihei; 800-275-8777

KAHULUI–WAILUKU AREA

Books ~ Waldenbooks, Kaahumanu Center, 275 West Kaahumanu Avenue, Kahului; 808-871-6112

Hospital ~ Maui Memorial Hospital, 221 Mahalani Street, Wailuku; 808-244-9056

Laundromat ~ W & F Washerette, 125 South Wakea Avenue, Kahului; 808-877-0353

Library ~ 90 School Street, Kahului, 808-873-3097; 251 High
Street, Wailuku, 808-243-5766

Pharmacy ~ Maui Clinic Pharmacy, 53 South Puunene Avenue
#120, Kahului, 808-877-6222; Wailuku Professional
Pharmacy, 1900 Main Street, Wailuku, 808-244-9099

Police Department ~ 55 Mahalani Street, Wailuku, 808-
244-6376

Post Office ~ 138 South Puunene Avenue, Kahului, HI, 800-
275-8777; 250 Imikala Street, Wailuku, 800-275-8777

HANA HIGHWAY

Library ~ 411 Hana Highway, Hana; 808-248-7714

Police Department ~ 4610 Hana Highway, Hana; 808-248-
8311

Post Office ~ 1 Mills Street, Hana; 800-275-8777

UPCOUNTRY AND HALEAKALA

Hospital ~ Kula Hospital, 204 Kula Highway, Kula; 808-
876-4331

Laundromat ~ Haiku Laundromat, 810 Haiku Road #134,
Haiku, 808-575-9274; Upcountry Laundry, 55 Pukalani
Street, Makawao, 808-573-1818

Library ~ 1159 Makawao Avenue, Makawao; 808-573-8785

Pharmacy ~ Paradise Pharmacy, 81 Makawao Avenue #21,
Makawao; 808-572-1266

Post Office ~ 770 Haiku Road, Haiku; 1075 Makawao
Avenue, Makawao; 800-275-8777

LANAI

Hospital ~ Lanai Family Health Center, 628 7th Street;
808-565-6423

Library ~ Fraser Avenue; 808-565-6996

Police Department ~ 312 8th Street; 808-565-6428

Post Office ~ 620 Jacaranda Street; 800-275-8777

MOLOKAI

Hospital ~ Molokai General Hospital, Kaunakakai Place,
Kaunakakai; 808-553-5331

Library ~ 15 Ala Malama Street, Kaunakakai; 808-553-5483

Police Department ~ 110 Ainoa Street, Kaunakakai; 808-
553-5355

Post Office ~ 102 Ala Malama Street, Kaunakakai; 800-
275-8777

Index

Lodging Index

Dining Index

HIDDEN GUIDES

Adventure travel or a relaxing vacation?—"Hidden" guidebooks are the only travel books in the business to provide detailed information on both. Aimed at environmentally aware travelers, our motto is "Where Vacations Meet Adventures." These books combine details on unique hotels, restaurants and sightseeing with information on camping, sports and hiking for the outdoor enthusiast.

THE NEW KEY GUIDES

Based on the concept of ecotourism, The New Key Guides are dedicated to the preservation of Central America's rare and endangered species, architecture and archaeology. Filled with helpful tips, they give travelers everything they need to know about these exotic destinations.